JUSTICE FOR MARCUS GARVEY

FOREWORD BY
TA-NEHISI COATES

JUSTICE FOR MARCUS GARVEY

LOOK FOR ME IN THE WHIRLWIND

EDITED BY THE SON OF MARCUS GARVEY
JULIUS GARVEY

BROADLEAF BOOKS
Minneapolis

JUSTICE FOR MARCUS GARVEY
Look for Me in the Whirlwind

30 29 28 27 26 25 24   1 2 3 4 5 6 7 8 9

Foreword © Ta-Nehisi Coates; "The Global Garvey Exoneration Effort" © Goulda Downer;
"The Legacy of Marcus Garvey in Publishing, Bookselling, and the Black Book Community
and the Movement to Exonerate" © W. Paul Coates; "Marcus Garvey Subtly Influenced
the Website Design of Aalbc.com" © Tory Johnson; "Black Bookseller MahoganyBooks
Rallied to Exonerate Marcus Garvey" © Ramunda Lark Young; "Marcus Garvey Taught
Self-Reliance That Blacks Have History Before and Beyond America" © Haki R. Madhubuti,
"The Importance of Marcus Garvey to Black Bookstores" © James Fugate; "Marcus Garvey
Is in Everything Related to Black Literature and Activism in the US, Europe, Africa, and the
Caribbean © Shirikiana Gerima; "Black Children's Book Publisher Modeled Marcus Garvey
as Institution Builder" © Wade Hudson; "The Legacy of Marcus Garvey Maintained" ©
Kassahun Checole, "The Garvey Movement" © Nkechi Taifa, Esq.; "Wading in the Great
River Garvey" © Karl B. Rodney, "The *Vindication* of Marcus Garvey" © Maulana Karenga,
PhD; "Global Garveyism in the Black Liberation Struggle" © Adam Ewing, PhD; "Travesty of
Justice" © Justin Hansford, Esq.; "Wrongful Conviction, Grave Injustice" © Anthony Pierce,
Esq.; "Howard University—A Century in Defense of Marcus Garvey" © Mwariama Kamau,
"Garvey Fights Racial Capitalism of the British Empire in Jamaica © Rupert Lewis, PhD;
"Lewis Ashenheim's Legal Defense of Marcus Garvey in Jamaica © Lynda R. Edwards; "Beyond
Trauma, the Whirlwind, and Redeeming the Soul of Humanity" © Linda James Myers, PhD

Library of Congress Cataloging-in-Publication Data

Names: Garvey, Julius W., editor. | Coates, Ta-Nehisi, writer of foreword.
Title: Justice for Marcus Garvey : look for me in the whirlwind / edited by
   Dr. Julius Garvey ; foreword by Ta-Nehisi Coates.
Description: Minneapolis : Broadleaf Books, [2024] | Includes
   bibliographical references and index.
Identifiers: LCCN 2023058875 | ISBN 9781506488721 (paperback) | ISBN
   9798889833376 (ebook)
Subjects: LCSH: Garvey, Marcus, 1887-1940. | Garvey, Marcus,
   1887-1940--Pardon. | Garvey, Marcus, 1887-1940--Trials, litigation, etc.
   | African American civil rights workers--Biography. | Pan-Africanism. |
   Judicial error--United States.
Classification: LCC E185.97.G3 J87 2024 | DDC 323.092
   [B]--dc23/eng/20240325
LC record available at https://lccn.loc.gov/2023058875

Cover design: Janay Nachel

Print ISBN: 978-1-5064-8872-1
eBook ISBN: 979-8-8898-3337-6

CONTENTS

II
Understanding the Legal Wrong and Efforts to Right It

FOREWORD

Garvey Began the Counter Narrative

Ta-Nehisi Coates

> We must canonize our own saints, create our own martyrs, and elevate to positions of fame and honor black men and women who have made their distinct contributions to our racial history. Sojourner Truth is worthy of the place of sainthood alongside of Joan of Arc; Crispus Attucks and George William Gordon are entitled to the halo of martyrdom with no less glory than that of the martyrs of any other race. Toussaint L'Ouverture's brilliancy as a soldier and statesman outshone that of a Cromwell, Napoleon and Washington; hence, he is entitled to the highest place as a hero among men. Africa has produced countless numbers of men and women, in war and in peace, whose lustre and bravery outshine that of any other people. Then why not see good and perfection in ourselves? We must inspire a literature and promulgate a doctrine of our own without any apologies to the powers that be.
>
> —Marcus Garvey

I GREW UP in a household where Malcolm X was Jesus, and I guess that would make Garvey God. Garvey was in many ways the inspiration, the forerunner for Malcolm X. Garvey was the elder of the Black power sensibility and Black pride that I was raised on. The colors red, black, and green, the colors of the Garvey Movement, were véry, very significant as was Garvey's notion that Africa was not a land of savages but a place to be proud of.

I spent a lot of time thinking about resistance to historical and cultural images of black people. That's what informs much backward politics. It was really important to me to recognize the history of black

folks. Garvey did that for me with his words "Up you mighty race!" I
know we don't use that language today, but that notion was important
in Garvey's time because it was a counter narrative to so much of American history, American society, American arts and culture.

Garvey's words countered what the world was telling me: "Down,
you weak creature." Garvey is and has been very important in my life.
I recited one of Garvey's speeches during high school. It was "Look for
me in the whirlwind" from when he was jailed in Atlanta. I related to
that, even at the time, and certainly now. I like the sense of ancestry,
his idea that we were part of something bigger. You are not alone. You
are never alone. That summarizes how I feel: the idea that the struggle
is, in fact, ancestral and not just limited to who you are right now and
where you are right now.

Marcus Garvey's thought and his work kind of define the world for
me. My whole notion of needing to provide a counter narrative really
begins there. It's not a matter of a quotation or a citation, but it defines
the world. It's the colors of my people. Among black people, Garvey is,
obviously, quite heroic. He's a symbol of resistance and a hero.

Garvey's legacy, for me, challenges the narrative of what black folks
are to a society that tries to reduce us to the subhuman. From Garvey I
keep going back to this idea of a counter narrative. That's what lasts for
me. The very notion of black folks wearing their hair natural, all that, is
Garvey. It all stems from the idea that you don't have to be ashamed of
who you are and how you look. Garvey's ideas are what we take into a
world where people wear natural hair as a normal thing. But people had
to struggle for that. We are still struggling for that right. Our struggle
is very much rooted in Garvey. He birthed all that.

Garvey's influence extends to the current generation of black
creatives. I think about "Halftime" by Nas all the time. There's
"Malcolm, Garvey, Huey" by Dead Prez; "The Blacker the Berry" and
"HiiiPoWeR" by Kendrick Lamar; and "Exhibit C" by Jay Electronica.
Garvey is in reggae. He is in our jazz, our art, our writing, our politics,
and our way of seeing the world.

Pursued by his enemies, railroaded on false charges, and facing a long prison sentence, Garvey seemed to know all of this. As he headed to jail, he remained confident, saying, "If I am apparently crushed by the system of influence and misdirected power, my cause shall rise again to plague the conscience of the corrupt. . . . I shall write the history that will inspire the millions that are coming and leave the posterity of our enemies to reckon with the hosts for the deeds of their fathers."

Garvey was prescient. I'm glad you're reading this book!

Ta-Nehisi Coates is an activist and award-winning author and journalist. He is the author of the best-selling books *The Beautiful Struggle, We Were Eight Years in Power, The Water Dancer* (a novel), and *Between the World and Me*, which won the National Book Award in 2015. He was a recipient of a MacArthur Fellowship and enjoyed a successful run writing Marvel's Black Panther (2016–21) and Captain America (2018–21) comics series. He gave his high school thesis speech on Marcus Garvey.

INTRODUCTION

Marcus Garvey—Preeminent Pan-Africanist of the Twentieth Century

Julius Garvey, MD

We are circumvented today by environments more dangerous than those in any other age. We are face to face with environments in a civilization that is highly developed; a civilization that is competing with itself for its own destruction; a civilization that cannot last, because it has no spiritual foundation; a civilization that is vicious, crafty, dishonest, immoral, irreligious and corrupt.

As by indication, a fall will come. A fall that will cause the universal wreck of the civilization that we now see, and in the new civilization the Negro will be called upon to play his part. He is called upon to evolve a national ideal, based upon freedom, justice, human liberty and true democracy.

—Marcus Garvey

MY FATHER, MARCUS Garvey, died on June 10, 1940, just short of his fifty-third birthday. During his lifetime, he defined Pan Africanism and led the largest mass movement of African peoples outside the continent of Africa. The organization that he founded in 1914 in Kingston, Jamaica—the Universal Negro Improvement Association and African Communities League (UNIA-ACL)—had at its height a membership variously estimated at between six million and eleven million, with 1,200 divisions in 40 countries, from America to Zambia.

The organizational newspaper, the *Negro World*, was the largest Negro weekly in the United States and was published continuously from 1918 to 1933. It was printed in three languages—English, Spanish, and French. Even though banned in many colonial African territories, it penetrated them all, from Kenya in the east, to South Africa, and to Senegal in the west.

He is considered the greatest Pan-Africanist of the first half of the twentieth century.

His main principles of organizational effort were

1. Unity. Garvey wanted all African people to unite in a fraternal bond based on a common identity, common source, common beliefs, common history, and common culture.
2. Nation-state. He believed that developing a nation-state in Africa that would lead to the future freedom, independence, and unity of other African states.
3. Self-reliance. He viewed self-reliance, and the paradigm for development, was African, not European. It was communal, inclusive, cooperative, and socially just. The economic policy was to regulate the use and flow of capital for the greatest good. There was no free market and no invisible hand. The market was constrained by ethics and driven by a social purpose. His form of capitalism was not voraciously driven by individual shareholder profit but by the African communal spirit of caring and sharing. It was opposed by the capitalist, industrialized, corporate system interested only in annually maximizing profits without regard to workers, society, or environment.
4. Education. He said, "We are going to emancipate ourselves from mental slavery, because whilst others might free the body none but ourselves can free the mind." He recognized that education began with the spiritual essence of the human being and had to be nurtured in order to guide scientific materialism, which on its own was leading to chaos and disaster.
5. Culture. He saw culture as the milieu in which people developed and, as such, could be used as an instrument to change the dependent psychology of the previously

enslaved and colonized African person. His use of titles,
symbols, images, propaganda, and parades are without
parallel in the motivation of the African.

His social and political philosophy was a major impetus for the
Harlem Renaissance in the 1920s. He had a similar influence in the
Caribbean in the 1930s. His theosophy and theology predate Black
Liberation Theology.

There is no area of African nationhood that he did not cover in his
organization's structure or philosophical teachings: psychology, culture,
education, religion, government, economics, business entrepreneurship,
trade, investment, character development, etc. He was completely dedicated to the unity and development of African people.

Marcus Garvey defined social enterprise before it had a name. His
answer to the social and economic exclusion of Africans worldwide was
to develop an organization and economic structure that made businesses
into social enterprises that, besides gaining a return on investment, had a
social dividend in the form of development and sustainability of desired
social goals such as the weekly *Negro World* newspaper, the Black Cross
Nurses, the educational institutions, the soup kitchens, the employment
agencies, the youth division, and the structure of the organization as
a whole.

His combination of economic independence with social cohesion
and progress were the pillars of his African Communities League. It
fired the imagination of Africans throughout the diaspora who wanted
their own independent communities and nations apart from the dehumanizing systems of white supremacy, slavery, and colonialism.

Garvey was opposed by white supremacists, Negro American integrationists, socialists, and communists. This unholy combination of
bedfellows conspired to charge and convict Marcus Garvey for using
the mails to defraud his own people.

The integrationists claimed that Marcus Garvey was disturbing
the amicable race relations between the races in America. The socialists and communists thought, as Marx and Engels taught them, that
the problems of the world were class problems and could be solved by

class struggle to gain control of the means of production and distribute the wealth this created. None knew the lessons that should have been learned by European expansion, enslavement of Black people, genocide of Brown people, and private appropriation of the earth's resources. Ignorance and miseducation joined white supremacy to oppose Black independence, while in the US South, an average of one black person per week was being lynched, and one of many attacks on Black progress was that the Greenwood section of Tulsa, Oklahoma—Black Wall Street—was burnt to the ground by a white racist mob in 1921.

As you will read in several of the chapters in this book, the trial of Marcus Garvey was a political one designed to destroy him and the UNIA-ACL. The judge should have recused himself, but he lied about his membership of and support for a rival organization. The prosecuting attorney coached the main witness in perjuring himself. The only evidence presented was an empty envelope without contents.

Yet Marcus Garvey was convicted in a jury trial of all white people. The ruling was based on the assumption that "something" that could have been in that envelope would have been enough to convict him of mail fraud, and for that reason, he should spend five years in prison.

The injustice is palpable.

The cry "Justice for Garvey" has been continuous, with petitions, marches and appeals since the conviction.

In 1987, the centenary of Garvey's birth, then prime minister of Jamaica, Edward Seaga, asked then president of the United States, Ronald Reagan, to grant Marcus Garvey a full posthumous pardon, because Marcus Garvey is the first National Hero of Jamaica.

Charles Rangel, former congressman from New York and head of the Congressional Black Caucus, introduced legislation to exonerate Marcus Garvey at every session of the Congress beginning in the 1980s.

Congresswoman Yvette Clarke, of the Ninth District of New York, along with twenty-two of her congressional colleagues, requested President Biden to back up his talk on racial justice and social equity by exonerating Marcus Garvey.

Such African American organizations as the National Association for the Advancement of Colored People (NAACP), the National Bar Association (NBA), the International Black Women's Congress (IBWC), the National Conference of Black Lawyers (NCBL), the Society of American Law Teachers (SALT), the Institute of the Black World 21st Century (IBW21), and a host of other organizations and prominent leaders such as former ambassador Andrew Young Jr. have supported the exoneration process.

The attempt on his life; his targeting by J. Edgar Hoover of the FBI; the collusion against him of British, French, Belgian, and Dutch colonial powers; his betrayal by many Negroes who were supposed to be leaders of their people and by those of Lilliputian intellect in the organization and outside the organization—nothing ultimately defeated Marcus Garvey.

My father, Marcus Garvey, said, "My firm purpose, my one purpose in life is to work for the salvation of my race." He understood his destiny to be that of a leader charged to unite all Africans worldwide. His vision was to redeem Black people from the morass of slavery and colonialism while building independent nation-states and ultimately a self-sufficient United States of Africa that would bring a new civilization to the world based on the brotherhood of man and the fatherhood of God.

The pressures of heading these organizations—the UNIA and ACL—were enormous. As a leader seeking real justice and true liberty for 400 million African people, Marcus Garvey sacrificed himself totally. He encountered scurrilous propaganda, wrongful conviction and imprisonment, deportation, an attempt on his life, as well as inducements to walk away and enrich himself. But he never wavered. His commitment was total, and his courage was unbreakable.

This book is a call to action for his posthumous exoneration. It also introduces Marcus Garvey and Garveyism to the current groundswell of social justice activists who may not be familiar with him.

Yet I must highlight that at my father's side was an equally courageous partner, one who never wavered in her loyalty to him and her commitment to the cause of African redemption—my mother, Amy Jacques Garvey. Together, my parents withstood all the blowback that a revolution creates and that revolutionaries must face.

Amy Jacques Garvey was a journalist, feminist, wife, and able custodian of his legacy. My mother was also someone who lived her whole life so that she might uplift and benefit the less fortunate. She helped run the UNIA and ACL office, beginning in 1919, contributing to the organization's *Negro World* newspaper, and editing the paper's women's section. Her tasks within the organization were as demanding as my father's, and my father depended on her to be his Rock of Gibraltar. She also ran our home and later, after our births, took care of my brother Marcus Mosiah Garvey III and me.

My mother was a diligent chronicler of the legacy of Marcus Garvey. She edited the four volumes of *The Philosophy and Opinions of Marcus Garvey*, all of which deal mostly with his ideas and his organizational work. My mother died in 1973 at the age of 77. Hers was a life well lived in the service of humankind.

I hope this book inspires you to join the effort to posthumously exonerate my father, Marcus Garvey, and to make your own contribution to the reconstruction of African civilization.

One Aim! One God! One Destiny!

Julius Garvey, MD, FACS, FRCS, is a retired board-certified cardiothoracic and vascular surgeon who practiced in New York. He is affiliated with Northwell Health System and is clinical associate professor of surgery at Albert Einstein College of Medicine. He was internationally schooled in England, Canada, Jamaica, and the United States. He has served educational and medical missions to Ghana, Senegal, Uganda, Mali, Sierra Leone, Jamaica, Haiti, South Sudan, and Ethiopia.

He lectures on the life and legacy of his father, The Honorable Marcus Mosiah Garvey. He delivered the 10th Annual Robert Sobukwe Lecture at Fort Hare University at Eastern Cape, South Africa, jointly sponsored by the Steve Biko Foundation.

I

THE EXONERATION EFFORT AND WHY

CHAPTER ONE

The Global Garvey Exoneration Effort

Goulda Downer, PhD, Global Effort Chair

> Marcus Garvey was the first man of color in the history of the United
> States to lead and develop a mass movement. He was the first man, on
> a mass scale, and level, to give millions of Negroes a sense of dignity
> and destiny, and make the Negro feel that he was somebody . . .
> He gave to the millions of Negroes in the United States a sense of
> personhood, a sense of manhood and a sense of somebodiness.
>
> —Martin Luther King Jr., who in 1965 visited Garvey's
> shrine in Kingston and laid a wreath.

Why the Need for a Posthumous Exoneration?

WE ARE THE beneficiaries of Marcus Garvey's vision. He clarified for us
the question of our identity and proudly proclaimed that it is grounded
in our African roots. He made Black people everywhere proud of themselves and proud of their African ancestry. Long before James Brown
sang it, Marcus Garvey proclaimed it: I'm Black and I'm proud.

A posthumous presidential pardon will provide some measure of
justice for Marcus Garvey and begin to right the wrong committed
against him and his family. It will discredit those who sought to demean
him, stain his good name, and disparage his memory.

What Is the Presidential Pardon Process?

The practice of pardons is a holdover from British colonial law. The
use of presidential clemency in the United States goes back to George

Washington's administration in 1795.[1] Andrew Johnson granted a blanket amnesty to soldiers who fought in the Confederate Army.

According to the US Constitution, only federal criminal convictions may be pardoned by the president. While the president's pardon power extends to convictions adjudicated in the Superior Court of the District of Columbia and military court-martial proceedings, the president cannot pardon a state criminal offense. The president alone is vested with the power to grant pardons.[2]

Once a pardon is granted, it cannot be overturned by Congress or the courts, no matter how controversial it may be.

Once an application is received, there is no hearing by the Department of Justice or the White House. Neither is there an appeal of the president's decision to deny a clemency request. Matters that pertain to the president's decision in a clemency matter are confidential and not available under the Freedom of Information Act (FOIA).

How Does the Pardon Process Work?

An online application must be made to begin the process of obtaining a presidential pardon. The application must be accompanied by one hundred thousand signatures. The signers need not be American citizens. Without the one hundred thousand signatures, a petition will not be presented to the president for their consideration. All signatures must be collected within a thirty-day period.[3]

In 2016, the last year of the Obama administration, the **Justice4Garvey** petition was launched to posthumously exonerate the Most Honorable Marcus Mosiah Garvey—to demonstrate against Garvey's wrongful conviction and false imprisonment by urging the public to sign the White House petition. At the helm of the petition drive was the CaribbeanAmerican Political Action Committee (C-PAC) mobilizing first those from the Americas. The effort fell short of the needed one hundred thousand signatures.

Relaunched in 2022, this time the appeal was global.

How Long Has This Process to Exonerate Marcus Garvey Been Going On?

Efforts to obtain a presidential pardon for Marcus Garvey began the day he was found guilty—June 21, 1923—and continue to this day. Dr. Julius Garvey, Garvey's youngest son, reached out to the C-PAC in August of 2016. He asked C-PAC to lead a renewed effort to obtain a pardon. As chair of C-PAC, I led the effort, and as mentioned, it fell short of the needed one hundred thousand signatures. It was relaunched in 2022, and unlike the 2016 effort, it was decided that the 2022 effort would be global in scope, since signatures are not restricted to American citizens and Marcus Garvey's ideas and impact are global. Special emphasis has been placed on the Americas and the Caribbean. With approximately 150 million people, this region has the largest concentration of people of African descent in the African diaspora. And Marcus Garvey, a native of Jamaica, is revered in the Caribbean. With this focus, we believed getting the one hundred thousand signatures, although challenging, would be highly likely. However, we found the thirty-day period daunting, especially since the use of electronic media was scant. Most people did not have laptops or other personal devices. That was only rectified during the COVID-19 pandemic, when more personal devices were made available as people worked at home.

The 2016 Effort

C-PAC invited Mr. Ayize Sabater, cofounder and CEO of Mentors of Minorities in Education Total Learning Cis-tem (M.O.M.I.E's TLC),[4] to partner with us in 2016. Together we developed the Students4Garvey initiative. It was launched in Washington, DC. Students of all ages, from elementary school to college engaged in a national campaign of letter writing to President Obama, requesting that he grant a posthumous pardon to Marcus Garvey. Dr. Julius Garvey attended the Students4Garvey event. He spoke to the students about his dad's unjust imprisonment, and he answered questions about his father's human rights work.

More than two hundred elementary and middle school students in the Washington, DC, area learned about Marcus Garvey and his work to uplift peoples of the world, especially those of African ancestry. Letters from more than one hundred children ages 6 to 12 in Jamaica and the US historically Black colleges and universities (HBCUs) were uploaded to the White House website and posted to a **justice4garvey. org** website.

The campaign also reached out to public and private media. Flyers and cards were handed out during the Congressional Black Caucus week-long meeting on the mall at the US capitol, as it prepared for the opening of the African American Museum of Natural History. Meetings were held with the Caribbean Corps of Ambassadors in Washington, DC, and with the prime minister of Jamaica.

Our efforts, although gallant, did not garner the required one hundred thousand signatures. We collected just under forty thousand signatures.

The 2022 Exoneration Effort

With a better understanding of the process, C-PAC tried again in 2022. This time was a global effort since the worldwide estimate was 1.4 billion people of African ancestry. A global effort would also inform the world anew about the pioneering Pan-African work of Marcus Garvey.

A focal point was chosen for each of five continents (Africa, Asia, Europe, North America, and South America), and a culturally sensitive marketing approach was developed for our outreach efforts.

Global Focus

Africa: Dr. Felicia Buadoo-Adade and Madia Logan served as vice-chairs for the Africa region. The campaign was supported by a myriad of advocacy groups and educational organizations, including the newly formed Obokese University of Excellence (OUE) in Ghana. Dr. Buadoo-Adade worked closely with Ms. Tomiko Duggan, executive director of the Universal Peace Federation (UPF), a non-governmental organization (NGO) in special consultative status with the Economic and Social Council of the United Nations. They disseminated information to the embassies of fifty African nations.

Asia: Mr. James Gordon, owner of CULTIVA, an internationally focused organization with outreach efforts in China, India, Vietnam, and Nepal, was the vice-chair for the Asia region. He and members of his subcommittee—in the US, India, and Japan—developed a social media campaign reaching out to universities, educational organizations, and student associations through such channels as WeChat and WhatsApp, local languages, and images identifiable by the targeted communities in each Asian region. The Asia campaign for Marcus Garvey reached over 620,000 people.

Europe: Sandra Campbell, who resides in England, served as the vice-chair for Europe. Fliers and Marcus Garvey quotes were circulated via social media and in person to thousands throughout Europe. Sixteen-year-old Damion Wint posted pictures and writings about the work of Marcus Garvey during Cultural Week at local colleges in Leeds and West Yorkshire in the United Kingdom. Young people used their wide social media platforms to reach thousands of their peers. They circulated petitions and urged their peers to sign them, raising awareness of the campaign to thousands. It is estimated that the White House received over twenty thousand signatures from this region.

South America: Dr. Elaine Knight served as the vice-chair for the South America region. As president of the Jamaican National Association of the Washington, DC, metropolitan area, she connected with a myriad of Caribbean American groups across the US and the Caribbean. Meetings were held with the Jamaican Embassy in Washington, DC, and with members of the Caribbean Community and Common Market (CARICOM) to promote the Garvey campaign in their countries and with their national associations in the US. Other participating entities included the Global Jamaica Diaspora Council Northeast USA, the Jamaican Association of Maryland, the Caribbean American Advisory Group of Montgomery County, and faith leaders, including the Iniversal Development of Rastafari (IDOR). This effort is estimated to have garnered at least thirty-one thousand signatures.

North America: Dr. Ayize Saboteur served as the vice-chair for the North America region. The outreach was conducted broadly within the United States, its territories, and Canada. Dr. Saboteur wrote, performed, and recorded a social media historical introductory clip to educate viewers about the significance of Marcus Garvey. More than one hundred media interviews—radio, television, blogs, newspaper articles, webinars—were conducted in February with Dr. Garvey and members of the exoneration committee. The campaign engaged with academic institutions, including historically Black colleges and universities (HBCUs); faith-based organizations, including Christian, Jewish, and Muslim groups; and national leadership organizations, including the Congressional Black Caucus. Conscious-minded millennial Jade Wiles focused on the southern states, with an emphasis on Georgia. Retired congresswoman Donna Christensen of the US Virgin Islands also worked with the campaign and reached out to twenty thousand individuals.

The campaign was notably supported by Black booksellers, publishers, and distributors under the auspices of W. Paul Coates. Black presses, booksellers, and distributors have enabled the writings of Marcus Garvey to remain in print, ensuring the continuation of his legacy.

Next Steps

The effort to keep the work and legacy of Marcus Garvey alive is almost as important as his exoneration. He indeed changed the world! We encourage you to keep his vision alive by acquainting or reacquainting yourself with his work and words.

Use the many resources, including those in this book and his many thoughtful sayings, that are available.

We encourage you to spread the word by holding learning sessions at faith-based settings, academic institutions, clubs, workplaces, etc.

Write to your local, state, and regional politicians, appealing to them to petition the White House.

If the Garvey global exoneration effort team has not gotten a positive response from the White House by spring 2024, we will

- follow up with the attorneys for the Garvey global exoneration effort to get a response to the petition from the White House;
- work to get a broader base of support for the effort among other national groups (e.g., by reaching out to the Jewish community, Native Americans, etc.); and
- work to get a formal involvement of the collective governments of the Caribbean and Latin America.

Goulda Downer, PhD, RD, LN, CNS, FAND, is president of the Caribbean American Political Action Conference (C-PAC) and chair of the Global Effort for *Justice4MarcusGarvey* and The Marcus Garvey Exoneration Effort. She is an associate professor in the College of Medicine at Howard University and at the helm of Howard University's Telehealth Training Center and Center of Excellence; she also directs the culturally focused Caribbean Clinicians Community of Practice HIV/HCV workforce strengthening program in twenty-six Caribbean island states. She has designed and directed several national programs of significance and has served as the principal investigator and project director for the federally funded National Minority AIDS Education and Training Center (NMAETC), the AIDS Education and Training Center-National Multicultural Center (AETC-NMC), the Capital Region AETC Telehealth Training Center (HU-CRTP), and the National HIV Curriculum Integration Project (H-NIP). Under her leadership, Howard University has been recognized locally, regionally, and nationally for strengthening the nation's HIV clinical workforce.

Within the past decade, her portfolio has expanded to include emergency disaster preparedness and management. She is a graduate of the US Federal Emergency Management Agency's National Emergency Management Advanced Academy and a National Community Emergency Response Team trainer and manager.

She has conducted research and published on HIV and emergency preparedness," developed training materials, and lectured on emergency disaster situations nationally and internationally. She also authored the chapters "How Climate Change Directly Affects Food and Nutrition Security" in the 2018/2019 edition of the *Caribbean/Latin America Disaster Readiness Manual* and "Climate Change and the Caribbean: Strengthening Preparedness Measures" in the 2021/2022 edition.

A recognized expert in the field of nutrition and food security, in 2011, she co-chaired the West Africa Region's Nutrition and Agriculture Steering Committee for the Comprehensive Africa Agriculture Development Program (CAADP). Dr. Downer has provided expert nutrition consulting services to the US Department of Justice, United States Agency for International Development, and the DC Superior Court judges. She has served as an advisory member on the Food and Drug Administration (FDA); expert HIV reviewer for the National Institute of Health (NIH); chair, Board of Nutrition and Dietetics, Department of Health, Health Regulation Administration, Washington, DC; HIV Nutrition Guidelines panel Member and co-leader of the Food, Water Safety and Other Issues group of the expert panel, Department of Health and Human Services (DHHS); chairperson, Washington, DC, Statewide Health Coordinating Council; and director of medical education for the National Organization on Fetal Alcohol Syndrome (NOFAS).

Notes

Epigraph: Brenda Haugen, *Marcus Garvey: Black Nationalist Crusader and Entrepreneur* (Minneapolis: Capstone, 2008), 98.

1. "The History of the Pardon Power," The White House Historical Association, December 2, 2020, https://www.whitehousehistory.org/the-history-of-the-pardon-power.
2. "The History of the Pardon Power."
3. According to https://www.justice.gov/pardon/apply-pardon, the number of signatures has varied over the years. During the Obama years, the required number of signatures increased exponentially. We the People was a website launched in September 2011 by the Obama presidential administration to provide a venue to encourage citizens to petition the government and exercise this fundamental right.

   The White House reported that in its first week, the We the People platform received more than thirty petitions that attained the five thousand signatures needed to receive an official response. Later that year, the required signature threshold figure was increased from five thousand to twenty-five thousand signatures that had to be collected in thirty days in order to generate an official response. The White House reported that in the first ten months of 2012, it took an average of eighteen days for a new petition to cross the twenty-five-thousand-signature threshold. In the last two months of that same year, average time was cut in half—to just nine days—and most petitions that crossed the threshold collected the required twenty-five thousand signatures within five days of their creation. The White House also reported that petition requests more than doubled during the last two months of 2012, when roughly 2.4 million new users accessed the We the People platform, 73,000 petitions were created, and 4.9 million signatures were registered. More than 60 percent of the petitions to cross threshold for required signatures in all of 2012 did so in the last two months of the year. As a result of the popularity of petition requests, in January of 2013—during Obama's second term—the White House raised the petition threshold from twenty-five thousand to one hundred thousand signatures, garnered in thirty days, to receive an official response from the White House.

In 2017 the Trump administration declared its plan to temporarily shut down the website and replace it with a less costly one. The platform was eventually kept in its initial form.

During the Biden administration, petitions are directed to the main whitehouse.gov domain. This marks the discontinuation of the We the People website.

4. M.O.M.I.E's TLC is a recipient of the National Arts and Humanities Youth Program Award for their innovative cultural storytelling technique. The award was presented at the White House by then first lady Michelle Obama and the President's Committee on the Arts and Humanities.

CHAPTER TWO

The Legacy of Marcus Garvey in Publishing, Bookselling, and the Black Book Community and the Movement to Exonerate

W. Paul Coates, Black Classic Press
with Apryl Motley

> Every time you see another nation on the African continent
> become independent you know that Marcus Garvey is alive. It
> was Marcus Garvey's philosophy of Pan Africanism that initiated
> the entire freedom movement, which brought about the indepen-
> dence of African Nations... independent nations in the Caribbean
> today ... All of the freedom movements taking place right here
> in America today.
>
> —Malcolm X

MORE THAN FIFTY years ago, poet and publisher Haki Madhubuti
issued a call for independent Black book producers and sellers to unite
and work for the common good of the Black community. That call
bore little immediate fruit, but recently a coalition of Black publishers,
booksellers, and distributors did just that. We mobilized to support
an endeavor many in the Black and global communities of color deem
critically important: the posthumous pardon of Marcus Mosiah Garvey
from all the charges the US government unjustly lodged against him a
hundred years ago.

Black leaders from Rev. Martin Luther King Jr. to Malcolm X have acknowledged Garvey's contributions, and it is impossible to examine Black empowerment efforts during the last hundred years and not see his imprint.

For me, Garvey represented Black nationalism. Support for Garvey was, in my view, a no-brainer. My growing interest in this legendary Black hero who preached Pan-African unity and independence in the early twentieth century began in the early 1970s, when I operated the Black Book, an independent Black bookstore in Baltimore. By 1978, when I transitioned from the Black Book to opening Black Classic Press, Garvey had become the most iconic of my Black heroes. My views were shaped by the reading and research I was doing on Black history, our struggles against white supremacy, and the activists who led and bled in those struggles. Marcus Garvey kept coming up, and as my awareness of Garvey and his accomplishments expanded, it did for my family as well. My children grew up listening to me read about him. Garvey is one of the largest personalities in our history. His conviction and imprisonment on trumped-up mail fraud charges in 1923 and later deportation to Jamaica have long unsettled the Black activist community. Calls for his exoneration have been continuous since his conviction.

Garvey Was a Publisher and Bookseller, a Model for Us Today

In addition to publishing the *Negro World*, the most widely read Black newspaper during his time, Garvey, a former printer's apprentice, had a burning interest in book publishing and bookselling. And we know, thanks to Garvey scholars like the late Dr. Tony Martin, that Garvey was a poet and astute literary critic who promoted a love for reading and the works of Black authors.

Books like those the Universal Negro Improvement Association (UNIA) published, promoted, and sold have become essential reading for serious students of the Black aesthetic and Black liberation struggles. These books include *The Philosophy and Opinions of Marcus Garvey*; his slim volume of poetry, *The Tragedy of White Injustice*; and volumes he encouraged his followers to read, like *From Superman to Man* by J. A. Rogers.

Garvey's enthusiastic and unapologetic promotion of positive Black images and literature is the model adhered to by the most enduring Black book publishers in the US: Third World Press (the oldest), Black Classic Press (my firm), Africa World Press, and Just Us Books. These legacy Black book publishers, after surviving decades of turmoil—financial, social, and otherwise—are witnessing renewed interest, growth, and stability.

In the wake of the Black Lives Matter movement and global COVID-19 pandemic, and with decades of publishing experience behind us, our operations have stabilized enough to spawn something that Garvey would be pleased with and that Madhubuti called for in the 1970s: a network of independent Black book distributors. Today, this includes Lushena Books in Chicago, Afrikan World Books in Baltimore, and the publisher and distributor Red Sea Press in Trenton, New Jersey.

Among US independent Black booksellers, Marcus Books, the oldest and a Garvey namesake, traces its origins back to the Garvey-inspired Black Power movement of the 1960s. Founded in Oakland, California, and supported and supplied for decades by Black publishers, distributors, and clientele, this store and other Black bookstores historically have served as centers of corrective information for Black people. Marcus Books is today joined by a rising number of up-and-coming Black bookstores, including MahoganyBooks in Washington, DC, and the Dock Bookshop in Fort Worth, Texas. These publishers, distributors, and booksellers are committed to producing and selling books by and about people of African descent. They are reflections in everyday life of Garvey's enduring call for Black people to build businesses and institutions that work in the interest of our community.

Just as Garvey's legacy gave sustenance to Black publishing, bookselling, and book distribution in the early twentieth century, key players from these three sectors joined together to fight on his behalf in the twenty-first. In early January 2022, a hastily forged coalition of Black publishers, booksellers, and distributors united to support efforts by

Garvey's surviving son, Dr. Julius Garvey, and others to obtain a presidential pardon for Marcus Garvey. This significant partnership sprang into action like Garvey, mobilizing grassroots and business participants on a virtual global stage.

Emails, calls, and press releases were hurriedly sent to rally the Black publishers, booksellers, and distributors. In less than twenty-four hours, more than thirty-five responded emphatically: Yes!

Ramunda Young of MahoganyBooks and Donya Craddock from the Dock Bookshop coordinated the booksellers. Representing Black Classic Press, my task was to keep the publishers and distributors engaged and informed. Everyone was encouraged to circulate the petition materials "by any means necessary" to their circles of influence— in-person, on their websites, and through social media. Individually and collectively, they hosted multiple Zoom meetings to spread the word to their customers and the general public.

In just days, participating bookstores created and distributed Marcus Garvey book lists and display materials, hosted in-store book talks, and held relevant discussion groups. MahoganyBooks topped the promotion efforts by creating a full-sized entryway graphic of Garvey, complete with a QR code linking scanners directly to the online petition.

That Marcus Garvey's legacy brought together the three publishing sectors is significant. It is a first, one that may open doors to combined future efforts. Each bookstore, publisher, and distributor has the capacity to reach and influence thousands of people as individual units. Combined, that singular power of communication is multiplied many times over. In essence, by working together we demonstrated that our traditional role as information providers can be coordinated with the potential of casting a unified national or even international message. Our community can be empowered by our collective emphasis on issues important to our community. As in the case of Garvey exoneration, our message might be one of social justice, but it also has the potential and could just as easily be a political message. This is new ground for community organizing, inspired by Marcus Garvey and his daring life.

For this volume, I thought it important to document the empowering experience of some of these booksellers and publishers through an oral history composite. I wanted to capture as well as I could the participants' motivations for, and lessons learned by, conducting the campaign to posthumously exonerate Marcus Garvey. Knowing the booksellers and publishers each came from diverse backgrounds, I especially wanted to know why they agreed so readily to join the campaign and what their interest was in Garvey and his legacy prior to joining the campaign. I was also interested in knowing about their customers' knowledge of Garvey, as a way to gauge Garvey's influence on everyday Black people. Almost one hundred years after his wrongful conviction, how did the memory of Marcus Garvey hold up in the minds of their customers?

What follows are edited versions of interviews with some of the Black booksellers (online and brick-and-mortar) and publishers who led our work to exonerate Garvey. Unsurprisingly, each interviewee relates a distinct experience of finding Marcus Garvey. The impact of discovering Garvey was life-changing for all of them. Each interviewee shares how and why Marcus Garvey remains relevant and important to their personal lives and their businesses.

As the founder of Black Classic Press and BCP Digital Printing, **W. Paul Coates** has dedicated himself to the republishing of obscure and significant works by and about people of African descent since 1978. BCP Digital Printing, established as a parallel entity of the press in 1995, stands out from other small publishing companies due to its state-of-the-art digital technology, which enables the company to produce books and documents on demand. By acquiring this technology, Black Classic Press has cemented its place in the forefront of twenty-first-century technology.

Visit www.blackclassicbooks.com and explore the many titles published by Black Classic Press on Marcus Garvey and his work.

Apryl Motley is a content creator/curator and a longtime beloved supporter of Black Classic Press.

Marcus Garvey Subtly Influenced the Website Design of Aalbc.com

Troy Johnson, Black Book Webmaster

Let no voice but your own speak to you from the depth.

Let no influence but your own raise you in time of peace and time of war.

Heal all, but attend only that which concerns you.

Your first allegiance shall be to your God then to your family, race and country.

There is no humanity before that which starts with yourself. "Charity begins at home."

First to thine own self be true, and thou canst not then be false to any man.

—Marcus Garvey

I started the African American Literature Book Club, which is better known as aalbc.com, back in 1997, and the official launch was in March 1998. That was only five years after the World Wide Web became available to the broader public—on April 30, 1993—which revolutionized the internet and allowed users to create websites filled with graphics, audio, and hyperlinks. It's been twenty-six years since I started creating this website, one of the first one for Black books. The primary target is to help people learn about Black culture through books and the written word. That's what motivates me. I am the biggest fan in terms of the content that's generated. I'm learning something new every single day.

A few things that are unique about aalbc.com. For my site, everything was coded by hand. All the web pages with design—for good, better, or worse—were designed by me, and because it's customized, I can do a variety of things pretty quickly that would take a lot more work or even some customization by a developer to get other off-the-shelf solutions to work. The customization on my site allows me to do rapid changes in terms of adding content design and determining how content is displayed. I can very easily accommodate pretty much any book and integrate audiobook platforms easily and seamlessly. That's an advantage and sometimes a big challenge. Every so often, I have to go through and do a massive upgrade.

I've been asked if there is anyone else in the Black or white world who is doing what I do, and I say no with some reservation, because I'm not completely aware of everything that's out there. But I'm aware of other books sites, especially those that focus on Black books. I probably have covered most of them on aalbc.com. They're all using Big Commerce or Shopify or some other off-the-shelf solution for their e-commerce platforms. Increasingly, independent bookstores aren't running their own e-commerce platforms; most Black-owned bookstores are using Bookshop as their e-commerce platform.

I built aalbc.com because it's important to not only sell Black books but also just as important to share information about the books, the authors, the publishers, and every element of the Black book ecosystem. When I started, no one else was doing that and I was not funded, but when the internet became public, it was really a great time. When the World Wide Web opened up, you could do almost anything you wanted to do. I had a small business creating websites for other small businesses. I said, "Let me try to figure out how to make money by selling things on the web." I'm still trying to figure that out with aalbc.com.

Aalbc.com is not just a bookstore. It's just as much, if not more, a content site. When you come to a page, the text in the book description is usually going to be hyperlinked. I'm going to link to important articles, videos, and other information about the book and its author. I do the same thing with Black bookstores. In fact, I've linked to every Black bookseller or store that I'm aware of—154 of them in the US. Some people think it's dumb to promote my competition. The real story is Black booksellers need to work together more rather than less because every bookstore is different with different people showcasing and selling books they like. Fortunately, once most people land on my site, they quickly recognize that I'm providing a service beyond just trying to sell books.

I posted a lot of content about Marcus Garvey during the campaign to exonerate him. I had long been aware of Garvey, but the information I had about him was superficial and probably a bit distorted. The scope of what he was doing was unprecedented. I discovered more about Garvey after I started the website, from reading articles or essays and watching videos about him from people who studied him, understood what he was doing, and had long been publishing information about him. But I wasn't aware of all this material until the exoneration effort.

But even before the campaign, Garvey's influence was in the design of the AALBC website in subtle ways. I embedded the black star throughout the website. Look at the home page and you will find a black star. You'll find a black star pretty much on every page. To me, that represents independence; it represents what Garvey was trying to do in terms of organizing Black people and getting all of us to work together, regardless of where we live.

For the exoneration effort on the site, I just did more of what I was already doing. I spread information through a video created to help people understand what I was doing and why I was doing it. My motivation for participating was that I believed in a lot of what Garvey was doing: self-sufficiency, Black people working together and being independent. Far too often, we look for others to validate what we're doing—what I call "the white cosign." We have to get past that point. Garvey did that somehow.

Troy Johnson is the president of the African American Literature Book Club (AALBC). His primary platform, aalbc.com, is the oldest, largest, and most frequently visited website dedicated to books by people of African descent. Through aalbc.com, Johnson sells, reviews, discusses, and publishes books. Aalbc.com is also a major platform for publishers to advertise and promote books. Johnson is also a recognized thought leader in the "Black book ecosystem."

Johnson has twenty years of corporate experience in roles ranging from designing wide area networks to managing international projects for major corporations, including Goldman Sachs and Deutsche Bank. As an educator, he taught information systems and web design at Baruch College's Zicklin School of Business. Mr. Johnson holds a BS and MS degrees in engineering and an MBA from New York University's Stern School of Business. He has three daughters and lives in Tampa, Florida.

Black Bookseller MahoganyBooks Rallied to Exonerate Marcus Garvey

Ramunda Lark Young

> Education is the medium by which a people are prepared for the creation of their own particular civilization, and the advancement and glory of their own race.
>
> If he is poorly educated he will fail in his duties as a man.
>
> —Marcus Garvey

We started MahoganyBooks in 2007 in the middle of a recession. Books have always been important to us. My husband, Derrick, is a huge lover of Black books. I loved books and was a voracious reader, but I was not necessarily aware of the vast number of Black authors when we first started, as my community did not have a Black bookstore, nor was I exposed to them readily in my home in Tulsa, Oklahoma, right near Black Wall Street. I never even knew Black Wall Street existed. It was never taught in my schools. It was never mentioned in my books. I had a tremendous love of reading, and I read everything else as a kid—but not Black books. I wasn't exposed to Black books until college. I attended an historically Black college and university (HBCU), Langston University in Oklahoma. Because of all the books and the history that I was exposed to in my late teen years, I developed a stronger sense of self-love and love of our culture.

My husband, on the other hand, grew up in Washington, DC. Black bookstores were there. His mom made sure he had access to Black books and read them throughout his childhood, often requiring book reports in the summertime on a variety of Black authors. After we married in 2002, we were searching for a vehicle to impact our community. Both of us, armed with our business degrees, yearned to make a difference. We shared a love of community, culture, and business. I'd been active in the National Association for the Advancement of Colored People (NAACP) throughout college and founded the inaugural section of the National Council of Negro on the campus of Langston University, so identifying a way to impact the community outside of myself was paramount. After five years of marriage, my husband and I were eager to continue this community impact—this time together. We began tossing around business ideas—from barbershops and restaurants to ultimately a bookstore. A Black bookstore resonated with both of us. It was personal for him because of what he was exposed to growing up. It was important to me because of my love of reading and my new discovery of Black books, which occurred as I matriculated through Langston. Two of the most influential books for me to this day that are guideposts as to how I move through this world are *Assata* by Assata Shakur and *Nile Valley Contributions to Civilization* by Anthony Browder.

We started MahoganyBooks online first. Because we had very limited access to capital to lease space, online was the most impactful option due the reach of the internet and the most cost-efficient, alleviating costs for warehouse and storefront leases, on-hand inventory, and employees. At that time, we had our one-bedroom apartment in Alexandria, Virginia, a laptop, and a dream. We wanted to make Black books accessible to people no matter where they lived. Growing up in Tulsa and not having exposure to Black books made it something that I wanted our people to have. I often imagined how much bolder and confident I'd be if I'd learned about the monumental contributions made blocks from my childhood home, on the sacred ground of Greenwood, fondly known to many as Black Wall Street. I didn't want anyone else to grow up and not know the historic pain of the massacre of this innovative community of entrepreneurs, thought leaders, professionals, and educators and ultimately the resounding resilience of Black people. Derrick wanted the same thing, to make Black books accessible no matter where folks lived in the world. The convergence of this focus on community and knowledge of our history with the desire to make Black books accessible across the nation drove us to create Mahogany-Books online. We wouldn't stop until it became a reality. Neither of us had created a website, but we knew folks were really beginning to shop online, especially our generation, who'd been exposed to the World

Wide Web in college and high school. In beginning our fledgling business, we were pretty nervous because of the recession and other factors, and we wondered, "Are people going to order from this unknown Black bookstore?" Our target demographic was just beginning to pay for things by putting their credit cards online, but we remained focused on the bigger vision. We didn't want to leave our history in somebody else's hands. History books were a driving force for us. When we visited general bookstores, we looked at the small shelf spaces allotted to Black books. If we waited for those stores to green-light our history, to say that it was worthy enough to be on their shelves, Black books might never be on their shelves.

We were exposed to Marcus Garvey—Derrick as a young man and even more so while working at a popular Black-owned bookstore in Maryland, but for me, I never saw any of his books on shelves of the main bookstores. What Derrick and I knew for sure was the power of knowing our history. That's why history books will always be a part of our mix at MahoganyBooks, not solely fiction. Urban fiction was out there when we started. Street literature was a hot category, and we were excited that folks were reading books. But we've rarely carried them in our bookstores. We felt history had a deeper rootedness, groundedness, so that's where we focused a large part of our inventory online and in our physical stores once we opened them. We knew the significance of our history—for example, how our community would be empowered by knowing the stances that Marcus Garvey took, the positions that a lot of our leaders took. We had to have knowledge of ourselves. Those books weren't in the general stores. We in turn made those books a priority for our quickly growing customer base. And we haven't veered from that after almost two decades in business. A lot of people think we should be more commercial in our inventory offerings or sell all the *New York Times* bestsellers. It's not important to us at all to sell top mainstream titles. It never has been, nor will be.

Derrick has had a lifelong love of Garvey and what he did. For me, it's probably been in the last five years or so that I connected to Garvey, to Black self-reliance. Growing up, I never understood the power of self-reliance. Although my dad was a great example, I still didn't fully grasp what it meant to generate income from an idea you created. My dad had a third-grade education, and he had his own business. He was the first entrepreneur I knew and saw up close and ultimately whom I credit with my desire to be an entrepreneur at a very young age. But growing up, I did not see my dad as the connection to what Marcus Garvey was talking about. Garvey insisted on the importance of working in our communities, and he stressed the importance of creating our own businesses. What connected me to Garvey was our bookstore business, trying to cultivate that space of self-reliance, loving who we are, no matter what other people think. To this day, we've fully funded our business without bank loans or funds from commercial organizations but instead from close friends, family members, and our own personal retirement savings. It's about community. I've loved that aspect about Marcus Garvey, who encouraged us to work in and with our community. He inspired economic independence. This ideology resonated with me deeply. It spurred me to cultivate connection and relationships among my community, my peers. I understood from Garvey that we could do this for ourselves.

It's not just about our business thriving; it's about other businesses thriving as well. It is about creating a supportive ecosystem. That's what I saw in Marcus Garvey. He taught us to ask, "How do we all come together?" How do we all get a win out of this and not just enrich somebody else's system? Our current business model assembles more than 95 percent of Black vendors across the nation and beyond to source our sideline business. Creating community amongst our own for ourselves struck a chord with me in a very deep place, and it still does.

Our appreciation of Marcus Garvey motivated us to lead the campaign among Black booksellers in support of his exoneration, but many of the newer Black bookstore owners were already aware of Marcus Garvey, selling many of his titles in their stores. It was an honor for us to be tapped by Paul Coates to participate in the exoneration efforts. We instantly knew MahoganyBooks would help any way we could. I immediately reached out to our Black book family—the Black

Bookstore Coalition, which I helped create in 2020 and is comprised of Black bookstore owners from across the nation. We had already been meeting, sharing, learning, and supporting each other for more than a year and a half. We'd built this beautiful community throughout the COVID-19 pandemic and cultivated a space of trust.

Many were excited to galvanize efforts. Some relatively new Black bookstore owners, opened in the last one to five years, yearned to get behind some movement that could represent Black booksellers and continue to solidify community amongst us. Supporting the Garvey exoneration was a way of connecting me to those bookstore entrepreneurs, as well as my ancestors and leaders like Garvey who came before me.

We have a great customer base, much of which is very aware of Garvey and his ideology and moral compass. We also have those who visit our stores who are not from the area. Quite a few were very familiar with Marcus Garvey, and even those who were not, for the most part, were excited to say, "Hey, we are part of this." People were not aware of the intricacies of his trial and conviction, but they were excited about being part of reshaping the Garvey narrative.

Our entire MahoganyBooks team is proud of our participation and ready to do it again until Garvey is fully exonerated. We ensured that everyone was armed with information crafted by the Justice4Garvey site and that everyone felt confident sharing our efforts and the importance of the overall effort to us with our customers.

Ramunda Lark Young is co-owner— MahoganyBooks in Washington, DC, with her husband, Derrick—of and National Harbor, Maryland.

Marcus Garvey Taught Self-Reliance and That Blacks Have History Before and Beyond America

Haki R. Madhubuti, Founder and Publisher of Third World Press

> Nationhood is the only means by which modern civilization can completely protect itself. Independence of nationality, independence of government, is the means of protecting not only the individual but the group.
> Nationhood is the highest ideal of all peoples.
>
> —Marcus Garvey

In 1967, along with several others, I founded Third World Press, now the oldest and longest running Black publisher in the US. I have been involved in Black struggle nationally and internationally for more than sixty-one years, actually all my adult life.

When I was fourteen years old, I read Richard Wright's *Black Boy*, and as a result of its impact on me, I read all his published books. Books became a haven for me, as I was pretty much on my own—my father was absent, and my mother was working in the sex trade and emotionally unavailable. Books helped keep me alive and tremendously aided in developing my Black consciousness and sense of self. Later in a Chicago library, I came across *The Philosophy and Opinions of Marcus Garvey* and grabbed it right away. As I began to read, what attracted me more than anything else was Garvey's approach to self-reliance and his insistence that we have history beyond this country. Garvey and his thinking and teaching stayed with me as I matured.

When I finished high school and ended up in the US Army—the poor boy's answer to unemployment—I felt isolated and used bookstores became my place of refuge, along with military base libraries and the public libraries of the cities where I was stationed. On one of my used bookstore visits, I found first editions and early editions of many books on the life and times of Marcus Garvey. I was influenced by Garvey primarily because he was a movement and institution builder, and I recognized early on how this government wronged him, as well as W. E. B. Du Bois, Paul Robeson, and many other Black women and men of the Garvey era.

Garvey was a major force. He allowed young boys, teenagers, and Black men and women like me to articulate to ourselves and others that there were possibilities for us in this country as whole Black human beings if we understood the racism and white supremacy we were fighting. I saw in him a leader controlling his own definitions and space while inspiring millions of Black people and others, resulting in the largest movement of organized Black people ever in the United States. Garvey was an inspiration for me in my early days of reading, study, and activism, and his concentration on African development has stayed with me to this day. Marcus Garvey's Universal Negro Improvement Association (UNIA) was a perfect example for all young activists of the 1960s and beyond. He stressed the absolute necessity of Africa as central to our activism and thought and institutional ownership as foundational.

I started Third World Press in 1967 with the help of Margaret Burroughs and Charlie Burroughs, who in 1962, in their home, started the DuSable Museum of African American History and Culture, the first Black museum in the US. Dudley Randall had founded Broadside Press in 1962, and he encouraged me to start Third World Press. I was completely aware of the phenomenal John H. Johnson, who built Johnson Publishing Company—*Ebony* magazine, *Jet*, and *Negro Digest* (soon renamed *Black World* magazine).

I said to myself, "I can do this." I started Third World Press in my basement apartment on the south side of Chicago with $400 and a used mimeograph machine. The first books to come out of Third World Press were poetry by Johari Amini and Carolyn Rodgers, who were also instrumental in the early founding of Third World Press. I published books that reflected the best that we had to offer, that provided direction, identity, and purpose, and showed us who we are and where we came from before enslavement in the West. Third World Press was one of the earliest Black publishing companies to publish a book on Garvey.

Garvey, Lumumba, and Malcolm: Black National Separatists by Shawna
Maglangbayan was published in 1972 and went into five printings. (It
is currently out of print, but we plan to bring it back in 2024 as a Third
World Press classic.)

Garvey understood how powerful we are as Black people, and he
wanted us to build our own institutions. At the turn of the twentieth
century, he fought and struggled against all persons, institutions, and
nation-states that disrespected African people. He was considered the
most dangerous Black man in America and a threat to white supremacy.
Patrice Lumumba, later in the Congo, using the ideas and principles
of Garvey and others, actively fought and struggled for the Congo's
independence until he was betrayed by his own Negro leadership, the
CIA, the United States, and European powers. Malcolm X, almost two
generations after Garvey, in this country and with the honorable Elijah
Muhammad and the Nation of Islam, worked 24/7 doing the same
type of liberation work until the CIA, FBI, New York Police Department, and Negro traitors brought him down. White supremacy and its
deadly effects are a monster that came down on the heads of Garvey,
Lumumba, and Malcolm X with a vengeance.

It is difficult to be psychologically and culturally Black and politically and economically serious in America and not have been influenced by Garvey's philosophy and actions. He was practical as well as
theoretical in his development of newspapers, businesses, and the Black
Star Line.

Garvey was not my color. Colorism, then as now, is central to the
culture and politics of America and most of the Western world. He
wasn't a yellow Black man like me. Garvey was a black Black man. That
pushed me more and more to Garvey. You looked at him and you'd
say that he was an Indigenous African. That appealed to me because
it reminded me that my beautiful, high-yellow mother and sister were
the results of rape and the evil use by white men. Black as a statement
of human possibilities, which would include color, culture, consciousness, and geography. In America, we have to add zip codes for all Black
people.

I'd like to see Black publishers and booksellers be more Garveyesque by moving toward complete ownership of spaces they occupy and becoming closer. Some of us who've been at this work for decades are close, but we need to support these young publishers, the new ones out there. I'm looking forward to the time that we can sit down, strategize, and listen to the young Black publishing professionals and see what they have on their minds. We have got to meet with young publishers and support them.

We have to include Black women in whatever we create to exonerate Marcus Garvey, not only because Amy Jacques Garvey was critical to him being remembered. But many Black women are leaders in book publishing and bookselling—for example, at Marcus Books in San Francisco and Oakland and the Dock Bookshop in Fort Worth, Texas. We cannot make the historical errors of the 1960s and 1970s that we made primarily due to ignorance—sexism, misogyny, anti-LGBTQ+. And certainly, there are thousands of independent white bookstores in this country that we need to bring into the campaign to exonerate the honorable Marcus Mosiah Garvey.

Professor Haki R. Madhubuti is a best-selling poet, author, publisher, and educator; is widely regarded as one of the architects of the Black Arts movement; and is founder and publisher of Chicago's Third World Press.

Madhubuti has published more than thirty-seven books and four albums/CDs with music, and his poetry and essays have been selected for more than one hundred anthologies. His first four Black Arts poetry books, *Think Black* (1967), *Black Pride* (with an introduction by Dudley Randall, 1968), *Don't Cry, Scream!* (with an introduction by Gwendolyn Brooks, 1969), and *We Walk the Way of the New*

World (1970), sold over 140,000 copies, making him one of the bestselling poets in the world. His book *Black Men: Obsolete, Single, Dangerous? The African American Family in Transition* (1991) was a national bestseller of over one hundred thousand copies. His poetry has been recognized by the National Endowment for the Arts and the National Endowment for the Humanities, and he has won the American Book Award, Illinois Arts Council Award, Studs Terkel Humanities Service Award, and the Hurston/Wright Legacy Prize in poetry for his book *Liberation Narratives*. His latest book, *Taught by*

Women: Poems as Resistance Language, New and Selected (2020), pays homage to women who have influenced him.

At the age of fourteen, he read Richard Wright's *Black Boy*, which redirected his young life. Between 1960 and 1963, Madhubuti (then Don L. Lee) served honorably in the United States Army. From 1962 to 1967 and beyond, as a college student, Black poet, and political activist, he was initiated into Black consciousness by the work and example of Malcolm X and was personally mentored by Margaret and Charlie Burroughs, Dudley Randall, Hoyt W. Fuller, Barbara Ann Sizemore, and the Pulitzer Prize–winning poet who was to become his cultural mother, Gwendolyn Brooks.

In 1967, Madhubuti founded Third World Press, the oldest continuously publishing Black-owned book publisher in the United States. In 2015, the publishing house expanded its mission as Third World Press Foundation. The Institute of Positive Education (1969) and Betty Shabazz International Charter Schools, which he cofounded, operate three schools in Chicago. He is cofounder of multiple institutions in Chicago.

Among his many awards, he has received the Literary Legacy Award from the National Black Writer's Conference for creating and supporting Black literature and for building Black literary institutions (2006). He was named by *Ebony* magazine twice as one of the "150 Most Influential Blacks in America" in the field of literature, *Chicago* magazine named him as a "2007 Chicagoan of the Year," and he received the President's Pacesetters Award from the American Association of Blacks in Higher Education in 2010. In 2015, the Chicago Literary Hall of Fame presented Madhubuti with the Fuller Award for Lifetime Achievement. In 2022, the National Association of Black Social Workers presented him with their Lifetime Achievement Award.

Madhubuti earned his master of fine arts (MFA) at the University of Iowa Writers' Workshop. He has taught at Columbia College of Chicago, Cornell University, University of Illinois at Chicago, Howard University, Morgan State University, University of Iowa, DePaul University, and Chicago State University (CSU), where he founded and directed the Gwendolyn Brooks Center for Black Literature and Creative Writing, which initiated Black Writers' conferences for over twenty years and brought every major Black writer in the nation to CSU. He cofounded the first MFA in creative writing program at a predominantly Black university and cofounded the International Literary Hall of Fame for Writers of African Descent, both at CSU.

Professor Madhubuti received his fifth honorary doctorate of literature from Knox College in May 2022 and was also named university distinguished professor emeritus at Chicago State University. He was a recipient of the Pegasus Lifetime Achievement Award from the Poetry Foundation in October of 2022. He has given poetry readings and literary, poetry, cultural, and political workshops in thousands of community and cultural centers, libraries, bookstores, colleges, and universities on four continents (multiple nations) and in over thirty-eight states in the US. Third World Press, the oldest independent continuous Black book publishing company in the world, will celebrate its fifty-sixth anniversary in October of 2023.

The Importance of Marcus Garvey to Black Bookstores

James Fugate, Eso Won Books, Los Angeles, California

Africa for the Africans.

—Marcus Garvey

We started Eso Won, maybe, in 1988. The name means "water over rocks" and is said to be an ancient African name for Egypt—known to be the valley of the kings at the Aswan River. We wanted a name for the store that would take people back to Africa. As water flows over rocks, so does knowledge flow through books.

One of our very first events was a program to honor Queen Mother Moore (Audley Moore), who was very much a Garvey person. And she was pretty old at that time. But we knew Dr. Anyim Palmer, who had a private school here that taught kids from an Afrocentric perspective— the Marcus Garvey School. We were asked to set up books there, and that turned out to be one of Eso Won's first events.

Dr. Anyim Palmer would allow a community group to meet at the Marcus Garvey School and discuss Black books. Three of us in that group that met at the Marcus Garvey School eventually formed Eso Wan.

I worked at the Compton College Bookstore, which had become known in the community as a store that had a great selection of Black history books. A community college bookstore should be more than just a college bookstore. Your kids read books, and you want to present them with books that reflect who they are. Every store I worked in became known for having a lot of Black history texts.

And when I came to Compton, it certainly became even more known. I met Tom Hamilton at that first store, and then we ended up being a part of the same community group, African Minds United, along with our third partner, Asamoa Nkwanta. We decided to form

a community bookstore that would sell Black books at events in the
community.

As Compton College Bookstore was owned by a private bookstore
leasing firm, a nationally known company, I did not feel comfortable
coming into the community and setting up a book display on the weekends representing the Compton College Bookstore, even though it was
presenting Black books. I felt uncomfortable that I was working on
my own time but representing a large white firm at Black community
events. When we were invited into the community to sell Black books,
although it was on my time, I chose to do it because I saw an opportunity
to expand the reach of Black books. But I did feel uncomfortable and
began thinking, "Perhaps you could do this on your own." I met Tom
and then Asamoa, and they indicated they wanted to start a bookstore.

When we first met, it wasn't feasible for Tom and Asamoa to start
a bookstore. Tom was married with three boys under the age of ten.
Asamoa worked at the Jet Propulsion Laboratory. I talked with Tom
and Asamoa about working just on weekends. Both had the extra funds
to start the bookstore, and Tom even built the tables that were needed
at some events.

We all worked on weekends selling books at Black community
events, although we were all working full-time at our other jobs. For
almost a year, we were known as Eso Won Books on wheels. Then we
found a small store not far from our current location, about a mile away.
Even though we ran the store only part-time, it gave us a place where we
could display all the books we had—about fifty milk crates of books.
We opened the store officially full-time, I think, in January 1990. After
that first Christmas, it made sense for one of us to quit his job, and since
I was not married and didn't have any kids, I quit my job at Compton
College Bookstore and started running the store full-time. Tom was the
co-owner of Eso Won and worked full-time, starting about 1993. Our
third partner, Asamoa, had left us at that point. His company wanted
him to get a PhD in mathematics, and they were willing to pay for it.
He and his wife actually went back east.

It's been an amazing thirty-five years or so since we started full-time. Our emphasis was on a Black historical vision of liberation and freedom. When our store started, as a new bookstore, there were authors not signed to major publishers who deserved to be heard in the community. Carrying books by Dr. John Henrik Clarke or Dr. Yosef Ben-Jochannan was important. Those people needed to be in the community and to give talks. Early on, we decided to bring out authors who might never be represented or heard of otherwise. The first one was Llaila Afrika, author of *African Holistic Health*.

The recent campaign for the exoneration of Marcus Garvey is, for me, one of the more significant activities at Eso Won in the last thirty years. Marcus Garvey wasn't taught when I was in Detroit public schools. The kind of thinking that Garvey had back in the early part of the last century was never taught. It was written out of history, even by Black people. It's very significant that we talk about it. Often people are afraid to talk about Garvey and his ideas, even Black people. It was institutions like the Marcus Garvey School here in Los Angeles that taught about Garvey, or in Detroit, the Shrine of the Black Madonna. Marcus Garvey was too radical.

The campaign to exonerate Marcus Garvey raises many significant issues Black bookstores should be focusing on and talking about, and I was happy to see that so that many bookstores were willing to lend their names to the campaign, along with many national figures who were willing to lend their names so that this topic would come forth in our community. That conversation leads people to come into a bookstore and ask, "What do you have on Marcus Garvey?"

For me, one of the most important books I read as a college student-activist was *Marcus Garvey and the Vision of Africa*, edited by Dr. John Henrik Clarke. It was an eye-opener because I knew of Marcus Garvey, but I didn't know much about him.

Books by John Henrik Clarke and Yosef Ben-Jochannan should be in our homes because they lay out pathways. Reading about people like Marcus Garvey will focus you. With this generation of young people who are coming of age now, there is no longer any question that Marcus

Garvey should be mainstream and be part of the community conversation at all times. Every bookstore should know about the campaign to exonerate Marcus Garvey and be talking about this.

When Tom and I officially announced that we were going to shut down at the end of the year in 2022, there was a huge outpouring of remembrance and thoughts of what we mean to bookselling, booksellers, and the community. Black bookstores bring information to Blacks in this country denied that information from others. I hope our store is remembered as a store that provided a wide range of information. Talking about Marcus Garvey is one of the most important subjects for Black bookstores.

James Fugate was co-owner of Eso Won Books in Los Angeles. He was born and raised in Detroit. After graduating from college, he worked for a short time at the Urban League and then at a small bookstore, which led to working in several college bookstores. When those stores became known for their large Black book selections, he cofounded EsoWon and worked full-time at the store from 1990 until he retired in 2022.

Marcus Garvey Is in Everything Related to Black Literature and Activism in the US, Europe, Africa, and the Caribbean

Shirikiana Gerima, Sankofa Video and Bookstore and Cafe

> Look for me in the whirlwind or the storm, look for me all around you, for with God's grace, I shall come and bring with me countless millions of Black slaves who have died in America and the West Indies and the millions in Africa to aid in the fight for Liberty, freedom and life.
>
> —Marcus Garvey

My husband, Haile Gerima, his sister, Selome, and I started Sankofa bookstore in 1997 and named it after our movie by the same name. Initially, the building was a place to create and distribute our movies. We created a space for both books and videos for a discerning audience. Haile and I were very clear that the bookstore would carry books and movies that we loved and that we were nurtured by. We felt we could participate in making Black books and films available to our community, particularly young people attending Howard. Over the years, that became our mission, and it still is today, twenty-five years later. Our space has been referred to as "liberated territory" because it is a place where people can feel comfortable to seek and share knowledge about their own culture. Our books, films, and even the food menu all have something to do with Black culture. We are really grateful to have a place where people from multiple backgrounds can grow and learn.

Sankofa was one of the Black bookstores working to exonerate Marcus Garvey. I was first introduced to Garvey in high school by a friend whose parents were immersed in the Garvey movement. Later I read books on Garvey that helped me realize Garvey's movement was incredibly advanced and influential. I'm still learning about the impact of Garvey on literature—for example, writers like Claude McKay and

Richard Wright. Garvey seeps into just about everything that has to do with Black literature and Black activism in the US, Europe, Africa, and the Caribbean. His impact has become central to my film work—for example in *Footprints of Pan Africanism*. His impact on the African independence movements is central to the actual shaping of those movements. *Footprints* points out how Kwame Nkrumah invoked Garvey at every turn, as can be seen in the creation of the Black Star shipping line, Black Star Square, and the black star on the Ghana flag. My favorite story is how Patrice Lumumba's parents would go to the river to see if Garvey was coming!

The exoneration effort has given us a chance to focus on his work and to pay attention to his contribution to so many layers of our existence. When we say we are going to exonerate Marcus Garvey, it does not mean we are allowing the system to say, "We forgive him." There is no need for Garvey to be forgiven. This country— the US government—needs to say it's sorry: "We are sorry for lying about Garvey; we're sorry for framing and setting him up and then convicting him in a sham trial." It's the government that should ask for forgiveness. Garvey needs none.

For the most part, our customers are very aware of Garvey. They come into the store quoting Garvey, or they ask for a particular book by Garvey. They are patient but very persistent about Garvey.

During the campaign to sign the exoneration petition, we had a banner on our web page to alert people and connect them to the petition. We also had physical banners in the store.

We sponsored an event with Dr. Julius Garvey, the last remaining son of Marcus Garvey, and held author events. Many of our readers have studied Garvey for years, so when we do events about Garvey, we get great participation. We are continuing to do this with authors of children's books on Garvey as well.

Some Garvey material we stock:

Marcus Garvey Coloring Book by Patrick Onwe

Marcus Garvey Activity Book; *Teach Me About Garvey* by Michelle Thomas

Marcus Garvey by Suzanne Francis-Brown

Footprints of Pan Africanism, DVD

It would be wonderful if we had an association of Black bookstores/publishers to reach out beyond the Black book community in support of this movement to exonerate Marcus Garvey. We could say to the community, "We are leading a charge for the exoneration of Marcus Garvey. Do you want to stand up with us?" Anybody who wants to get on board can join the charge. Such an association could take on other urgent issues like books in prisons and banned books.

Whether Garvey is exonerated or not, my interest is that the next generation knows more about Garvey's struggle as a result of this campaign. Then we've done our job. The exoneration process may never work. If it does, great. Either way, our job is the same: to make sure that what the US government did, with the help of its antiblack allies, is not forgotten. And that the work of Garvey lives on. If we do that, then we've succeeded.

Shirikiana Gerima is co-owner of Sankofa Video and Bookstore and Cafe in Washington, DC, located across from Howard University, on Georgia Avenue, historically a thoroughfare for Black residents and businesses.

Haile Gerima, her husband and business partner, is a filmmaker from Ethiopia. He came to the United States to study film in 1967. He changed his focus from acting to filmmaking, producing, and directing. He has made a number of award-winning films that have garnered attention locally,

nationally, and internationally and has made a number of important contributions to the Black film aesthetic. He is especially noted for re-analyzing the thinking, the language, and the possibilities for cinema when it comes to telling Black stories. He has, through his craft, mentored and been a model for a number of young filmmakers.

When he went to the University of California, Los Angeles (UCLA), he was part of a cohort of young Black filmmakers. As a result of the rebellions during the 1960s against brutality and racism, institutions like UCLA were beginning to open up their doors to quell some of that tension. Halie's cohort included young filmmakers who would go on to accomplish new aesthetics in Black filmmaking. Haile was classmates with Black and Brown people who questioned every standard precept of Western cinema. They viewed and criticized each other's films. They expanded the notion of films and taught themselves the art of making films that reflected their genuine experiences from within those communities. They encouraged each other to challenge static aesthetics and stereotypes of Blacks in cinema.

Haile came to Washington, DC, after graduating and began teaching at Howard University. He treated students, teachers, and community members as equals in a search for understanding the impact of film on our lives, our choices, our human relationships, and our history. Many would meet on Saturday mornings to view films in the auditorium and compare and contrast film language, aesthetics, and social impact, questioning choices in lighting, casting, camera angles, and music and how these choices enhanced or weakened the story, questioning whether they mimicked commercial films and, if not, how they were genuinely representing the filmmaker's own world and artistic view. Just as importantly, those gathered looked at how these choices impacted the viewer. Students and teachers and community members worked on productions where they went into the community and produced films like *Wilmington 10—USA 10,000*. It was a wonderful time to be at Howard and working with Haile and other instructors.

The same year that Haile came to Washington, DC, Shirikiana transferred to Howard University from Wayne State University in Detroit, where she had been working in radio news, pursuing a degree in mass communications. The Detroit she left behind was a very politically active place. There was the free South Africa movement, the political prisoners movement, the Free Angela Davis movement, labor movement, and the anti-war movement. She came to Washington, DC, with a solid base of political thinking that helped attract her to filmmaking. She gravitated toward Haile's work and the classes he was teaching and was intentional about going into mass media, making it a tool that could help Black people say what really needed to be said and replacing the twisted ways in which the media intentionally misrepresents Blacks.

Black Children's Book Publisher Modeled Marcus Garvey as Institution Builder

Wade Hudson, Just Us Books

> A people without the knowledge of their past history, origin and culture is like a tree without roots.
>
> —Marcus Garvey

When I was growing up, in a small, segregated town—Mansfield, Louisiana—I did not know Marcus Garvey even existed. The white school board determined what Black schoolchildren could read. There were no bookstores in our area. And certainly no Black bookstore, so I didn't have access to Black literature.

My first introduction to Marcus Garvey was when I went to Southern University for undergraduate school. That was 1964. Black students were beginning to transform institutions that utilized an old, traditional, white Western European model of educating and preparing Black students for various professions. Black students started to protest and call for an approach that included who we are. We wanted Black history and Black culture. A number of Black professors were on the cutting edge, introducing students like me to our history and culture. One of those instructors was Dan Davis, from whom I first learned of Marcus Garvey.

What resonated with me about Garvey was that he was an institution builder. In a way, Garvey reminded me of Black people in Mansfield and the institutions they tried to build for themselves, although until recent years racist whites tried to block them. I began to read articles about Garvey at that time, and I was ready for his message to focus on building our community. I was embracing my Blackness and my Africanness. Dan Davis loved Marcus Garvey. We used to go to his apartment—five or six of his students. We'd sit on the floor. He'd sit in his little chair and talk about Marcus Garvey and share history that we did not know.

Southern began to change because students like me started to push, protest, and call the administration on the carpet. We protested even though we knew much of what the administration could do was determined by white folks downtown. But we still fought. Here again, Marcus Garvey was a role model for me and others. Garvey and Malcolm X became more important to me as I grew in the Civil Rights Movement and engaged in it. I started to see that the Civil Rights Movement, although important, was lacking, that what we were fighting for was much bigger than integration. Self-determination and institution building became important goals—being in control of our own destiny, determining our own value, getting to know and understanding our history. We needed to be more connected to our history rather than floundering and floating because of our disconnection.

For example, one of the first Black publishing companies in America was started by the African Methodist Episcopal (AME) Church in Philadelphia. The church wanted curriculum material that spoke to its members' own experiences rather than the white ones in the books it was receiving. That's why my wife, Cheryl, and I started Just Us Books in 1988, nearly two hundred years later. A year before, we had self-published an alphabet concept book Cheryl had created. We had submitted Cheryl's manuscript along with manuscripts that I had written to major publishers in New York. They told us there was no market. In fact, one editor said, "Black people don't buy books."

Rather than complain about what publishers were not doing, Cheryl and I stepped out on faith to publish the *AFRO-BETS ABC Book* ourselves. We identified a market for it, direct mail marketed it, and reached out to sororities, fraternities, and other community organizations. We printed five thousand copies of that first book. In less than three months, we had sold all five thousand copies. We went back to print another five thousand.

That's the way the company was launched. In 1988, we officially incorporated as a publishing company, Just Us Books.

We were concerned about literacy and reading and passing on our history, our culture, to our children.

The next books that we published were by Cheryl, and then I authored *AFRO-BETS Book of Black Heroes*, which featured biographical sketches of important Black achievers, historical as well as contemporary. We then began publishing Black authors and illustrators who were looking to get a start in the industry and were drawing little interest from major publishing houses.

At the time, a handful of Black book writers and illustrators were creating books for children about the Black experience and Black history and culture—for example, Walter Dean Myers and Eloise Greenfield. But their books were not getting visibility in the mainstream market, and those that were selling mostly reached only the educational and library markets. Because of my background in public relations and marketing, we recognized early on that we had to get into the retail market. So, we did. We went directly after accounts at Toys R Us and Kmart. During our first couple of years, we were fairly successful in getting our books placed in their stores. Our marketing approach included going directly to the people. We took our books to festivals, church events, national conferences, schools, and libraries. In the late 1980s and the 1990s, there were still TV programs oriented toward Black history, life, and culture, and we sought them out and were able to get interviews and coverage on some of those programs. We set up book tours for the authors of each book we published.

We became so successful that some of the major publishers wanted to hire us as consultants. Walter Dean Myers asked us to help him set up tours for two of his books. He had never done a book tour.

We were getting greater visibility and, like Haki Madhubuti with Third World Press back in the 1960s, concentrating on institution building. We were building Just Us Books as an institution rather than solely as a business. And to be quite honest, we didn't have the revenue or the finances to open it solely as a business anyway. Building it as an institution enabled us to make connections with other Black folks, other Black organizations. Marcus Garvey is a model for institution building.

Paul Coates at Black Classics Press, Haki at Third World Press, Glen Thompson at Writers & Readers, and Kassahun Checole at Africa World Press all started before Just Us Books, but the focus was on the adult market. Children's and young adult books were—and still are—our focus. That set us apart from what other Black publishing companies were doing at the time. Now, thirty-five years later, Cheryl and I are still very much involved and engaged in the company, along with our daughter, Katura, and our son, Stephan. We depend on both of them a lot. Cheryl and I are old school. Katura and Stephan bring fresh new approaches, using technology in book design, social media, and many other aspects of our operations. Katura also works in the editorial department and has acquired manuscripts. Two of my brothers, Willie and Major, also work with the company. Willie handles our sales, and Major handles shipping. They've been with us twenty-five years. Just Us Books really is a family operation. Institution building means including others, giving them opportunities. Garvey certainly modeled that for us.

Marcus Garvey is so important, as are other forerunners and forefathers and foremothers. That's why Just Us publishes books for children and young adults wrapped in historical content. We get to readers at an early age. We want historical figures like Garvey to have a place in publishing for children. That was one reason Just Us Books participated in the campaign to exonerate Marcus Garvey. Getting him exonerated is paramount. But this campaign also gave me the opportunity to introduce Marcus Garvey to a lot of folks who did not even know he existed. A lot of people signed the petition and got to know who this important Black man was. People would say, "Oh my God, he did all of that." A whole lot of people just did not know. This campaign gave me, Cheryl, Katura, and Stephan the opportunity to introduce Garvey to others, including members of my church who were interested in and fascinated by Garvey's accomplishments. If we don't lift up those who have been important in our journey and our struggle, people forget that those important people ever existed. It's like the old saying, "As long as there's someone to call my name, I live." Being able to call Marcus Garvey's name means he continues to live.

Wade Hudson is president of Just Us Books, a children's and young adult book publishing company he and his wife, Cheryl, founded in 1988. He is also the author of many books for young readers. His published books include the anthologies *We Rise, We Resist, We Raise Our Voices* and *The Talk, Conversations about Race Truth & Love*, both with Cheryl Willis Hudson; *Journey, Poems by Wade Hudson*; *Defiant, Growing Up in the Jim Crow South*; and *Invincible, Fathers and Mothers of Black America.* He resides in West Orange, New Jersey.

The Legacy of Marcus Garvey Maintained

Kassahun Checole, Black Book Distributor and Publisher

> The Negro will have to build his own industry, art, sciences, literature, and culture before the world will stop to consider him.
>
> —Marcus Garvey

Africa World Press and the Red Sea Press are sister companies—a book publisher and a book distributor—started in 1983 and 1985, respectively. The objective and mission are informing and empowering African peoples about their history and politics, as well as their social interests and concerns.

Garvey was taught to me early in the school system in Eritrea/Ethiopia and through our parents telling us about great personalities and reading activist materials on the Pan-Africanist movement that were being sent to us from all over the world. We were informed by our teachers about Garvey and his presence as a great man. Marcus Garvey was talked about often as one of the main leaders who saw that there was only one Africa.

We were young and highly affected by reggae music and the Rastafarians. Awareness of Garvey and the Rastafarian movement was the initial spark that helped us understand and appreciate the Pan-Africanist movement that talked about "United Africa." This movement was an opening for a Pan-Africanist awareness that was further influenced by the ideology and activism of Kwame Nkrumah, Gamal Abdel Nasser, and the African martyr, Patrice Lumumba. We were not fully aware at that time of how significant Garvey was, but that was the start of awareness about him and his incredible impact on the general anti-colonial and anti-imperial movement.

I went through a short politicization period at Haile Selassie University reading radical Marxist material and African authors, and

Malcolm X became a very strong influence on me; his speeches, activism, and stand against the whole system of oppression I appreciated.

This was a formative period for me. I was reading books about the Vietnam War, Cuba, the struggle against oppression around the world, and at the same time, the struggle for civil rights and equality in the United States. Angela Davis came into the picture while I was in high school in Eritrea/Ethiopia, as did the Jackson Brothers, George and Jonathan. I can never forget the essential role of Muhammad Ali's defiance and his anti-war stand. All these became part of my learning process about the Pan-African struggle and my overall radicalization.

I came to the US from my birth country, Eritrea. One of the first places I visited was Harlem in New York City, where I was introduced to the National Memorial Bookstore on 125th Street, owned by a very unique person, Mr. Louis Michaux. While at that store, I met a man who saw me picking up books and looking at them like I was a kid in a candy store. He said to me, "You must be an African."

"Aren't we all?" I responded. That man happened to be John Henrik Clarke. I didn't know who he was at the time. But he took me under his wing. This guy who knew everything about Africa better than I did was telling me which books to read. I took his name and phone number. Neither he nor I knew that one day I would become one of his publishers. About a week or so later, I left New York City to go to school in upstate New York at the State University of New York (SUNY) Binghamton.

When I went to upstate New York, the first thing I did was join the activist movement in the Cornell-Binghamton area. My first week, I joined a demonstration against the Vietnam War. Not that I was knowledgeable or had people who told me what this was about. It was my knee-jerk reaction to join this anti-war demonstration. By chance at that demonstration, I met other people, and they were members of a collective called Glad Day Press, which I joined. Glad Day Press or the collective printed everything needed to inform people about the Vietnam War. They printed books, posters, maps, and every imaginable kind of informative material and distributed it around the country. They had a small printing press. I became a helper there, collating and binding books, which was, at that time, done mostly by hand. I did those kinds of things and learned more about printing.

In Binghamton, I started studying African liberation movements, including my own country's liberation struggle. Almost every day at lunch, I would set up a table at the student center and provide information that I got from New York and other places about liberation movements. I started the first day I came to Binghamton and continued until I finished my studies there in 1977.

The liberation movements that I was enthused about were the anti-colonial movements in former Portuguese colonies—Angola, Guinea-Bissau, Mozambique—but also in Namibia (colonized by Germans), South Africa (colonized by the Dutch and British), and Zimbabwe (colonized by the British). These movements were linked to the larger anti-apartheid movement, which was an important issue that galvanized the African American liberation struggles.

Also, at this time in the early 1970s, I got engaged in the Black Student movement. The leading concern of Black students at that time was to advocate for Black studies and the need for a more vibrant Black staff and faculty to nurture the growing desire for a proud self-identity. That linked up with the larger civil rights issues that increasingly become internationalized and radicalized.

My activism in the Black Student movement was a bit troubled because my activity with the larger left-leaning movements in the radical white groups was viewed suspiciously. My activism broadened to include diverse anti-imperialist and anti-colonial struggles of the Vietnamese and other Asian movements like that of East Timor and even on the question of Palestine.

I looked at my white friends and comrades from a lens of whether they were anti-imperial and anti-colonial and their overall "progressive stand."

I did not view "race" and the horrible racial history of white subjugation of Black and Brown people as a major factor in relation to the class struggle. I learned quickly that the "race" issue has a unique dimension in the US setting. My interaction with my Pan-Africanist and radical Black activist friends brought me closer to the struggle for Black liberation, to understanding the critical/central role of race in the context of America. It also helped to have met my wife in Binghamton, who was active in the Black auto workers movement in Detroit.

Garveyites had a foothold in Binghamton. My exposure to Caribbean activists and intense reading of scholars like C. R. L. James, Jan Carew, and Walter Rodney—and eventually engaging with them personally—further shaped my view of Garvey and his impact on the world.

The movement to exonerate Marcus Garvey recognizes his importance to people of African descent and humanity as a whole. Garvey was a lot of things to many people, but he was not a criminal. It's important for us to recognize and fight for his exoneration because he was speaking for us. He created a community of Africans, one of the largest communities of Africans to demand that Africa should be free, Africa should be for Africans, and Africa should be united.

He encapsulated the many studies and work that had been done earlier to say that Africa is the mother of civilization. And he strived, in many ways, to make sure that we, children of the Pan-African movement, understand that we have nothing to be ashamed of. Our history should energize us. It ought to be a reason for pride, if only we knew ourselves and our history. Garvey wanted us to know that Africa is the founding of human civilization and that our history should never be forgotten. To be a part of the exoneration movement to clear this man's name, to separate Garvey from the false charges that were hung on him so long ago, is one of the more important things I could have done and will do again.

Kassahun Checole, founder and publisher of Africa World Press and the Red Sea Press in Trenton, New Jersey, was formerly a professor of sociology and political economy. He is currently a senior fellow at Tilburg University in the Netherlands.

CHAPTER THREE

The Garvey Movement

Personal, Powerful, Political

Nkechi Taifa, Esq.

> We are circumvented today by environments more dangerous than
> those which circumvented other peoples in any other age. We are face
> to face with environments in a civilization that is highly developed:
> a civilization that is competing with itself for its own destruction, a
> civilization that cannot last, because it has no spiritual foundation;
> a civilization that is vicious, crafty, dishonest, immoral, irreligious
> and corrupt.
>
> —Marcus Garvey

OF ALL THE movements that began in the twentieth century, it was
the Garvey movement and its Universal Negro Improvement Association (UNIA) that was the most personal to me. Was it because it was
the most successful mass organization during its time, and probably
afterward, for instilling pride, confidence, and hope in the Black community? Was it because the association uplifted the critical importance
of economic independence and the patronization of Black businesses?
Was it because the movement laid the seeds and served as the foundation
for just about every Black movement to come? No—although all these
statements are true, it was for none of those reasons.

The Garvey movement was most personal to me because it touched
my grandfather, James Albert McIntosh, an immigrant to New York
from the Caribbean islands in the late 1800s—like Garvey—who later

taught his son, my uncle Ambrose, who was born in 1910 and passed the spirit down to me.

I never knew my grandfather, because he transitioned when I was a baby, but I did know my uncle Ambrose, who was a youth during the height of the Garvey movement of the early twentieth century. My uncle was neither a radical nor a revolutionary. He was not a militant or a race man, at least as far as I know. But like thousands of his contemporaries growing up in Harlem during the first part of the twentieth century, involvement in the Garvey movement was part of the ordinary course of affairs.

It was commonplace to see politicians, preachers, and others honing their oratorical skills, propped up on street-corner soapboxes, and Garvey, who preached to the Black masses, was no different. My uncle Ambrose, as a youth growing up amidst it all and being guided by his Caribbean-born father, drank it all in.

Marcus Mosiah Garvey was a powerful Black man, and ultimately, he was punished severely for it—a punishment that down to this day has not been rectified. While still in Jamaica, Garvey declared, "I read *Up from Slavery* by Booker T. Washington and then my doom—if I may so call it—of being a race leader dawned upon me. I asked, where is the Black man's government? Where is his king and his kingdom? Where is his president, his country, and his ambassador, his army, his navy, his men of big affairs? I could not find them," he said, "and then I declared, I will help to make them."

One of Garvey's main vehicles for helping to achieve a political, economic, and military infrastructure was through the creation of the UNIA on August 1, 1914. The motto of the group was short but strong—"One God, One Aim, One Destiny." The UNIA had a robust communication arm, the *Negro World*, a publication Garvey initiated in January 1918. This newspaper quickly became a leading one and a very important vehicle for the promotion of his philosophy and opinions. At its height, the *Negro World* had a regular circulation of at least fifty thousand, with a national and international readership several times that number. Although I never saw an original copy, I can only presume that my granddaddy regularly read the publication back in the day, and I'm sure it likely spurred my uncle's love for the written word, making him a frequent visitor to New York's Schomburg Library throughout his life.

Each issue of the *Negro World* carried a lengthy front-page editorial from Marcus Garvey addressed to the Fellowmen of the Negro Race. The paper stressed pride in Black history and continuously uplifted the red, black, and green banner of the UNIA—the colors of the flag that eventually inspired flags around the world. Rather than run the advertisements of the day, which promoted Eurocentric toy brands, the paper encouraged the sale and production of Black dolls.

Indeed, the first large-scale production of a positive item Black children could identify with dates to this period during the 1920s. This was a revolutionary toy development in this country and was encouraged and marketed by the UNIA. A caption under a UNIA picture of a young Black child proudly carrying her Black doll read, "Little Thelma Miller, 8 years old, is very fond of her little colored doll. She is a real Garveyite." I wish I could tell you that one of those little Black dolls made it down to me as a little girl growing up in the 1950s, but alas, I can't. I can fantasize, however!

Garvey and the UNIA were also at the forefront for economic independence. In his collection of speeches, Garvey states, "A race that is solely dependent upon another for its economic existence sooner or later dies." Marcus Garvey urged his followers to patronize their own businesses and coined the expression "Buy Black." One of the businesses Garvey established was the Negro Factories Corporation, in 1919, which was capitalized at one million dollars. Offering stock to Blacks at $5 a share, the company planned to provide loans and executive or technical assistance to Blacks who needed help establishing their own small businesses. The UNIA established retail stores and provided services on a cooperative basis. The organization developed a chain of cooperative grocery stores, a restaurant, steam laundry, tailor and dressmaking shop, millinery store, and publishing house. In concert with UNIA values, my grandfather had a very successful carpentry business in

Harlem that people flocked to. My uncle continued the business, which included patronization by notables such as the Harlem Renaissance poet Langston Hughes.

During 1919 and 1920, the UNIA grew spectacularly as masses of Black people responded by the thousands, due to disillusionment with the empty promises of America. By 1919, enough money was raised to purchase a large auditorium, renamed Liberty Hall. Marcus Garvey started organizing in support of a fleet of Black-owned and Black-operated steamships that would link all African peoples and unite the Black diaspora. This fleet of ships was called the Black Star Line, whose purpose, he declared, was "to serve as a commercial and spiritual tie among Blacks wherever its ships traveled." The ships were for trade and travel as opposed to being used as a vehicle for mass emigration back to Africa, as many erroneously believed. And yes, family lore has it that my granddaddy had shares in the Black Star Line, although unfortunately I never was able to find a certificate.

Garvey's vision was not limited to the United States. In 1920, he called for the first international convention of the UNIA that included delegates representing all parts of the world. Several thousand Black delegates came from the then all forty-eight states and from more than a score of countries spanning three continents. I cannot say definitively that my granddaddy took my uncle to this historic 1920 international convention in Harlem, but it is a fact that amongst those in attendance were Vietnam's Ho Chi Minh, Ghana's Kwame Nkrumah, India's Mahatma Gandhi, the Reverend Earl Little (father of Malcolm X), and Elijah Muhammad—all of whom would draw upon the teachings of the Honorable Marcus Garvey from this convention in later years, fashioning struggles for victory around the world. Indisputably, all dots lead back to Garvey.

The huge parades galvanized by the UNIA included units of African Legionnaires, the military arm of the organization. Although unarmed, many had World War I experience and were skilled, and their presence made it plain that they believed in self-defense. Indeed, my proudest revelation concerning Garvey, discovered not too long ago, was the testimony from my elder cousin Lee, who often heard her mother say that our grandfather "was an officer in Marcus Garvey's army and that when they marched, he would march too!" I can even envision my uncle as a youth, propped on my grandfather's shoulders, gazing with pride at the thousands of Blacks who dotted the streets of Harlem during Garvey's spectacular parades.

Another uniformed regiment of the UNIA at the Harlem parades was the Black Cross Nurses. The existence of the Black Cross Nurses indicated the readiness of the UNIA to come to the aid of suffering people all over the world. My grandmother, being a midwife, was likely involved in the movement as a Black Cross Nurse. I've often wished that more family lore, even as recent as my grandparents' time, had been preserved for our family's future generations. The trauma as well as the glory, however, rests within our collective genes. And although personal recollections are scarce, there is no question that the spirit of the Garvey movement, infused with all its pomp and pageantry, succeeded in elevating the nearly crushed Black pride, esteem, and self-confidence of the era.

For instance, as mentioned earlier, Kwame Nkrumah participated in Garvey's international convention and went on, forty years later, to liberate Ghana. Mahatma Gandhi later developed his own movement in India. Ho Chi Minh subsequently rose to prominence in Vietnam. Elijah Muhammad and the Reverend Earl Little also attended the UNIA's 1920 international convention. Just a cursory glance at the discipline and order the UNIA generated and the discipline and order that is the hallmark of the Nation of Islam reveals similar roots. From the Reverend Earl Little and Elijah Muhammad sprang Malcolm X, and from Malcolm X sprouted many movements. Among them were the Black Panther Party for Self-Defense, the Provisional Government of the Republic of New Afrika, the New Afrikan Independence Movement, the National Black United Front, the Independent Black School movement, the Buy Black movement, and the Reparations movement, to name a few. Again, it is not too exaggerated to say, all dots lead back to Garvey.

Another ardent follower of Marcus Garvey later became known as Queen Mother Audley Moore. Born in 1898, she, too, participated in the UNIA's 1920 international convention in Harlem and was a catalyst in getting the issue of reparations included on the platforms of multitudes of organizations active during the twentieth century. Queen Mother Moore praises Marcus Garvey for raising her consciousness about Africa and the Caribbean. In her own words, "Garvey brought us a message the likes of which I'd never heard. He told us about the splendors of our ancient history and culture, of the great kings and queens that we had been. Of the riches of Africa, and of the kind of people that we were. And we were just enthrived to no end." Queen Mother Moore credits the Garvey movement with laying the groundwork for her life's work spreading the gospel about reparations.

On May 19, 2022, I testified before an Oversight Hearing on Clemency and the Office of the Pardon Attorney before the House of Representatives' Judiciary Committee. Clemency includes both commutation of sentences and pardons. Part of my testimony called for a posthumous pardon for Marcus Garvey. The general position of the Garvey family is that the grant of a pardon is insufficient and misplaced, that Marcus Garvey deserves to be completely exonerated. I totally agree with that perspective; however, there currently exists no mechanism for exoneration within the Office of the Pardon Attorney. As such, advocacy has advanced using the terms *pardon* and *exoneration* interchangeably. Today's UNIA has taken the position that the organization is "self-exonerating" Marcus Garvey. That stance is admirable, but the United States government should not be left off the hook. The government must be held accountable for its role.

I stated in my testimony that the quest for a posthumous pardon for Marcus Garvey has been a multi-decade effort, spanning several administrations, to right a wrong committed by the US government nearly a hundred years ago. I stated that, considering the politically motivated biases and prosecutorial misconduct at the root of Garvey's trial, his exoneration is warranted to rectify a gross miscarriage of justice that has persisted for far too long. The following represents excerpts from my congressional testimony:

> Marcus Mosiah Garvey was one of the most prominent leaders of the civil rights movement in the first half of the 20th century. In 1923, Mr. Garvey was wrongfully convicted in U.S. federal court on a bogus charge of using the mails in furtherance of a scheme to defraud and sentenced to five years in prison. The facts, however, demonstrate that Marcus Garvey was targeted because of his race and political beliefs, that he received an unfair trial, that he nonetheless made extraordinary contributions to the community and the civil rights movement, and that a full pardon is warranted to remedy this significant miscarriage of justice.

Marcus Garvey was not just a wrongfully convicted person. His unjust conviction involved racial and political motivations intended to stifle a growing movement among Black people that even today requires rectification and redress.

Mr. Garvey's vision of racial justice and anti-colonialism has been honored by governments around the world. The thirty-two member nations of the Organization of American States unanimously passed a resolution naming its Hall of Culture in his honor in 2008. Moreover, his native country, Jamaica, has designated him as its first National Hero, and his likeness appears on the nation's currency.

The modern organized effort to exonerate and restore Mr. Garvey's reputation has lasted for over thirty years. Dr. Julius Garvey and his late brother, Marcus Jr., testified before the House Judiciary Committee in 1987 alongside several historians and luminaries. The Honorable Charles Rangel, then chairman of the House Ways and Means Committee, annually cosponsored house resolutions for Mr. Garvey's exoneration.

While there is no question that pardons are most beneficial for those who are living, there are times when the granting of exceptional posthumous petitions are valuable and necessary to show that discredited values of the past are no longer the values of the present. Such is the case with Marcus Garvey. Although most of the posthumous pardons have been issued by governors on the state level (e.g., then Virginia governor Ralph Northam granted posthumous pardons in August 2021 to the Martinsville Seven, young Black men electrocuted seventy years ago for the purported rape of a white woman), there is precedent across party lines for posthumous pardons granted by the president.

In 1975, President Ford granted a posthumous pardon to Confederate General Robert E. Lee, restoring full citizenship rights removed because of his military leadership of the Southern succession.

In 2008, President Bush issued a posthumous pardon to Charles Winters, who served eighteen months for smuggling B-17 bombers to the state of Israel, in violation of the Neutrality Act of 1939.

In 1999, Lieutenant Henry O. Flipper received a posthumous pardon from President Clinton, 117 years after his dishonorable discharge from the military on specious charges. Flipper was the first African American graduate of West Point, and the first African American commissioned officer in the regular US Army. Although found not guilty during his court-martial for embezzlement of funds, he was nevertheless dishonorably discharged. Lieutenant Flipper's posthumous pardon gave a semblance of closure to the family, restored his good name and reputation, and removed yet another appalling stain from this country's system of justice.

For more than a hundred years, Jack Johnson's legend as the first Black heavyweight boxing champion has been undisputed, but his legacy had been tarnished by a 1913 racially tainted criminal conviction for transporting a white woman across state lines, in contravention to the Mann Act. Since his death in 1946, there had been advocacy for a posthumous pardon, which was granted by President Trump.

Posthumous pardons, though symbolic, serve to affirm this country's commitment to righting wrongs and ending injustice, regardless of when it occurred.

Marcus Garvey is an exceptional candidate for a posthumous pardon. International organizations, members of Congress, local governments, and countless civil society groups have mobilized in support of his exoneration. Congressional resolutions have been introduced in support of a presidential pardon. Monuments and landmarks have been dedicated to his memory. The Honorable Marcus Garvey has been designated as Jamaica's first National Hero; his image adorns Jamaican currency; and the Jamaica government has bestowed upon him the title of "Right Excellent."

My family connection to the legacy of Marcus Garvey is similar to the connections of countless Black people across the country and throughout the Pan-African world. Thus, it is not only fitting but also very personal to me that the name of the Honorable Right Excellent Marcus Garvey be cleared and his powerful legacy uplifted.

Nkechi Taifa, Esq. (preferred pronunciation: Neh KEE Chee Tah EE fah) is a civil and human rights attorney, scholar-activist, talk show host, and author. She is president of The Taifa Group LLC and serves as senior fellow for the Center of Justice at Columbia University and as a power, innovation and leadership graduate of Harvard Kennedy School. A visionary thought leader and nationally recognized expert and commentator on race and justice issues, Taifa is convener emeritus of the Justice Roundtable Coalition and served as commissioner and chair of the DC Commission on Human Rights. She has worked for the Open Society Foundations, Howard University School of Law, the American Civil Liberties Union, Women's Legal Defense Fund, and National Prison

Project and as an attorney in private practice. She has testified before the United States Congress, the Inter-American Commission on Human Rights, the US Helsinki Commission, the DC City Council, the Maryland Legislature, and the California Reparations Task Force.

Nkechi is founder and executive director of the Reparation Education Project, Inc., an inaugural commissioner on the National African American Reparations Commission, and a founder of the National Coalition of Blacks for Reparations in America. She delivered a powerful TEDx talk, "Reparations, An Issue Whose Time Has Come." A native Washingtonian, Nkechi is the author of the best-selling memoir *Black Power, Black Lawyer: My Audacious Quest for*

Justice and the author of several books for children. Her most recent book, *Reparations on Fire: How and Why it's Spreading Across America*, has been described as "part historical analysis, part revolutionary manifesto, and part political red-alert."

In addition to her five published books, Nkechi Taifa is the author of scores of scholarly works, including law review articles, book chapters, and white papers. She has been featured in major print and electronic media and has received numerous honors and awards for her work, including *ESSENCE* magazine's WOKE 100 Black Women Advocating for Change.

For the complete Nkechi Taifa experience, visit www.NkechiTaifa.com.

CHAPTER FOUR

Wading in the Great River Garvey

Karl B. Rodney, Publisher, *Carib News*

> The ends that you serve that are selfish will take you no further than
> yourself but the ends you serve that are for all in common will take
> you into eternity.
>
> —Marcus Garvey

THE GARVEY PHILOSOPHY, the Garvey drive, and the Garvey prophecy are like a great river that flows through the continents of the world, flooding us with a philosophy, a set of values, a way of thinking and living that changes the lives of Black people wherever we are. For some, we have just dipped our feet into this water; for others, we have waded knee-deep into this great river, absorbing all the teachings of this great prophet and putting them into practice in the way we conduct our lives.

The concept of the river came to me through a discussion I had with the great entertainer, humanist, and civil rights icon Harry Belafonte, who talked about the source of the Nile River in Africa. The source, Jaloba, and what flows from that source is the history of humankind. And it's developed throughout the world, and that source feeding the Nile has also fed great rivers around the world with respect to civilization: the Mississippi, the Amazon, and even the rivers and gullies in the Caribbean. And so it is for Marcus Garvey, who floods many shores around the world, impacting so many lives unnumbered and unnamed and delivering the great message everywhere, no matter the boulders and other diversions along the riverside.

The river keeps flowing. Garvey's teaching and philosophy continue to flow abundantly. The entire world benefits from the Garvey river. My connection with the Garvey movement and the Garvey philosophy continuously brings increased awareness and consciousness. I have come to the Garvey philosophy and prophecy in many ways, but meeting and working with his sons—through the personal and professional connection with the Garvey sons, Marcus Jr. and Julius, over the many decades—was what riveted it for me. They were so aligned to the message, so dedicated and focused, that I not only admired them but also was drawn to work with them. Marcus Jr. and his wife Jean were close friends with my wife, Faye, and me. We traveled to Africa together and worked with them in his effort with the Universal Negro Improvement Association (UNIA), even printing the paper for a period of time. Julius, with a distinguished medical career, stuck to his father's mission. Both sons were brilliant in their own right. I have known a lot of children of famous people, and these two men were disciplined, dedicated, and dignified in their pursuit of their father's mission.

Jamaica

In my early years in Jamaica, I was vaguely exposed to Garvey as a child. Garvey was spoken of in the household and spoken of knowingly because the Garvey headquarters in Jamaica was on Stipe Road, in Kingston and St. Andrew, which was known as the corporate area, and that is where my family lived. The Garvey UNIA headquarters was located at Elderwese Park. As a result of this proximity, my family members were in relatively frequent contact with members of the Garvey association. I was told by one of my older siblings that my grandfather, George Rodney, owned stock in Garvey's Black Star Line and was a strong supporter of the Garvey movement, particularly around the effort to generate trading partnerships among the Black people of Africa, the Caribbean, and America.

My older sister, Hazel Rodney-Blackman, a well-known fashion designer in the New York area, was also a very talented painter and quilter. She was a pioneer in showcasing African fabric, African arts, and African design and had two boutiques that specialized in African wear, so her consciousness of us coming together with Africa, the diaspora, and Africa collaboration that Garvey represented and so diligently pursued was part of her own drive and commitment. In the 1960s, she led a group of quilters who developed a quilt that depicted Garvey and the Ethiopian emperor Haile Selassie with a backdrop of the Black Star Line ships.

Professor Rex Nettleford, vice-chancellor of the University of the West Indies, on one of his visits to New York, saw the quilt and was moved by it and suggested to my sister that it would be a good idea to donate this quilt to the newly renovated Liberty Hall in Kingston, Jamaica. Working with the director at the time, Elaine Melbourne, the quilt was shipped to Jamaica and currently hangs in Liberty Hall, a legacy of Garvey, Haile Selassie, and the dream of the Black Star Line.

My older siblings were quite familiar with the Garvey presence, and after I migrated to New York, I was further exposed to the writings of Garvey and to the awareness of Garvey's philosophy in the Black community. In the Black world, you couldn't help but be drawn to it. Scholars like John Henrik Clarke were well known on the lecture circuit for talking about the power of Garvey.

Jamaica Progressive League

As I left college and started in the corporate world, the Garvey message reached me again in 1970 when I became involved with the Jamaica Progressive League (JPL). An organization formed in 1936 by Black American and Jamaican scholars, its primary mission was to develop political awareness and create a political movement for independence in Jamaica and in the Caribbean countries. W. A. Domingo, one of the founders of the JPL, was also the founding editor for the Garvey newspaper, the *Negro World*. Domingo and Marcus Garvey were close in their philosophy and in their drive to build awareness within the Black community. When I took leadership of the JPL in 1972, we embarked on a significant project in New York City to establish a Jamaica House where the offices and organizations of Jamaica and other Caribbean countries could be housed and where services could be provided for the growing Jamaican immigrant group. Our plan was to put a stake in the ground to develop an economic center, a cultural center, that Jamaicans, Caribbean folks, and African Americans would have as a gathering place, and that we would own, manage, and maintain. We had the audacity to establish this Jamaica House on West Fifty-Seventh Street between Fifth and Sixth Avenues in what is called the Tiffany/Carnegie Hall District—at one end the famed Tiffany store and at the other the famed concert hall, right in the heart of Manhattan. Jamaica House was established, and the fourteen-story building had to be tenanted. You can well imagine the emerging wrath of the white tenants and the ensuing saga of the ten-year battle against racism that poured from every imaginable angle, as we managed this major commercial property in the heart of New York City. Our version of Garvey's struggles.

Carib News

In 1982, I left corporate America and the JPL to establish *Carib News*, a weekly newspaper looking at the Caribbean American community in a way that connected this growing community with the larger Black community.

The power and the significance of Garvey's publication the *Negro World* and how it informed and inspired Black communities inspired me on this publishing mission. Garvey's the *Negro World* was one of the largest circulated and most influential publications of its time and became known as a guide to the Harlem Renaissance and the thinking of Blacks.

Launching *Carib News* brought me in alignment with the Garvey movement and with Solomon Goodridge, who was also a journalist and who joined in this effort to bring the kinds of news and information of significance to a growing community. Goodridge became a contributing editor to *Carib News*. Goodridge's involvement in the Garvey

organization was deep and that was brought to bear at *Carib News*. I
was getting deep in the Garvey river—foot, knee, and torso. The motto
of a Garvey exhortation: "Free your mind from mental slavery" was the
basis of the motto we embraced at *Carib News*: "Free Your Mind, Read
Carib News."

I was now reading more of Garvey, collecting Garvey's books,
listening to Garvey lectures, coming to fully appreciate the value of
this prophet and what he meant. I met Ken Jones, a journalist serving as
information officer in the Jamaica New York Consulate General Office.
A Garvey scholar, Ken was instrumental in providing a grounding for
activities and discussions that amplified the Garvey philosophy and
made it accessible to the general public.

Ken's book *Marcus Garvey Said*, which *Carib News* helped to
produce and publish, featured a collection of Garvey quotes that was
widely circulated among the community. Ken Jones was the conduit that
led me to Harlem stalwart, enduring legislator, and former congressman
Charles Rangel.

Charles Rangel Introduced Legislation to Exonerate Garvey

The former congressman took the issue of Garvey's exoneration as a
serious matter and one worthy of consideration in the US Congress.
Year after year, Rangel appealed in Congress, introducing legislation
around the exoneration of Garvey. It became his passion. *Carib News*
became a partner in that effort, constantly quoted and placed in the
Congressional Record. For eighteen years, former congressman Rangel
introduced legislation for Garvey's pardon and exoneration.

Gil Noble Advocated for Garvey on TV

Another pivotal connection that served as a catalyst through the years
with respect to the Garvey movement was Gil Noble, the TV journalist,
commentator, and activist known for his *Like It Is*, airing on Sunday

afternoons on WABC-TV in New York. Gil, born in Jamaica, had a particular interest in reconnecting to the home he had left at an early age. As president of the JPL, I was able to facilitate that connection with Gil Noble and Jamaica and with Michael Manley and Gil, who turned out to be one of the strongest advocates for Garvey, as Sunday after Sunday, in his typically tenacious and deliberate fashion, he would advocate, expose, and amplify all aspects of the Garvey mission.

Connecting with Garvey through Art

The New York artist Leonard Morris painted a portrait of Marcus Garvey and his wife Amy Jacques Garvey in the early 1980s that is a wonderful, full-size portrait of a renowned couple. This portrait of Marcus and Amy Jacques Garvey was the centerpiece of an exhibition. Of course, it was well, well executed and, of course, quite expensive also. At the end of the exhibition, Leonard Morris came to my wife, Faye Rodney, and offered us the privilege of housing this portrait of the Garveys as a complement to us. We were very touched and so, of course, accepted the offer. For years, this beautiful portrait of Marcus and Amy Jacques Garvey hung in prominence at our home. We lived with the portrait for years. It was a pleasure, privilege, and inspiration to have it in our home to share with our family and friends.

Like Garvey, We Become a Target

In 1995, we conceived and executed the Caribbean MultiNational Business Conference, inaugurated in Jamaica to bring together businesspersons, civic leaders, cultural icons, and elected officials from the Caribbean, Africa, and the United States to contemplate our common international values and to work directly together. We sustained the Caribbean Multi-National Business Conference for twentyseven years. We were indeed deep in the river Garvey.

It is no surprise that we and the conference attracted unwanted attention from naysayers and outright spies. Radio programs carried many of the sessions live. BET carried taped sessions for a while. Sessions were open. But the National Legal Policy Council (NLPC), an outgrowth of the John Birch Society and funded by dark-money billionaire funders, decided this coming together of Black folks was objectionable. This right-wing group targeted Jesse Jackson, Al Sharpton, Rep. Maxine Waters, former representative Charles Rangel, the National Action Network (NAN), the Association of Community Organization for Reform Now (ACORN), Planned Parenthood, and other groups.

We sought the counsel of Harry Belafonte, a long-time supporter and participant in the conference. As a seasoned civil rights activist who has been at the front lines of similar attacks and charges, he was always supportive of our efforts, not only lending his name to the conference but also graciously hosting us in his private villa in St. Martin. He said: "Tell me all about this investigation." After we did, his response was: "You came to America; you went to college and got a degree; you worked in corporate America; you raised your children to be responsible citizens; you and your wife started a small business. And this is your reward—you are being investigated by a corrupt government. Welcome to America." Then he detailed to us what the FBI does. They destroy organizations; they destroy individuals. Indeed, they tried to destroy him, Dr. Martin Luther King Jr., the entire Civil Rights Movement, and of course Marcus Garvey.

Belafonte made it real for us that the effort we had joined for exoneration and pardon for Garvey made us the targets—even when a Black president and a Black attorney general were at the helm of the leadership of this country. Belafonte said: "This is what they do. Even when you have a black president, this is what they do, and this is how they have destroyed us. This is America." Belafonte made it clear, and it came home to me, tears in my eyes, the forces we were up against. This is America.

At that moment in Harry Belafonte's home, I came to understand what we are facing as a people, the importance of Garvey, and the importance of achieving the exoneration. We left Mr. Belafonte's home with a different perspective on what Marcus Garvey experienced and what he means to us and so many others. We, too, face decades later what Garvey faced. Three long, weary, destructive years and the Ethics Committee could find nothing the Caribbean Multi-National Business Conference did wrong—a box they claim was checked and that was done on the advice of the Ethics Committee. They did not care for the truth; they just wanted to destroy. The Garvey exoneration became personal; it was no longer abstract. It was not history; it became an experience.

Exoneration Is Only a Stream in the River of Garvey

We accelerated our efforts. We recommitted ourselves to the effort to push for Garvey's exoneration. The mighty river Garvey will overcome. It gets stronger and stronger as it builds. Its momentum reaches out to its people. No FBI, no political leaders can stop the flow of that river. In this latest drive we, at *Carib News*, are driven to bring exoneration to this great man. We conduct seminars, we hold conference sessions, we have special Zoom meetings, we carry editorials, we carry front-page stories, we carry digital stories, and we are laser-focused—from presidential action to action within the federal legal system. No stones will be left unturned. We will continue the fight because the fight for Garvey is a fight for ourselves, survival, destiny.

The constant battle for pardon and exoneration of Garvey, the need to clear his name, must be pursued aggressively. The racism of the American judicial system gives it no credibility. The effort was, yes, to destroy Garvey but more to destroy the implementation of the Garvey business and economic model, to drive the Black Star Line out of business, to block Black people who acted to determine their own destiny, and to prevent the awakening of Africa and the Caribbean, all part of the Garvey dream. This was what the authorities were afraid of. This was their motivation for pressing charges against Marcus Garvey.

Every legal scholar will point to the unsubstantiated charge and the lack of any legal basis for charges. Yes, we need to marshal our resources in fighting for exoneration, but we must also fight for reparations for the Garvey family, the Garvey organization, and the Garvey investors that the United States of America treated so dastardly. We must seek redress in the courts. Part of that redress should be a civil suit against the United States of America for the destruction of the properties of the shareholders of the Black Star Line, the UNIA, and the rights of families of Garvey to the riches that would have been acquired through the enterprise. We need to rectify the Garvey economic model, not just Garvey's wrongful conviction.

This implementation will need the support of academic institutions and business organizations around the world. Together we can restore Black people to the path that Garvey had created. That path is one of economic empowerment and unity. This mighty river of Garvey will get over the reparation barriers. If pursued, Garvey's dream can be realized. People of color around the world must come together to see his vision realized.

What is needed now is a full baptism in the Garvey river. Every major learning institution should have a Marcus Garvey studies and in the business schools, a Garvey business module. Private equity funds can be developed through existing financial mechanisms and institutions to realize the Garvey vision. The movement forward now is to make the investment. The several billionaires of color can come together to be a part of the Garvey economic model and make the investment engine that will drive us. The mighty Garvey river keeps flowing stronger and stronger. And if the Garvey movement vision is unleashed and flows downstream, it will refresh, reinvigorate, and restore. We can then truly look to see Garvey in the "whirlwind" on the banks of the great river.

Karl B. Rodney and **Faye A. Rodney** founded the New York *Carib News* forty-two years ago to fill a recognized void in communication of the growing Caribbean American community. *Carib News* was designed to provide consistent, timely, accurate, and reliable information on the Caribbean region and the Caribbean American communities in the United States. It has since grown into the largest circulated publication serving the Caribbean American community. The mission of *Carib News* is to provide a medium for dialogue and information that would serve as a bridge to the larger community, assist in the assimilation process, and to promote values and contribution of the community.

Because of the pioneering efforts of Karl and Faye Rodney, *Carib News* is now a recognized institution of the community, playing a significant role in projecting the importance and potential of the community.

Carib News has become the publication of record for the Caribbean American community, hosting several prime ministers, presidents, governors, mayors, members of Congress, and other elected and civic leaders at editorial board meetings exploring issues of interest to the community and the region. As founder and sponsor of the Annual Multi-National Business Conference in the Caribbean, *Carib News*, for the past twenty-eight years, has hosted the most successful business conference, bringing together African American entrepreneurs, elected officials, and civic leaders to explore opportunities of business, health, education, and information in the Caribbean and between our American friends. Both the political and economic impact of the community have been enhanced and regional issues of consequence addressed through the efforts of the Rodneys.

Carib News's community outreach program goes the full extent, from celebrating mothers in a unique program for the past forty years to organizing the Caribbean Expo at Lincoln Center in New York, which presents the culture and business of the Caribbean in a positive light in the Americas. *Carib News* founded the now famous breakfast before the New York Labor Day Parade and the corporate luncheon during the parade, which bring corporate sponsorship and political clout to the parade. Other outreach programs include information seminars on various issues, sports awards, and cultural enrichment, all organized through the Carib News Foundation, a not-for-profit 501(c)(3) entity.

Prior to the founding of *Carib News*, Karl Rodney served as a senior corporate executive at Equitable Life Assurance Society in their Systems Development Department, responsible for several major national computer conversion projects, rising to the position of senior division manager over an eighteen-year career.

Karl Rodney also served in a volunteer role as president of the Jamaica Progressive League for ten years, the longest-running Caribbean American organization in the US, founded in 1936. The league was instrumental in advising the independence of Caribbean countries.

During Karl Rodney's tenure as president, the league acquired a fourteen-story commerce building on Fifty-Seventh Street between Fifth and Sixth Avenues in New York as its headquarters, the first and only Black organization or company to own commercial property in the downtown of any major US city.

Karl B. Rodney, publisher and CEO, is active in several organizations. Some are:

- The New York United Way—Board Member, Member Governance Committee
- The United Way International—Board Member, Member Resource Committee
- American Foundation for the University of the West Indies—Chairman
- The New York City Partnership—Past Board Member
- Caribbean Tourism Organization Foundation—Chairman
- The New York Urban League—Past Board Member
- The New York Sport Foundation—Past Board Member
- Brooklyn Center for the Performing Arts at Brooklyn College—Vice President
- Caribbean American Chamber of Commerce & Industry—Founding Member
- Black Equity Alliance—Vice Chair/Founding Member
- New York Police Foundation—Past Board Member
- National Association of Black Publishers—Regional President
- Caribbean American Chamber of Commerce—Founding Member
- Martin Luther King Living & Dream Foundation—Board Member
- The Greater Harlem Chamber of Commerce—Board Member, Executive Committee
- Sigma Pi Phi Fraternity—Member, Beta Zeta Boulé

A magna cum laude graduate of Hunter College City University of New York in economics, he completed the coursework toward an MA degree from the same institution. He has completed several professional-level courses in economics and finance management.

He has received an honorary doctorate from the University of the West Indies and the City University of New York, Medgar Evers College, and has been awarded the Jamaican government's Order of Distinction, Commander Class.

CHAPTER FIVE

The *Vindication* of Marcus Garvey

Maulana Karenga, PhD

> Long before many of us were even conscious of our own degradation, Marcus Garvey fought for African national and racial equality. I think that of all the literature I studied, the book that did more than any other to fire my enthusiasm was *The Philosophy and Opinions of Marcus Garvey*, published by his wife.
>
> —Kwame Nkrumah

IN SPITE OF the empire's and oppressors' propaganda and suppressive acts against him, Marcus Garvey weighs heavy in the scales of history and stands tall as a model, mirror, and monument to us and humankind. As I have noted, "*Kawaida*" contends in this regard that one of the greatest powers in the world is the ability to define reality and cause others to accept it. Also, our oppressor cannot be our teacher, for as Malcolm taught, the logic of the oppressed cannot be the logic of the oppressor if they want liberation. Therefore, in spite of the oppressor's constant pernicious propaganda, Garvey's awesome and enduring record is etched in the stone and steel of uncompromising struggle for liberation of his people in the interest of African and human good.

To talk of exoneration for Marcus Garvey, then, is not simply a legal matter but more correctly a larger ethical and human rights one, a matter of freedom, justice, and the righteous and victorious liberation struggle of a people, the world community of African people. The term *exoneration* does not capture or contain the expansive and complex character of the issue and our needed response to it. It is more appropriate and fruitful to talk in a larger and an expansive sense of the *vindication* of Marcus Garvey in various truthful and worth-affirming ways, rather than simply of his legal exoneration. The legal initiative is only a part of the struggle, even though it is an important part. The larger struggle is to vindicate the continuing value of his life's work and struggle; that of his copartner, Amy Jacques Garvey; and that of all their co-combatants in the struggle to liberate, redeem, and raise up Africa as a force for good in the world. It is to vindicate, prove right and worthy, his faith in his people and in the righteous victory of his cause. To vindicate his work, struggle, and faith is to honor his legacy of liberative good in the world by emulating it, living it, and advancing it.

Marcus Garvey remains present and powerful in the hearts, minds, and liberation movements of his people, who are the whirlwind and storm in and through which he prophesied and promised to return.

Struggle for Garvey Exoneration Vindicates the Global Africans

The global struggle to legally exonerate the Honorable Marcus Garvey must be seen and engaged in at the same time as a struggle to vindicate the world African community. This is especially true in a context of systemic racism where crime is racialized and whole races are criminalized, especially the Black race, African peoples. We do not escape this blanket racialized and racist indictment and ongoing threat of targeting, mass incarceration, and termination. The violence of systemic racism continuously and menacingly hangs over our heads, not only in our political work and struggle for liberation but also in our daily lives as we walk down the street; drive or sit in our cars; study in our educational institutions; work at our places of employment and business; pray in our churches, mosques or temples; play in the park; and rest or sleep in our homes. This injustice committed against Garvey is not only committed against him, but it is also a shared injustice committed against us, the world African community. For justice, like freedom, for us, is indivisible. Anywhere and anytime any African is denied their rights and due respect, all of us are somehow denied and injured. As Sekou

Toure (1959) explained, "We are aware that as long as the whole of Africa is not liberated, Guinea will not feel safe." For African freedom and security are indivisible, inseparably linked. And thus, he argues that the pain and suffering of unfreedom and insecurity of African persons and people are shared. It is, he says, as if a person has a cut finger: "The finger itself does not feel the pain alone, it is the whole body of that person that registers it." Therefore, each and all of us feel the pain of this injustice and all similar violations of African human rights and human dignity; we suffer because of them and seek to overcome and end them.

The global struggle to legally exonerate Garvey from these false charges and this wrongful conviction is to resist racist uses of the law to criminalize and suppress rightful resistance. Garvey was a Pan-Africanist liberator and leader, a teacher, a global organizer of the largest number of Black people in history, an institution builder, a journalist and writer, and a speaker of liberating and uplifting truth. His central message and mission was African redemption, African self-determination, and African liberation and upliftment from unfreedom and oppression. His battle cry was, "Up you mighty race. You can accomplish what you will." He stressed education and organization of the masses of our people in self-reliant, self-authorizing, and cooperative projects and practices. For him, African liberational redemption was a collective project and practice in which all Africans should participate.

Garvey's project is important not only for African self-formation and redemption but also to human freedom. Garvey (1967, 1:54) said that members of the Universal Negro Improvement Association (UNIA) "have decided that we shall go forward, upward and onward toward the great goal of human liberty" and "to lift ourselves and to demand respect of all humanity." Thus, "we declare to the world Africa must be free, that the entire [Black] race must be emancipated from industrial bondage, peonage and serfdom." Linking this inclusive libera-tion to the larger struggle for human freedom, Garvey asserts, "We have a program we believe to be righteous; we believe it to be just. And we have made up our minds to lay ourselves down on the altar of sacrifice for the realization this great hope of ours, based upon the foundation of righteousness." And therefore, "we make no compromise, we make no apology in this our declaration."

Teaching against vulgar individualism and self-seeking at the expense of the people, Garvey (1967, 1:2) said, "The ends you serve that are selfish will take you no further than yourself, but the ends you serve that are for all in common, will take you into eternity." Thus, the call is for *ujima*, collective work and responsibility in building the good communities, societies, and world we all want and deserve to live in and leave for future generations. Such a liberative, redemptive, dignity-affirming, and life-enhancing message—messenger and mission should not be criminalized and suppressed. We are morally obligated to engage in righteous and relentless resistance to this and, in addition, to join in and wage the struggle to legally exonerate Marcus Garvey.

Our effort is to seize the pen of history and rescue African history from the falsification imposed on it by colonialists, imperialists, racists, genocidists, and other oppressors. It is to set the record straight, correct the distortions and falsifications they thrive on. Our oppressors thrive on a falsification of history that indicts the oppressed and exonerates the oppressors. As Malcolm taught, the oppressor, through manipulation and falsification of history and current events, as well as through various media "can make the criminal look like he's the victim and make the victim look like he's the criminal." We must, then, through righteous and relentless struggle, seize the pen of history, lived and written history, and rewrite truthfully in word and struggle the real history of our people and leaders and humanity as a whole. Thus, we set the record straight. In this new history, struggled for, rewritten, and achieved, not only will Marcus Garvey, our other leaders, and our people be legally exonerated and vindicated in real and relevant ways, but so will the whole of humanity. It is what Cheikh Anta Diop (1991) calls reconciling African civilizations and history with human history, ending "the deliberate falsification of the history of humanity" as a whole.

In a letter from an Atlanta prison during his political imprison-ment, Garvey (1967, 2:324) calls on us to continue the struggle, to be "co-workers in the cause of African Redemption" and to not lose hope, be dispirited, or diverted from the struggle. He says that even if it seems our oppressors and the enemies of human freedom "have seemingly triumphed for a while," we must continue the struggle, for "the final battle when staged will bring us complete success and satis-faction." Thus, he concludes his letter from Atlanta urging us to, "Hold fast to the faith. Desert not the ranks. But as brave soldiers march on to victory" through righteous and relentless struggle (327). For he says a redeemed and liberated Africa has a vital role to play in reconceiving and rebuilding the world. Africa will pose, he asserts, a new "way to life and peace, achieved not by ignoring the rights of our brother [and sister] but by giving to everyone [their] due." Indeed, "the hand of justice, freedom and liberty shall be extended to all [hu]mankind" (54)

Whirlwind and Storm Are Part of the Struggle for Reparations and Liberation

The global struggle for the exoneration of the Honorable Marcus Garvey must be understood and pursued as part and parcel of our overall strug-gle for reparations and liberation. Garvey's concept of African redemp-tion can be understood as a reparative and uplifting liberation. This calls for a reparative justice for great and grievous injury—the holocaust of enslavement, the savagery of segregation, and continuing systemic racism.

Garvey (1967, 1:17) notes that people who are endeavoring to get freedom are, of necessity, radical. For "they cannot be anything else because they are revolting against the conditions that exist." He continues arguing that "conditions as they exist reveal a conservative state, and if you desire to change these conditions, you must be a radical. I am therefore satisfied to be the same kind of radical, if through radi-calism I can free Africa." And one of his most illustrious students, Malcolm X, reaffirms this teaching, saying that "I know of no group that is promising unless it's radical. If it's not radical it is in no way involved effectively in the present struggle."

Anticipating Frantz Fanon's (1968) concept of Europe as a civilization against itself, "swaying between atomic and spiritual disintegration," Garvey poses a similar critique of the current world powers and again stresses our critical role in a massive world transformation in the interests of ourselves and all humankind. He says:

> We are circumvented today by environments more dangerous than those which circumvented other peoples in any other age. We are face to face with environments in a civilization that is highly developed, a civilization that is competing with itself for its own destruction; a civilization that cannot last because it has no spiritual foundation, a civilization that is vicious, crafty, dishonest, immoral, irreligious and corrupt. (Garvey 1967, 1:25)

In a word, it will fall from its own internal contradictions, from the weight of its own unworthiness, imploding from its failure to respect the rights, dignity, and interests of all involved and build social systems that serve the common and greater good.

But he knows there is also a need for righteous and relentless struggle to bring this global system of oppression to an urgently needed end. Thus, Garvey states that "the masses of the human race on the other hand [are] dissatisfied and discontented" with the current "arrangement of human society" (1967, 1:25). Indeed, humanity as a whole "is universally disturbed because of the injustices inflicted upon the masses by the dominant powers" and "determined to destroy the systems that hold up such a society and prop up such a civilization." At this critical juncture of conflict and radical social change, Africans "are called upon to play their part," wage righteous struggle, and "evolve a national ideal, based on freedom, human liberty and true democracy."

He finds common ground with Mary McLoed Bethune (2008, 124) who teaches us that "our task is to remake the world. It is nothing less than that."

But for African peoples to play this vanguard world-transforming role, united in struggle with other oppressed, struggling, and progressive people, we must, he teaches, continue to build and strengthen ourselves and our capacity for victorious struggle. Thus, Garvey tells us that as self-determining Africans and human beings, we must put aside illusions, break through the mystifications of established order propaganda and cultural hegemony, and dare to remake ourselves and our world. He (1967, 1:1) states, "CHANCE has never yet satisfied the hope of a suffering people. Action, self-reliance, the vision of self and the future have been the only means by which the oppressed have seen and realized the light of their own freedom." Indeed, we are to resist our oppression on all levels and every site and undo through struggle all the damage it does to us, healing ourselves, raising ourselves, and renewing our lives in and for ourselves and our community, and struggle mightily for the good of the world and all in it. And this means thinking freely, reconceiving and reconstructing a new society and world, and struggling audaciously and victoriously to bring them into being. As Garvey (1967, 2:126) said, sharing his vision: "I saw before me, then, as I do now, a new world of Black people . . . , a nation of sturdy people, making their imprint on civilization and causing a new light to dawn on the human race."

This requires that we truly know ourselves in expansive ways, love each other and our people, and struggle boldly and tirelessly for African liberation. Garvey calls on us to deepen our love for our people and each other. He tells us that "the time has come for those of us who have the vision of the future to inspire our people to a closer kinship, to a closer love of self, because it is through this appreciation of self that we will be able to rise to that higher life" and unite "into one mighty bond so that we can successfully pilot our way through the avenues of opposition and the oceans of difficulties that seem to confront us" and achieve freedom, justice, peace, security and other goods of life (1967, 1:47). This stress on love and respect for the people and a profound belief in them and their capacity to free themselves and build good and meaningful lives is reaffirmed in the teachings of one of his contemporary freedom fighters and educators, Dr. Mary Mcleod Bethune. It is one of her fundamental teachings that "the measure of our progress as a race is in precise relation to the depth of the faith in our people held by our leaders" (Bethune 2008).

Molefi Asante recognizes and respects Garvey as a philosophical forerunner to his Afrocentric initiative, which stresses agency, victorious self-assertion in the world. In his seminal work introducing his theory of Afrocentricity, Asante praises Garvey as an intellectual inspiration for his own work and describes his philosophy as a "brilliant ideology of liberation in the first half of the 20th century." In fact, he says, "In no nation in the world was there a philosophical treatment of oppressed people any more creative than Garveyism." He concludes his analysis of Garvey's thought by posing it as a contribution and precursor to his own, saying, "His vision foreshadowed the Afrocentric road to self-respect and dignity."

In his stress on African and human agency, Garvey (1967, 1:55) wants us to practice a radical self-determination and tells and teaches us that "we must realize that upon ourselves depend our destiny, our future and we must carve out of that future, that destiny." And he also teaches us that our liberation will come "not from the will of others to see us rise, but from our own determination to rise, irrespective of what the world thinks" (31).

This is not to deny the need for cooperative relations of mutual respect and mutual benefit but to stress that we are essentially and ultimately our own liberators. Therefore, he calls for initiative, originality, creativity, and self-determination in all things. He says, "The race needs workers at this time, not plagiarists, copyists and mere imitators; but men and women who are able to create, to originate and improve, and to make an independent racial contribution to the world and civilization" (Garvey 1967, 1:24). Indeed, Nana Garvey (1967, 1:23) says, "The reliance of our race upon the progress and achievement of others, [or] for a consideration in sympathy, justice and rights is like a dependence upon a broken stick, resting upon which will eventually consign you to the ground." Thus, self-determination and self-reliance must be practiced "not only in one essential, but in all those things that contribute to human happiness and well-being."

Garvey (1967, 2:12), recognizing that liberation is a political practice as well as the freeing of mind and spirit, argued that strength through knowledge, organization, and unity is key to achieving justice, liberation, and respect among the peoples of the world. He stated that "if we must have justice, we must be strong; if we must be strong, we must come together; if we must come together, we can only do this through the system of organization." Furthermore, he said, "Point to me a weak nation and I will show you a people oppressed, abused, taken advantage of by others. Show me a weak race and I will show you a people reduced to serfdom, peonage and slavery." But "show me a well-organized nation and I will show you a people and a nation respected by the world" (Garvey 1967, 2:12–13).

Amy Jacques Garvey

It is important to emphasize here the commitment of Amy Jacques Garvey (2016, 1963), Marcus Garvey's wife and co-combatant in the struggle, to creating and expanding space for the women of the movement to live their lives, do their work, and wage the liberation struggle in what she calls "copartnership" with men based on mutual respect, equality, and interdependence. Reading the signs and requirements of the times as interpreter, teacher, frontline leader, and soldier, she spoke of the critical coming into consciousness and active commitment of African women, Black women, in the struggle, saying, "The wide-awake woman is forging ahead prepared for all emergencies, and ready to answer any call, even if it be to face the cannons on the battlefield."

Recognizing and severely criticizing sexism and pointing out the Black woman's extreme and ongoing suffering from various structures and practices of oppression, external and eternal, she notes the strength in struggle and unbreakable courage under fire of Black women, asking, "Who is more deserving of admiration than the Black woman, she who has borne the rigors of slavery, the deprivations consequent on a pauperized race, and the indignities heaped upon a weak and defenseless people?" In spite of this, she states, "She has suffered all with fortitude, and stands ever ready to help in the onward march to freedom and power." And she urges African women to always self-consciously present themselves as "intelligent. Independent human beings [able] to assert and maintain their rights in co-partnership with their men," demonstrating they "are great thinkers as well as doers" (111).

Amy Jacques Garvey (2016, 251–52) reasoned and taught that "the exigencies of this present age require that women take their places beside their men" and made an essential and important contribution not only to Garveyism but also to womanist, Black radical nationalist, anti-colonialist, and anti-imperialist thought and discourse. In her writings during her husband's political imprisonment, she urged members of the UNIA to continue the struggle, keep the faith, and continue the work necessary to carry on "the grand noble task of [Black] uplift and the redemption of Africa" (153–61). Linking service to humanity with service to one's people, she calls for service and sacrifice as central practices in the redemption and liberation of Africa. She says in one of her lectures,

> the call of service to humanity, and particularly to one's race means sacrifice and the men and women who are not prepared for sacrifice had better not shoulder the thing called service to the race. We at this time must be prepared to give our all to this organization. If we are not prepared for such service and such sacrifices, we cannot hope to get anywhere. It is not merely a matter of attending meetings, or paying dues to the organization, but it is question of giving one's whole life to the cause. (198)

Moreover, she continuously holds Marcus Garvey as a model of service and sacrifice that all should emulate. She says,

> Take a leaf from Garvey who could be free today living in luxury if for one moment he would have agreed to surrender

his principles, to retract and go back upon his word, to cease active service to his race. But Marcus Garvey is not a man that can be bought, and I have made up my mind to go the whole way with Marcus Garvey. And what Marcus Garvey can do for his race you also can do. If you die, serving your race, you have died well, but if you die serving another race, you have died pretty low. (201–02)

She is a leader and teacher in her own right and again embodies the spirit and aspirations of her copartner in love and struggle, Marcus Garvey, in all she does to achieve the redemption and liberation of Africa. Garvey praised her for her great sacrifice and extensive service and asked during his political imprisonment that she be provided for and protected and given "the consideration that is due a faithful and devoted wife who gave up her husband for the cause of human service." For indeed, "she has suffered and sacrificed with me for you" and for the redemption and liberation of Africa and its people throughout the world African community (238).

Reading of Garvey's attitude in the context of the US government's political imprisonment of him and the intention to crush the movement, one witnesses his deep-rooted resolve, his audacious defiance, and his steadfast faith in our people. In his first letter in captivity, he says, "I am delighted to inform you that your humble servant is as happy in suffering for you and our cause, as is possible in the circumstances" (Garvey 1967, 2:257). In the second letter, he greets his "co-workers in the cause of African Redemption," saying, "It is with feeling(s) of deep love and thoughts of a great future for the [Black] race that I address you" (324). And he assured them that months of political imprisonment, "being imprisoned as a punishment for advocating the cause of our real emancipation, have not left me hopeless or despondent," but instead, he sees victory and freedom coming. Then, he tells them they are not to read setback as defeat, saying, "Our enemies have seemingly triumphed for a while, but the final battle when staged will bring us complete success and satisfaction." And it is here that Garvey challenges his people as always to understand and assert themselves in audacious and radically transformative ways to achieve their liberative goals, and he uses the metaphor of whirlwind and storm to relate not only to what he promises to do, but also to be critical of the heavy history-changing responsibility of continued and expanding struggle he places on us, his people.

Maulana Karenga, PhD, is professor and chair of the Department of Africana Studies at California State University, Long Beach. He holds two PhDs: his first doctorate is in leadership and human behavior/political science with focus on the theory and practice of African American nationalism (United States International University), and his second doctorate is in social ethics with a focus on the classical African ethics of ancient Egypt (University of Southern California). Professor Karenga, an ethical philosopher, is the leading exponent of Maatian ethical thought, having developed over the last three decades a creative and scholarly *Kawaida* interpretation of ancient Egyptian ethical thought as a living tradition and a useful philosophical option for critical reflection on the urgent issues of our time. His second dissertation, a major work of 803 pages titled "Maat, The Moral Ideal in Ancient Egypt: A Study in Classical African Ethics" and submitted in 1996, was the most requested work from UMI out of forty-five thousand dissertations and theses worldwide of that year. Published as a book in 2002, it has received praise from the Africana studies and Egyptological communities as a seminal and defining

work that has opened up a valuable new dialogue with ancient Egyptian thought and culture.

Dr. Karenga is the author of 17 books and monographs, 4 coedited books, 57 journal articles, 42 book chapters, over 650 columns and commentaries on critical issues, and numerous encyclopedia entries. Included in this list of books are *Introduction to Black Studies*, the most widely used introductory text in Black/Africana studies; *Selections from the Husia: Sacred Wisdom of Ancient Egypt*; *The Book of Coming Forth By Day: The Ethics of the Declarations of Innocence*; *Kawaida: A Communitarian African Philosophy*; and a translation and ethical commentary on the classical Yoruba text, *Odu Ifa*, titled *Odu Ifa: The Ethical Teachings*. His most recent publications, in addition to *Introduction to Black Studies*, fourth edition, are *Maat, the Moral Ideal in Ancient Egypt: A Study in Classical African Ethics*; *Handbook of Black Studies* (co-authored with Molefi Kete Asante); *Kawaida and Questions of Life and Struggle*; *Essays on Struggle: Position and Analysis*; *The Message and Meaning of Kwanzaa: Bringing Good in the World*; and *The Liberation of Ethics of Malcolm X: Critical Consciousness,*

Moral Grounding and Transformative Struggle.

An activist-scholar of national and international recognition, Dr. Karenga has had a far-reaching effect on Black intellectual and political culture since the 1960s. Through his intellectual and organizational work, his organization, Us, and his philosophy, *Kawaida*, he has played a vanguard role in shaping the Black Arts movement, Black studies, the Black Power movement, the Black Student Union movement, Afrocentricity, ancient Egyptian studies and the study of ancient Egyptian culture as an essential part of Black studies, Ifa ethical studies, rites of passage programs, the Independent Black School movement, African life-cycle ceremonies, the Simba Wachanga Youth movement, Black theological and ethical discourse, and the Reparations movement.

Moreover, he is the executive director of the African American Cultural Center and the Kawaida Institute of Pan-African Studies, Los Angeles, and national chairman of Us, a cultural and social change organization—so named to stress the communitarian focus of the organization—and the National Association of Kawaida Organizations (NAKO). Dr. Karenga has also played a key role in national united front efforts, serving on the founding and executive committee of the Black Power Conferences of the 1960s, the National Black United Front, the National African American Leadership Summit, the Black Leadership Retreat, NAKO,

and on the executive council of the national organizing committee of the Million Man March/Day of Absence, as well as authoring the mission statement for this joint project.

Dr. Karenga is also internationally known as the creator of Kwanzaa, an African American and Pan-African holiday celebrated throughout the world African community on every continent in the world. He is the author of the authoritative book on the subject, *Kwanzaa: A Celebration of Family, Community and Culture*, and lectures regularly and extensively on the vision and values of Kwanzaa, especially the Nguzo Saba (the Seven Principles), in various national and international venues. In addition, he has lectured on the life and struggle of African peoples on numerous campuses of the US and in Senegal, Nigeria, Egypt, South Africa, the People's Republic of China, Cuba, Trinidad, Britain, and Canada.

He also served as chairman of the African American delegation to the Second World Black and African Festival of Arts and Culture, Lagos, Nigeria; spokesman for a delegation of African American Educators of Independent Schools to the People's Republic of China; member of the planning committee for the Pan-African Festival of Arts and Culture, Dakar, Senegal; chairman of the delegation of educators/activists of the Us to Cuba; co-planner and co-convener of the Annual Ancient Egyptian Studies Conference of the Association for the Study of Classical African Civilizations, Cairo, Egypt; inaugural lecturer for the initiation of Black History Month, London, England; honorary doctorate recipient and commencement speaker, University of Durban-Westville, South Africa; official guest and keynote lecturer, 160th Anniversary of Emancipation, Port-of-Spain, Trinidad and Tobago; presenter of the Annual Stephen Glanville Memorial Lecture for Egyptology 2010 at the Fitzwilliam Museum at the University of Cambridge; and inaugural lecture, The Masizi Kunene Lectures, the University of Kwa-Zulu Natal, South Africa.

A highly respected senior scholar in Black/Africana studies and a board member of the National Council for Black Studies, the preeminent professional organization of the discipline, Dr. Karenga has played a major role in the founding and development of the discipline and is the recipient of numerous awards and honors for scholarship, leadership, and community service from the preeminent professional organizations, departments, and programs in the field and from various other organizations and institutions.

His fields of teaching and research within Black studies are Black studies theory, history and pedagogy; Africana (continental and diasporan) philosophy; ancient Egyptian (Maatian) ethics; ancient Yoruba (Ifa) ethics; African American intellectual history; ethnic studies; multiculturalism; and the socio-ethical thought of Malcolm X. He is currently writing a book on deep thinking in Africana Studies titled *Djaer, Deep Thinking in Africana Studies: Cultivating Critical, Creative and Ethical Reflection*. Dr. Karenga is the subject of the book *Maulana Karenga: An Intellectual Portrait* by Dr. Molefi Kete Asante, which is the definitive text on his intellectual and organizational work.

References and Further Reading

Alexander, Michelle. 2012. *The New Jim Crow: Mass Incarceration in the Age of Colorblindness*. Revised Edition. New York: The New Press.

Asante, Molefi. 1988. *Afrocentricity*. Trenton, NJ: Africa World Press.

———. 1998. *The Afrocentric Idea*. Philadelphia: Temple University Press.

Bethune, Mary McLeod. 2008. *Mary McLeod Bethune: Words of Wisdom*. Edited by Chiazam Ugo Okoye, Bloomington, IN: AuthorHouse.

Brown, DeNeen L. 2021. "Descendants of Marcus Garvey Press Biden for Posthumous Pardon." *Washington Post*, December 4, 2021. https://www.washingtonpost.com/history/2021/12/04/marcus-garvey-biden-pardon/.

Césaire, Aimé. 1972. *Discourse on Colonialism*. New York: Monthly Review Press.

Diop, Cheikh Anta. 1991. *Civilization or Barbarism: An Authentic Anthropology*. New York: Lawrence Hill.

Fanon, Frantz. 1968. *Wretched of the Earth*. New York: Grove.

Garvey, Amy Jacques, ed. 1963. *Garvey and Garveyism*. New York: Octagon Books.

———. 2016. *Selected Writings from the Negro World, 1923–1928*. Edited by Louis J. Parascandola. Knoxville: University of Tennessee Press.

Garvey, Marcus. 1967. *Philosophy and Opinions of Marcus Garvey or Africans for the Africans*. 2nd ed. 2 vols. Edited by A. J. Garvey. London: Frank Cass.

———. (2004). *Selected Writings and Speeches of Marcus Garvey*. Mineola, NY: Dover Publications.

Hill, Robert, ed. 1983–2006. *The Marcus Garvey and Universal Negro Improvement Association Papers*. 7 vols. Berkeley: University of California Press.

Karenga, Maulana. 1984. *Selections from the Husia: Sacred Wisdom of Ancient Egypt*. Los Angeles: University of Sankore Press.

———. 1997. *Kawaida: A Communitarian African Philosophy*. Los Angeles: University of Sankore Press.

———. 2006. *Maat, The Moral Ideal in Ancient Egypt: A Study in Classical African Ethics*. Los Angeles: University of Sankore Press.

———. 2008a. *Kawaida and Questions of Life and Struggle: African American, Pan-African and Global Issues*. Los Angeles, University of Sankore Press.

———. 2008b. *Kwanzaa: A Celebration of Family, Community and Culture*. Los Angeles: University of Sankore Press.

Hill, Marc Lamont. 2016. *Nobody: Casualties of America's War on the Vulnerable*. New York: Simon and Schuster.

Lewis, Rupert. 1988. *Marcus Garvey: Anti-colonial Champion*. Trenton, NJ: Africa World Press.

Malcolm X. 1965a. *The Autobiography of Malcolm X*. New York: Grove.

———. 1965b. *Malcolm X Speaks*. New York: Merit.

———. 1970. *By Any Means Necessary*. New York: Pathfinder Press.

———. 1968. *The Speeches of Malcolm X at Harvard*. New York: William Morrow and Company.

Martin, Tony. 1976. *Race First: The Ideological and Organizational Struggles of Marcus Garvey and the University Negro Improvement Association*. Westport, CT: Greenwood.

Toure, Sekou. 1959. *Toward Full Re-Africanization*. Paris: Présence Africaine.

CHAPTER SIX

Global Garveyism in the Black Liberation Struggle

Adam Ewing, PhD

> Marcus Garvey was one of the first advocates of Black Power, and is still today the greatest spokesman ever to have been produced by the movement of black consciousness. . . . . He spoke to all Africans on the earth, whether they lived in Africa, South America, the West Indies or North America, and he made blacks aware of their strength when united.
>
> —Walter Rodney

GARVEYISM WAS A global phenomenon. The movement spread with unprecedented success, reaching every continent and touching Black people wherever they lived. It did so with the ambition of remaking the world: breaking the grip of European power and erecting a new international order founded on the equitable distribution of the world's resources—Europe for the Europeans, Asia for the Asians, and Africa for the Africans. Garveyism emerged from and galvanized the rich tradition of pan-African resistance that had nurtured Black communities in the Americas since the dawn of the Atlantic slave trade. By carrying this message across the world, Garveyites sparked a revolutionary thrust in the Black liberation struggle that would reach its climax in the 1960s and 1970s and that would become one of the central dramas of the twentieth century.

A Politics of Refusal

Marcus Garvey was born in 1887, in the seaside town of St. Ann's Bay, Jamaica. The colony was dominated by the demands of the plantation system, which had arrived with the British more than two centuries earlier and had survived slavery largely intact. Erected on land brutally cleared of its inhabitants, fueled by the labor of enslaved Africans and their descendants, and arrayed to support the prosperity and stability of Britain, the Jamaican plantation was a symbol of Europe's imperial vision, a cog in its larger ambition to remake the world in its own image and to establish global white supremacy.[1]

Garveyism emerged out of a long tradition of resistance in Jamaican society that defied the logics of the plantation system and European supremacy and that fought to sustain and reestablish African-centered societies. In the Americas, Africans from all over the western and central regions of the continent were bound together under the common signs of "Black" and "slave." A shared identity—a pan-African identity—developed within these communities that found points of contact in things that many African societies shared, from modes of worship to family structure to social values.[2] Pan-Africanism in this sense was a politics of connection.[3] But pan-Africanism was also a politics of refusal. These communities rejected the ambition of the colonial project to strip Africans of their identity and to absorb them—as servants and subordinates—into a Euro-centric world order.[4] They escaped into the mountains and formed maroon settlements. They organized island-wide rebellions against the slave system in 1760 and 1831. They rejected European faiths in favor of African-derived religions like Myalism, or they adapted Christianity within the framework of an African cosmos. In 1865, one of the practitioners of these faiths, the Native Baptist deacon Paul Bogle, led a major rebellion against British rule that was quelled only by a campaign of brutal repression. Marcus Garvey's father, who claimed maroon heritage, was a participant in the political agitation leading up to the rebellion.[5]

Marcus Garvey grew up hearing these stories in the shop of his godfather, Alfred "Cap" Burrowes.[6] When he launched the Universal Negro Improvement Association (UNIA)—first in Kingston in 1914 and then, to greater effect, in New York in 1918—he sought to marshal the tradition of Paul Bogle, of Tacky and Sam Sharpe, of Nanny and Cudjoe and the spirit of the thousands of unknown Jamaicans who had risked their lives to win autonomy in the teeth of white power. "Africa for the Africans, those at home and those abroad," was not merely a slogan, explained Amy Jacques Garvey in her pioneering work, *Garvey and Garveyism*. It was "the pulsating heart of Garveyism"—the demand that European hegemony be shattered, that Black land be reclaimed, that Black sovereignty be reestablished, that African societies thrive outside of and resistant to European power.[7] Garveyism was both an anti-colonial movement and a revival. It proclaimed that Africa would be free when Black people realized the futility of bargaining with their white captors and awakened to the need to reclaim their own civilization, their own cultures, their own *spaces*.

The Accepted Voice of an Awakened Race

The catalyst for Garvey's movement was the global devastation of the Great War. The bloody conflict shattered the German, Russian, Austro-Hungarian, and Ottoman Empires and sparked protest and rebellion throughout Asia, the Middle East, Africa, and the Caribbean.[8] In East Africa, a report from the British War Office warned that the protracted East Africa campaign—which brought Africans from every corner of the continent around the same campfires—had engendered new solidarities, a politics of "Africa for the Africans," and "a conscious feeling of the possibilities of a black Africa." White propagandists like J. Lothrop Stoddard warned that the war had critically weakened the ramparts of world white supremacy, which now faced the specter of a "rising tide of color" across Asia, Africa, and the Americas.[9] The war indeed had a galvanizing effect on the millions of Africans, West Indians, and African Americans who served in the Allied armies and were repaid with a torrent of racist abuse. It also had a galvanizing effect for those facing hunger, rising prices, disease, violence, and repression on the home front. In Harlem, then emerging as a great mecca of the African diaspora, stepladder orators and organizers like Hubert Henry Harrison announced the growing popularity of a militant race-conscious, anti-racist, and anti-colonial politics—what Harrison dubbed the "New Negro Manhood Movement." New Negro activists demanded that Black people cease shedding blood in European wars and mobilize instead around the struggle for Black liberation.[10]

Marcus Garvey arrived in Harlem in 1916, and by the war's end, he had shifted the gravity of the New Negro movement toward the UNIA. Garvey argued that the war was a lost opportunity and a wake-up call. It had come at a moment when Black people were disorganized and disunited, unable to capitalize on Europe's vulnerability. The critical task of the moment was to build a movement that could unite the scattered sons and daughters of Africa, awaken them to their collective destiny, and mobilize their shared resources toward the liberation of the African continent.[11] To bring this about, the UNIA launched a series of ambitious economic and political projects. In 1919, Garvey announced the launch of the Black Star Line Steamship Company, a transatlantic shipping venture supported by and connecting Black shareholders in North America, Central America, the Caribbean, and Africa. By the end of the year, the UNIA was publicizing plans to move the central operations of the organization to Liberia and to engage in diplomatic negotiations with the Liberian government to make the independent West African nation the staging ground for the UNIA's efforts to liberate the rest of the continent. In August 1920, the UNIA hosted the first of its international conventions in Harlem, during which tens of thousands of supporters marched through the streets, and delegates adopted the Declaration of Rights of the Negro Peoples of the World.

News of the arrival of Garvey's great new organization—gathering strength, resolved in its demand for Africa's liberation—spread like wildfire across the African diaspora, carried on the lips of sailors and migrant workers and transmitted on the pages of Garvey's newspaper, the *Negro World*. UNIA divisions proliferated across the United States: in the urban centers of the north and Midwest, in the soil-rich lands of the Missouri Bootheel and the Mississippi Delta, in the port cities of the Chesapeake and the Gulf of Mexico, and wherever else Black people found a home.[12] Alarmed officials watched helplessly as enthusiasm for Garveyism swelled on the banana plantations of Central America, in the sugar region of Cuba, and in all the lands touched by the Caribbean sea.[13] In Africa, Garveyite organizers traveled throughout the continent—from the upper Guinea coast to the Congo River, from the Cape of Good Hope to the Swahili Coast, and deep into the interior—announcing the arrival of the great global movement and winning new participants. An observer in the British colony of the Gold Coast (present-day Ghana) remarked that Garveyism had "gripped the coast and many of the towns are seething with it." French agents in West Africa worried that Garveyism was "more dangerous than rifles" but conceded that there were "no walls thick enough" to stop its spread. In South Africa, the moderate educator and activist, Davidson Don Tengo Jabavu, complained that Garveyism had "made a deep impression on our illiterate people so that even from backwoods hamlets rings the magic motto, 'Ama Melika ayeza' (The Americans are coming)." "Today the *Negro World* stands out as the accepted voice of an awakened race," observed Garveyite Samuel Haynes in 1927. "It is translated into scores of dialects twenty-four hours after arrival in Africa, and carried by fleet runners into the hinterland, up the great lakes of Southeast Africa, and the uncharted reaches of the Nile, the Congo, the Zambesi and the Niger, where millions of our fellowmen wait in silence for its arrival."[14]

During the early years of its spread, Garveyism crackled with revolutionary possibility. In July 1919, a major rebellion erupted in Belize, British Honduras, during which thousands of women and men marched through the streets, destroying white-owned property and chanting, "This country belongs to the blacks." British investigators noted that a larger insurgency had been prevented by quick-thinking officials, who locked and removed weapons from the Drill Hall before it was encircled by a group of five hundred. They blamed the spread of

Garveyite literature—the *Negro World* and the pro-Garveyite paper, the *Belize Independent*—for "inflame[ing] coloured men against white men by describing real or imaginary injustices to coloured men in other countries."[15] In November 1919, island-wide uprisings in Trinidad were sparked by organizers of the Trinidad Workingmen's Association (TWA), whose leadership read passages of the *Negro World* at meetings and circulated information about Garvey and his shipping company, the Black Star Line.[16] In February 1920, an estimated sixteen thousand workers went on strike in the Panama Canal Zone, led by Garveyites Eduardo Morales, William H. Stoute, J. L. Seymour, Samuel Radway, and F. S. Ricketts. "The white man thinks that we can never do any good, for he says that we are disorganized[,] that some are Jamaicans[,] some are Barbadians, Spaniards, Trinidadians, and that we have grievances with one another and also hate ourselves, and by such means can never come to any conclusion," declared the Panamanian-born Morales at a workers' meeting. "Let us show them different. Let us [make them aware] of the fact that we are no more different nationalities in this cause." The strike was put down with a massive display of force by Canal Zone authorities: drawn bayonets, the eviction of striking workers from their homes, and the deportation of strike leaders.[17]

In Africa, the arrival of Garveyism likewise sparked a series of mobilizations against European rule. In the Eastern Cape, the Israelite movement, led by the prophet Enoch Mgijima, was radicalized by news of the UNIA's First International Convention of the Negro Peoples of the World, in 1920, and Garvey's supposed declaration—relayed to Mgijima by his nephew in Queenstown—that a war for Africa was coming and that Africans must lift up their swords. When the Israelites did raise their swords against the state—on May 24, 1921—they were met by a hail of machine-gun fire from police and armed forces, and nearly two hundred members of the movement were slaughtered.[18] In the Belgian-occupied Congo, a massive religious revival, inaugurated in the spring of 1921 and led by the prophet Simon Kimbangu, was likewise radicalized by Garveyite organizing in the region and by rumors that a Black American army would arrive in a great ship, sail up the

Congo River, and expel the Europeans.[19] That same year, in Kenya, Harry Thuku launched an extensive organizing tour of the African reserves, preaching a message of pan-African unity and resistance to white rule. Thuku was inspired by his connections to—and correspondence with—both the Indian nationalist movement and the UNIA. Like other mobilizations of the period, Thuku and his followers found themselves outgunned by colonial authorities willing to defend their rule with violence. After Thuku was arrested, on March 15, 7,000–8,000 supporters marched to the police station in Nairobi, and a group of 200–250 women urged the men to push forward. According to a witness, one of the organizers, Mary Muthoni Nyanjiru, "leapt to her feet, pulled her dress right up over her shoulders and shouted to the men: 'You take my dress and give me your trousers. You men are cowards. What are you waiting for? Our leader is in there. Let's get him.'" As the crowd surged forward, the *askari* opened fire, killing Nyanjiru and many more. After an investigation, the government claimed a death toll of twenty-one. A mortuary worker sympathetic to Thuku's movement counted fifty-six bodies in the morgue.[20]

Quiet and Peaceful Penetration

In the fall of 1919, the Washington Counsel for the United Fruit Company sent an urgent message to the US secretary of state Robert Lansing, warning that if the spread of Garveyism was not quelled, it threatened to replicate the "French experience in Haiti."[21] The subsequent repression meted out to the movement by colonial and state authorities prevented a geopolitical explosion comparable to the Haitian Revolution. Marcus Garvey was surveilled, prosecuted, imprisoned, and deported by the US government. He was denied entry to Africa. The UNIA and the *Negro World* were banned across most of sub-Saharan Africa.[22] Efforts to claim the right to Black sovereignty, self-determination, and autonomy in the colonies of Africa and the Caribbean—by Garveyites and others—were viewed as subversive to good order and met with violence. From the colonial perspective,

Africans and their descendants must undergo a period of tutelage—for hundreds if not thousands of years—during which they would be "civilized" under the firm guidance of European rule. To claim otherwise was to invite social disintegration and chaos. In the mind of the Belgian colonial government, the claim of African sovereignty was nothing short of anti-European chauvinism—*des sentiments xenophobes*.[23]

But if the rise of Garveyism did not precipitate another Haitian Revolution, it nevertheless announced a similar turning point. As in Haiti, the backdrop for Garveyism's emergence was a bloody imperial war, which inaugurated what C. L. R. James called "a period of world-wide revolutionary change" and opened up new opportunities to challenge white supremacy.[24] Garveyism broadcast this message relentlessly: that the European empire was in decline, that a rising tide of anti-colonial resistance would soon reorder the world, and that local organizing efforts—far from futile in the face of powerful colonial governments—were contributing to a global movement certain of success.[25] The primary message conveyed by Garveyism during the 1920s and 1930s was not one of insurrection but rather one of *preparation*. Garvey presciently argued that another major conflict was on the horizon in Europe. He stressed that when this new war came, Black people must be prepared to "strike a blow in Africa" for their liberation. "The last world war brought the opportunity to many heretofore subject races to regain their freedom," Garvey observed. "The next world war will give Africa the opportunity for which we are preparing."[26]

The goal of the UNIA was thus organization itself: spreading the message of Garveyism to every corner of the Black world and establishing centers of Garveyite activity wherever Black people lived. As the radicalism of the wartime and postwar period gave way to the reactionary 1920s, Garvey called for a focus on "quiet and peaceful penetration": a turn away from grand provocations and toward the patient and essential work of consciousness raising, networking, and institution building. In the words of Garveyite leader William Sherrill, the organization would strive to "organize the Negro, to bring about a better relationship between Negroes everywhere; to arouse

Negroes to a sense of loyalty to themselves and to their race." Amy Jacques Garvey celebrated the "men and women who will take *Negro World* into certain districts of Africa, where to be caught with one is a death sentence," and praised "those who translate the philosophy and opinions of Marcus Garvey by sections into different dialects and carry their parchment from village to village spreading the gospel of Garveyism."[27] In *Garvey and Garveyism*, Jacques Garvey revealed that during the 1920s, the UNIA established a clandestine network of representatives in Paris and London who maintained contact with African agents working for freedom on the continent. "Both seamen and students have been indoctrinated in Garveyism in England, France, and the U.S.A.," she wrote, "and on their return home, quietly and secretly, spread the gospel of Unity and Freedom." Jacques Garvey observed that the full scope of the movement in Africa would be revealed only in the "secret reports in the archives of the colonial offices," which she predicted would demonstrate the extent to which European states worried about and surveilled the movement—a prediction that has been thoroughly confirmed by subsequent research.[28]

In the Americas, the UNIA organized hundreds of divisions—stretching south to Guayaquil, Ecuador, and north to Edmonton, Canada—on the message that Black people must awaken to their common cause and mobilize to prepare for their liberation.[29] "We are entering into a period of constructive awakening, when we will have to buckle down to the tasks which are before us, and build as we have never done before, so that the strength and position of the race may be assured," declared Garveyite organizer R. T. Brown at a UNIA meeting in Costa Rica in 1923. Garveyites were encouraged by Marcus Garvey to "go out as missionaries and preach" the doctrine of the UNIA, to "let all the world know that this is the hour; this is the time for our salvation." Garvey cast his movement as a "spiritual force" that was carried by the strength of divine prophecy—that "princes shall come out of Egypt and Ethiopia shall stretch out her hands unto God" (Ps 68:31). But prophetic power was made manifest through worldly struggle. "Prayer alone will not save us; sentiment alone will not save us," he warned. "We have to work and work and work if we are to be saved."[30]

The work performed by Garveyites was one of self-definition. Garvey called for Black people to release themselves from the thrall of "mental slavery": to reject "the doctrine of other men," to "[see] everything from the African viewpoint," and to thereby become "creators of their own needs."[31] This was a pan-African politics of refusal—a rejection of the limitations of the European assimilationist project—that required a parallel project of *articulation*. The UNIA crafted a new flag (the red, black, and green tricolor), a national anthem (the Universal Ethiopian Anthem),[32] and new religious rites (the Universal Negro Ritual and the Universal Negro Catechism).[33] The organization encouraged Garveyites to understand their work, however modest, as part of a global, shared project. On the pages of the *Negro World*, Garveyites learned of the activities of divisions all over the world, read letters from far-flung supporters, and were exposed to a steady stream of news reports—carefully curated by the editors—sharing information about anti-colonial movements and uprisings throughout Africa, Asia, the Middle East, and the Americas. Many Garveyites came to see their work, as Miami-based Garveyite Samuel Alonzo Culmer put it, "on a larger scale." And they also came to see it as moving the tides of history. "The UNIA is a powerful factor and is not only entrenched in the lives of the Negro people of America and the West Indies, but also in the very lives of the Negroes at home in the motherland," wrote Leo Porter in the *Negro World*. "Hence, the redemption of Africa is only as far distant as Negroes abroad, big and small, keep away from the unification of this association."[34]

Garveyism was successful as a mass politics because it joined this global vision with a focus on the necessities of local organization. Garveyism was, as Michael O. West and William Martin have suggested, a "pan-African potter's clay" that could be molded to fit the diverse circumstances of the African diaspora.[35] In the Caribbean, Garveyism became an important influence on the region's developing labor movement.[36] For entrepreneurs in West

Africa, the UNIA was appealing because of its potential ability to thwart British shipping and trading monopolies.[37] For far-flung supporters—such as Aboriginal activists in Australia—Garveyism offered an inspiration example for their own political mobilizations.[38] Garveyites were empowered, as Ernest Wallace, a UNIA organizer working in Lesotho, put it, to "cook [their] own pot."[39] This allowed Garveyism—a movement born in Jamaica, rooted in the particular experiences of Caribbean pan-Africanism, and carried around the world by the "transmission belt" of West Indian migration—to spread widely among African Americans throughout the United States and to nearly every corner of sub-Saharan Africa. It allowed Garveyism to make important inroads among Haitians, Afro-Cubans, and other Hispanic speakers in the Caribbean region despite cultural, political, and language barriers.[40]

Garveyism's flexibility was particularly important in colonial Africa, where Garveyism was banned and heavily surveilled. In British-occupied Malawi, Zambia, and Zimbabwe, activists developed secret channels of communication with Garveyites in South Africa and the United States, read smuggled copies of the *Negro World*, and organized seemingly innocuous, government-approved "Native Welfare Associations," through which to promote the Garveyite message of race pride, unity, and self-help.[41] In central Kenya, Jomo Kenyatta and other members of the Kikuyu Central Association (KCA) maintained the ties with the UNIA, first established by Harry Thuku, well into the 1930s and translated Garveyite pan-Africanism into a dynamic politics of Kikuyu anti-colonial nationalism. Kenyatta, who was detained during the Mau Mau Emergency and later became the first president of independent Kenya, later told C. L. R. James that "in 1921 Kenya nationalists, unable to read, would gather round a reader of Garvey's newspaper, the *Negro World*, and listen to an article two or three times. Then they would run various ways through the forest, carefully[,] to repeat the whole, which they had memorized, to Africans hungry for some doctrine which lifted them from the servile consciousness in which Africans lived."[42]

Wherever it took root, the UNIA developed what the Black Panther Party would later call "survival programs": services and support designed to sustain oppressed communities while they prepared for revolution. Garveyites operated loan banks, schools, and health clinics and ran laundries, groceries, restaurants, and barber shops. UNIA auxiliaries like the Black Cross Nurses offered assistance to the sick, to the needy, and to young mothers. Following the model of the West Indian friendly society, UNIA members paid sickness and death benefit dues, making the organization a social insurance agency. Beyond the services they provided to the community, UNIA divisions were centers of community life, hosting musical performances, dances, holiday celebrations, parades, beauty pageants, religious services, and literary events.[43] They proliferated in major centers of West Indian migration—Cuba, Panama, Costa Rica, and elsewhere—where they created an important organization stability for mobile workers and families.[44] And they emerged on the frontiers of Black settlement, where they served as a vital lifeline of news, information, and connection. "Liberty Halls, wherever located, served the needs of the people—Sunday morning worship, afternoon Sunday Schools, public meetings at nights, concerts and dances . . . on holidays and Saturday nights," recalled Amy Jacques Garvey.

> Notice boards were put up where one could look for a room, a job, or a lost article. In localities where there were many members out of work during the winter the Black Cross Nurses would organize soup kitchens, and give them a warm meal daily. The [Universal African] Legions would make portable screens for a corner of a hall, where men who could not be temporarily housed with fellow members, could sleep on benches at night. In the freezing winter days stoves had to be kept going to accommodate the cold and homeless, until they 'got on their feet' again."[45]

Within UNIA communities, Garveyites negotiated the terms of their "internal boundaries," reconceptualizing their relationships with each other.[46] The UNIA offered a radically democratic standard for participation in the organization—African ancestry and a willingness to work for the liberation of the race—that cut across class lines and redefined notions of respectability.[47] These norms of respectability placed powerful demands upon Black women and stressed masculinist conceptions of the Garveyite nation-in-formation.[48] But Garveyite women fought hard—and achieved some notable success—in winning leadership positions and broadening definitions of Black womanhood within the organization. According to Honor Ford-Smith, the UNIA served as an incubator for the emergence of the Jamaican feminist movement in the 1930s and 1940s. Robert Trent Vinson has demonstrated the extent to which African women dominated the Garveyite "American" movement in South Africa's Transkei region in the 1920s and 1930s.[49] Across the world, in the daily life of local UNIA divisions, Garveyite women carved out dynamic spaces within which to express their visions of liberation—what the scholar Ula Y. Taylor calls "community feminism."[50] This was because the UNIA was a community in the making, a space where, as R. A. Bennett, president of a local division in Cuba, put it, "we must build a foundation for ourselves."[51] Garveyites worked diligently toward the moment of opportunity when those foundations would become the basis of new, self-determining nations.

Legacies

Garveyism was brought into existence by the brilliant and determined organizing work of Garveyites, Marcus Garvey chief among them. But it was also much more than that. "If you study Garvey because you see Garvey as an absolute or an end unto himself, then you will not understand very much," observes Robert A. Hill. "It is the people who made Garvey. . . . It is our struggle for survival as a people that is the source of which everything comes."[52] Garveyism resonated because, as Hubert H. Harrison once remarked, it held up to Black people the world over "those things which bloom in their hearts."[53] It tapped into popular traditions of pan-Africanism, resonated with local experiences, and joined Black communities in conversation with each other. By giving a global platform to these traditions, Garveyism left an impact that far exceeded the organizational reach of the UNIA. As Garveyism spread through the world, it escaped its own boundaries, sparking movements and mobilizations that long outlived Garvey himself.

With its prophetic language of African liberation and its celebration of a Black God, Garveyism galvanized Black-centered religious revivals throughout the diaspora, sparking a pan-African Great Awakening.[54] The interwar period witnessed a flowering of new Black faiths founded by followers of Marcus Garvey and rooted in the Garveyite dictum, echoed in Robert Athlyi Rogers's *Holy Piby* (1924), to "be ye not contented in the vineyard or household of others . . . prepare ye rather for yourselves a foundation."[55] In the United States, Rogers's Afro Athlican Constructive Church, Noble Drew Ali's Moorish Science Temple, and W. D. Fard's Nation of Islam each viewed Garvey as an apostle or a prophet.[56] Likewise, several of the early followers of the Jamaican-based Rastafarian movement were either Garveyites or had been influenced by Garvey's message. They took seriously Garvey's characterization of himself as a "John the Baptist in the wilderness" and understood his 1923 warning to his enemies that "a greater and more dangerous Marcus Garvey is yet to appear" as foretelling the coronation of Ethiopian Emperor Haile Selassie, the king of kings, less than a decade later.[57] In Malawi, mission-educated Garveyites were involved in the formation of a series of independent churches: the Providence Industrial Mission (1926), the African National Church (1929), and the Blackman's Church of God, which is in Tongaland (1933). Yesaya Zerenji Mwasi, who led the Black Man's Church of God, accused white missionaries of thwarting efforts to unify Black Africans and attempting to subjugate Africans as "perpetual subjects under their permanent control." He called instead for a "Christianity of the soil" rooted in the worship of an "indigenous and personal God."[58]

In the Caribbean, Garveyism played a critical role in preparing the ground for the revolutionary struggles that erupted during the labor rebellions of the 1930s and that were carried forward to the assassination of Walter Rodney in Guyana in 1980 and the fall of Grenada's People's Revolutionary Government in 1983. Many of the leaders of the labor rebellions—who later became the leaders of an era of national independence—were current or former Garveyites. Those leaders, and many others, brought to those struggles "not only the ideas of Garvey . . . but also the experience of public speaking and organising and of recognising the need for unity, self-reliance, and solidarity."[59] When the Black Power movement erupted in the Caribbean in the late 1960s, movement activists likewise drew inspiration from the politics of Garveyism. They argued that the newly independent nations of the Caribbean required something more than independence alone— that their Black-majority countries must not be mere appendages of a Western-dominated international order but rather centered in their own needs, rooted in the popular will and the cultural traditions of the Black majority. When Robert A. Hill and other members of the Abeng collective launched their pioneering Black Power journal, *Abeng*, in Jamaica in 1969, they emblazoned Marcus Garvey's words across the paper's masthead: "We want our people to think for themselves."[60]

In Africa, Garveyism likewise played a critical role—as Zambian independence leader Harry Mwaanga Nkumbula put it—in "creat[ing] the nucleus for the freedom and independence" of the continent. In the aftermath of World War II—the great European conflict that Garvey had foreseen—African women and men touched by the "quiet and peaceful penetration" of Garveyism during the interwar period emerged at the forefront of the nationalist struggle. Nnamdi Azikiwe, the first president of Nigeria, recalled that "Marcus Garvey's motto"— One God! One Aim! One Destiny!—"gave me the ambitions to be of service for the redemption of Africa." Kwame Nkrumah, the first leader of Ghana, recalled, "Of all the literature I studied, the book that did more than any other to fire my enthusiasm was *Philosophy and Opinions of Marcus Garvey*." When Ghana won its independence in 1957, Nkrumah invited William Sherrill, the president-general of the UNIA, to the raucous celebrations, telling Sherrill that "his life and work had been largely influenced by the Philosophy of Marcus Garvey and the

UNIA." Sherrill met with many of the assembled African leaders, who also shared their appreciation for the work of the organization. T. D. T. Banda, president-general of the Nyasaland African Congress, explained to Sherrill: "Most of my people in Nyasaland (Malawi) have read and heard quite a lot about the philosophy of your Founder and the 'Aims and Objects' of your great and wonderful association and we are all very happy that we have come to see each other at last."[61]

The revolutionary projects of the twentieth century ultimately failed to achieve Marcus Garvey's ultimate objective: the dismantling of the Western-dominated world system. We continue to live with the fallacy of Eurocentric universalism and in a global order straining under the weight of stark inequality and racial hierarchy. So long as this injustice prevails, Garveyism's project of refusal and articulation—the refusal of European domination, the articulation of self-determining African societies—will remain the beating heart of the ongoing and unyielding Black liberation struggle.

Adam Ewing is an associate professor of African American studies at Virginia Commonwealth University. He is the author of *The Age of Garvey: How a Jamaican Activist Created a Mass Movement and Changed Global Mass Politics* (Princeton University Press, 2014) and the co-editor (with Ronald J. Stephens) of *Global Garveyism* (University Press of Florida, 2019).

Notes

Epigraph: Walter Rodney, *The Groundings with my Brothers* (London: Bogle-L'Ouverture Publications, 1969), 20.

1. George Beckford, *Persistent Poverty: Underdevelopment in Plantation Economies of the Third World* (1972; Jamaica: Maroon Publishing House, 1983), 13, 215; George Beckford and Michael Witter, *Small Garden . . . Bitter Weed: The Political Economy of Struggle and Change in Jamaica* (Morant Bay, Jamaica: Maroon Publishing House, 1982), 14–18; George Beckford, "Plantation Society: Toward a General Theory of Caribbean Society," *Savacou: A Journal of the Caribbean Artists Movement* 5 (June 1971), 13–15; Sidney W. Mintz, "From Plantations to Peasantries in the Caribbean," in *Caribbean Contours*, eds. Sidney W. Mintz and Sally Price (Baltimore: The Johns Hopkins University Press, 1985), 128–29; O. Nigel Bolland, *The Politics of Labour in the British Caribbean: The Social Origins of*

Authoritarianism and Democracy in the Labour Movement (Kingston: Ian Randle Publishers, 2001), 9–10.

2. Edward Kamau Brathwaite, *The Folk Culture of the Slaves in Jamaica* (1971; London: New Beacon Books, 1981), 5–34; Wynter, "Jonkonnu in Jamaica: Towards the Interpretation of Folk Dance as a Cultural Process," *Jamaica Journal* 4, no. 2 (1970), 45–46; Sidney W. Mintz and Richard Price, *The Birth of African-American Culture: An Anthrological Perspective* (1976; Boston: Beacon Press, 1992), 10–19.

3. George Shepperson usefully separates "Pan-Africanism" with a capital letter, which he associates with the specific political movement associated with the Pan-African Congresses of Du Bois and Nkrumah, and "pan-Africanism," which he describes capaciously as "all those all-African movements and trends which have no organic relationship with the capital 'P' variety." I define "pan-Africanism" as the assertion of a global Black identity that cannot be, and refuses to be, assimilated into European universalism. It is critical to understand, as I express above, that pan-Africanism is fundamentally a project of refusal, a rejection of the assimilationist logic of colonization and the effort to reconstitute a foundation for the flowering and full expression of Blackness. Unlike the political formation that developed out of the Pan-African Congresses, pan-Africanism was a popular politics—one, as Cedric J. Robinson argues, that was "discovered" by Western-educated Black intellectuals in the twentieth century. See Shepperson, "Pan-Africanism and 'Pan-Africanism': Some Historical Notes," *Phylon* 23 (Winter 1962), 346; Robinson, *Black Marxism: The Making of the Black Radical Tradition* (1983; Chapel Hill: University of North Carolina Press, 2000), 5.

4. The colonial project, observes Talal Asad, is the effort to build a "single, shared world," to create—in Edouard Glissant's words, the "notion of a single History." As Aimé Césaire bitterly remarked, European colonization meant "societies drained of their essence, cultures trampled underfoot . . . extraordinary *possibilities* wiped out." Pan-Africanism was a popular tradition embodied in the search for what Mīcere Gīthae Mūgo calls "liberated zones," physical, intellectual, and artistic spaces forged by Black communities outside of colonized landscapes of power. This was an implosive project because, as Glissant writes, its participants fought for the "right to opacity": to represent themselves outside of the universalizing logic that gave European colonialism its coherence and its legitimacy. If colonialism sought to reduce the world to a single center, pan-Africanists demanded a plurality of centers; as Ngugi wa Thiong'o puts it, "the right to name the world for ourselves" (3). See Asad, "Conscripts of Western Civilization," in *Dialectical Anthropology: Essays in Honor of Stanley Diamond*, vol. 1, ed., C. Gailey (Gainsville: University Press of Florida, 1992), 333–34; Édouard Glissant, *Caribbean Discourse: Selected Essays*, trans. J. Michael Dash (Charlottesville: University of Virginia Press, 1993), 93; Aimé Césaire, *Discourse on Colonialism*, trans. Joan Pinkham (New York: Monthly Review Press, 2000),

43; Mīcere Gīthae Mūgo, "Art, Artists and the Flowering of Pan-Africana Liberated Zone," in Wole Soyinka et al., *Reimagining Pan-Africanism* (Dar-es-Salaam: Mkuki na Nyota, 2015), 183–90; Édouard Glissant, *Poetics of Relation*, trans. Betsy Wing (Ann Arbor: University of Michigan, 1997), 190–91; Ngũgĩ wa Thiong'o, *Moving the Centre: The Struggle for Cultural Freedoms* (London: James Currey, 1993), 3. For a trenchant discussion of Black material and social space, see Katherine McKittrick, *Demonic Grounds: Black Women and the Cartographies of Struggle* (Minneapolis: University of Minnesota Press, 2006).

5. Horace Campbell, *Rasta and Resistance: From Marcus Garvey to Walter Rodney* (1981; Trenton: Africa World Press, 1987), 19–39; Barry Chevannes, "Introducing the Native Religions of Jamaica," in *Rastafari and other African-Caribbean Worldviews*, ed. Barry Chevannes (New Brunswick, NJ: Rutgers University Press, 1998), 1–9; Jean Besson, "Myal, Revival and Rastafari in the Making of Western Jamaica: Dialogues with Chevannes," in *The African-Caribbean Worldview and the Making of Caribbean Society*, ed. Horace Levy (Jamaica: University of the West Indies Press, 2009), 28–29; Wynter, "Jonkonnu in Jamaica," 36; Mimi Sheller, *Democracy After Slavery: Black Publics and Peasant Radicalism in Haiti and Jamaica* (Gainsville: University Press of Florida, 2000), 238–39; Holt, *Problem of Freedom*, 289–303.

6. Amy Jacques Garvey, "The Early Years of Marcus Garvey," in *Marcus Garvey and the Vision of Africa*, ed. John Henrik Clarke (New York: Random House, 1974), 27–32.

7. Amy Jacques Garvey, *Garvey and Garveyism* (1963; Baltimore: Black Classic Press, 2014), 272. Jacques Garvey was the wife of Marcus Garvey and an important leader in the UNIA. After Marcus Garvey's death, she remained a critical voice of the Pan-Africanist movement and the chief preserver of her husband's legacy. In the view of this author, Jacques Garvey inaugurated the field of Garveyism studies with the publication of *Garvey and Garveyism*, which she published at great personal expense and is now a classic in the field. See Ula Y. Taylor, *The Veiled Garvey: The Life and Times of Amy Jacques Garvey* (Chapel Hill: University of North Carolina Press, 2002), 223–24.

8. Erez Manela, *The Wilsonian Moment: Self-Determination and the International Origins of Anticolonial Nationalism* (Oxford: Oxford University Press, 2007), 4.

9. J. E. Philipps, "Africa for Africans and Pan-Islam," 1917, British National Archives (BNA), WO/106/259; Lothrop Stoddard, *The Rising Tide of Color against White World Supremacy* (1920; New York: Charles Scribner's Sons, 1922).

10. Barbara Foley, *Spectres of 1919: Class and Nation in the Making of the New Negro* (Urbana: University of Illinois Press, 2003); Jeffrey B. Perry, *Hubert Harrison: The Voice of Harlem Radicalism, 1883–1918* (New York: Columbia University Press, 2009); Chad L. Williams, *Torchbearers of Democracy: African American Soldiers in the World War I Era* (Chapel Hill: University of North Carolina Press, 2010); Adriane Lentz-Smith, *Freedom Struggles: African Americans and World War I* (Cambridge, MA: Harvard University Press, 2009); Winston James,

Holding Aloft the Banner of Ethiopia: Caribbean Radicalism in Early Twentieth Century America (London: Verso, 1998); Melvin E. Page, ed., *Africa and the First World War* (New York: St. Martin's Press, 1987).

11. Article in the *West Indian*, Grenada, 28 February 1919, *MGP*, 11:174–76; Report of UNIA Mass Meeting at Madison Square Garden, 30 October 1919, in *Marcus Garvey and Universal Negro Improvement Association Papers (MGP)*, ed. Robert A. Hill (Vols. 1–10: Berkeley: University of California Press, 1983–2006; Vols. 11–13: Durham, NC: Duke University Press, 2011–2016), 2:128–31.

12. Adam Ewing, *The Age of Garvey: How a Jamaican Activist Created a Mass Movement and Changed Global Politics* (Princeton, NJ: Princeton University Press, 2014), 131–32.

13. Testimony of Captain William Caile Price before the Riot Commission, Belize, British Honduras, BNA, CO 123/296/65699; Eyre Hutson, Governor of British Honduras, to Secretary of State for the Colonies, BNA, FO 371/4467/A5761; Stewart E. McMillin to Robert Lansing, 21 December 1919, *MGP*, 11:471; Henry A. Baker to Secretary of State, 9 December 1919, and Baker to Secretary of State, 6 December 1919, U.S. Department of National Archives (DNA), RG 59, File 844G.

14. A.W. Wilkie to J. H. Oldham, 8 December 1920, quoted in Arnold Hughes, "Africa and the Garvey Movement in the Interwar Years," in *Garvey: Africa, Europe and the Americas*, eds. Rupert Lewis and Maureen Warner-Lewis (Kingston, Jamaica: Institute of Social and Economic Research, University of the West Indies, 1986), 111; Lieutenant Governor of Côte d'Ivoire to Martial-Henri Merlin, 4 December 1921, *MGP*, 9:251–56; D. D. T. Jabavu, "Native Unrest in South Africa," *International Review of Missions* 19, no. 42 (April 1922), 250; S. A. Haynes in the *Negro World*, August 20, 1927, 4. For more on the spread of Garveyism in Africa, see Ewing, *Age of Garvey*, 91–93, 164–68.

15. Report of the Riot Commission, 21 October 1919, BNA, CO 123/296/65699.

16. G. H. May to Colonial Secretary, 5 August 1919, BNA, CO 295/522/50042; Report by Major H. de Pass, 12 March 1920, and Report by L. H. Elphinatono, 12 March 1920, CO 295/527/17716.

17. Carla Burnett, "'Are We Slaves or Free Men?': Labor, Race, Garveyism and the 1920 Panama Canal Strike" (PhD diss., University of Illinois at Chicago, 2004), 46, 68–74; Carla Burnett, "'Unity is Strength': Labor, Race, Garveyism, and the 1920 Panama Canal Strike," *The Global South* 6, no. 2 (2012): 39–64; see also J. A. Zumoff, "Black Caribbean Labor Radicalism in Panama, 1914–1921," *Journal of Social History* 47, no. 2 (2013): 429–57.

18. Robert Edgar, "The Prophet Motive: Enoch Mgijima, the Israelites, and the Background to the Bulhoek Massacre," *International Journal of African Historical Studies* 15, no. 3 (1982): 420–21; Frederick Hale, "Fear and Support of an African Independent Church: Reactions to the Bulhoek Massacre of 1921," *Fides et historia: Official Publication of the Conference on Faith and History* 26, no. 1 (1994): 77; "Article in *Christian Express* (Lovedale, South Africa)," 1 July 1921, in

MGP, 9:54; *Interim and Final Reports of the Native Affairs Commission . . . relative to 'Israelites' at Bulhoek and Occurrences in May, 1921* (Cape Town: Government Printers, 1921), 3–10; Robert Edgar, *Because They Chose the Plan of God: The Story of the Bulhoek Massacre* (Johannesburg: Ravan Press, 1988).

19. Adam Ewing, "Kimbanguism, Garveyism, and Rebellious Rumor Making in Post-World War I Africa," *Souls: A Critical Journal of Black Politics, Culture, and Society* 20, no. 2 (2018): 149–77.

20. Muchuchu's recollections are recorded in Carl G. Rosberg Jr. and John Nottingham, *The Myth of 'Mau Mau': Nationalism in Kenya* (New York: Meridian, 1966), 51–52. For Harry Thuku's connections to Garveyism, see Ewing, *Age of Garvey*, 95–106.

21. Washington Counsel for the UFC to the Secretary of State, Washington DC, September 1919, quoted in Tony Martin, *Race First: The Ideological and Organizational Struggles of Marcus Garvey and the Universal Negro Improvement Association* (Westport, CT: Greenwood Press, 1976), 98.

22. By the end of 1922, the *Negro World* had been banned in Malawi, Nigeria, the Gambia, the Gold Coast, and all of French West Africa. It was "strictly controlled" in Sierra Leone. See Robert A. Hill, "Introduction," *MGP*, 9:xlviii; Pierre Jean Henri Didelot to Governor-General of FWA, 4 July 1922, *MGP* 9:510; PRO, CO 267/600/26912, Acting Governor, Sierra Leone, to Duke of Devonshire, 28 May 1923; Henri Jaspar to Louis Franck, 30 June 1921, *MGP*, 9:49–50; Report by Special Agent J.T. Fourney, 7 June 1921, *MGP* 3:459. For British efforts to deny Marcus Garvey entry to Africa, see BNA, CO 533/294/32018; Nyasaland Register of Correspondence, 15 May 1923, CO 703/7; Register of Correspondence, Gold Coast, 17 May 1923, CO 343/28; Nigeria Correspondence, CO 583/118/34197; Acting Governor to Duke of Devonshire, Freetown, Sierra Leone, CO 267/600/28912.

23. Caroline Elkins, *Legacy of Violence: A History of the British Empire* (New York: Knopf, 2022); Rapport no. 322 du 17.5.21 de A. T. Thysville à CDD, in Paul Raymaekers and Henri Desroche, eds., *L'Administration et le Sacré: Discours Religieux et Parcours Politiques en Afrique Centrale (1921–1957)* (Brussels: Acadamie Royale des Sciences D'Outre Mer, 1983), 51–55.

24. C. L. R. James, *Nkrumah and the Ghana Revolution* (London: Allison and Busby, 1977), 66. This chronology is also suggested by Michael O. West, "Like a River: The Million Man March and the Black Nationalist Tradition in the United States," *Journal of Historical Sociology* 12, no. 1 (1999): 81–100.

25. Ewing, *Age of Garvey*, 133–36.

26. "Another War in Europe and the Negro," *Negro World*, January 13, 1923, 1; Garvey, "The Negro's Place in World Reorganization" (March 24, 1923), in *The Philosophy and Opinions of Marcus Garvey or Africa for the Africans*, 2 vols, ed. Amy Jacques Garvey (London: Frank Cass, 1967), 2:36.

27. Speech by Garvey, 16 November 1924, *MGP*, 6:42–46; *Negro World*, February 6, 1926, 3; *Negro World*, March 17, 1923; *Negro World*, February 20, 1926, 7.

28. Jacques Garvey, *Garvey and Garveyism*, 272–74.

29. For the UNIA branch in Guayaquil, see *Negro World*, September 16, 1922; for Edmonton, see *Negro World*, April 16, 1921, 9. For a compiled list of UNIA locals from the mid-1920s, see Tony Martin, *Race First*, 361–73.

30. R. T. Brown, Report to Siquirres, Madre de Dios, Cedar Creek and Germana Divisions, Costa Rica," *Negro World*, January 13, 1923, 7; "Monster Audience at Sunday Night Meeting in Liberty Hall," *Negro World*, February 19, 1921, 3–4; Speech by Marcus Garvey at Liberty Hall, *Negro World*, April 28, 1923, 2; Speech by Marcus Garvey at Liberty Hall, *Negro World*, April 14, 1923, 2.

31. *Negro World*, November 24, 1923, 4; "Another War in Europe and the Negro," *Negro World*, January 13, 1923, 1; Garvey, *Philosophy & Opinions*, 2:24–25.

32. The Universal Ethiopian Anthem was composed by Arnold J. Ford, and its lyrics were written by Ford and Benjamin E. Burrell (quoted from *MGP*, 1:280):

Ethiopia, thou land of our fathers,
Thou land where the gods loved to be:

REFRAIN.
As storm cloud at night sudden gathers,
Our armies come rushing to thee.
Shall we in the fight be victorious
When swords are thrust outward to glean?
For us will the vic'try be glorious
When led by the red, black and green?

CHORUS.
Advance, advance to victory!
Let Africa by free!
Advance to meet the foe
With the might
Of the red, the black, the green.

Shall aliens continue to spoil us?
Shall despots continue their greed?

REFRAIN.
Will nations in mock'ry revile us?
Then our keen swords intercede!
And tremblings shall fall on the nations,
As eyes of mankind hath not seen,
Defeat shall meet their preparations,
And vic'try the red, black and green.
And when the great battle is ended,
The swords and the spears be laid down:

REFRAIN.
The land which their might had defended,
Shall once more become as our own.
And peace and prosperity bless us,
Our standard shall float far above us:
With warfare not sorrow between us;
The red, and the black, and the green.

33. For more on the Universal Negro Ritual and the Universal Negro Catechism, see
    W. Gabriel Selassie I, "Rethinking Garveyism as Religion: The UNIA Universal
    Negro Ritual and the UNIA Universal Negro Catechism," *Journal of African
    Religions* 8, no. 2 (2020): 266–91.
34. Samuel Alonzo Culmer, "Why I Am a Garveyite?" *Negro World*, November
    6, 1926, 5; Leo Porter, "Ladies of Jamaica Division Lead Men in Constructive
    Effort," *Negro World*, April 7, 1923, 8.
35. Michael O. West and William G. Martin, "Contours of the Black International:
    From Toussaint to Tupac," in *From Toussaint to Tupac: The Black International
    since the Age of Revolution*, eds., Michael O. West, William G. Martin, and Fanon
    Che Wilkins (Chapel Hill: University of North Carolina Press, 2009), 10–11.
36. Adam Ewing, "Caribbean labour politics in the age of Garvey, 1918–1938," *Race
    & Class* 55, no. 1 (2013): 23–45; O. Nigel Bolland, *The Politics of Labour in
    the British Caribbean: The Social Origins of Authoritarianism and Democracy in
    the Labour Movement* (Kingston: Ian Randle Publishers, 2001); Rupert Lewis,
    Marcus Garvey: Anti-Colonial Champion (Trenton, NJ: Africa World Press
    1988), 255–73.
37. A. G. Hopkins, "Economic Aspects of Political Movements in Nigeria and in the
    Gold Coast, 1918–1939," *Journal of African History* 7, no. 1 (1966): 133–36; Ian
    Duffield, "Pan-Africanism, Rational and Irrational," *Journal of African History*,
    18, no. 4 (1977): 608–11; Alex Harneit-Sievers, "African Business, 'Economic
    Nationalism,' and British Colonial Policy: Southern Nigeria, 1935–1954,"
    African Economic History 24 (1966): 25–30; J. Ayodele Langley, *Pan-Africanism
    and Nationalism in West Africa, 1900–1945* (London: Oxford University Press,
    1973), 91–92; "Article in the *West African Mail and Trade Gazette*," 24 September
    1921, in *MGP*, 10:718; Letter from Sierra Leone by 'Dorn," *Negro World*, March
    26, 1921, 4; Right Oh! to John E. Bruce, 1 November 1920 and A. Agbebi to
    Bruce, 15 May 1920, in John E. Bruce Papers, Group B, Box 2, Items 188 and
    258, Schomburg Center for Research in Black Culture, New York Public Library.
38. John Maynard, "'In the interests of our people': The influence of Garveyism
    on the rise of Australian Aboriginal political activism," *Aboriginal History* 29
    (2005): 1–22; Maynard, "'The Age of Unrest, the Age of Dissatisfaction': Marcus
    Garvey and the Rise of Australian Aboriginal Political Protest, 1920–1929,"
    in *Global Garveyism*, eds. Ronald J. Stephens and Adam Ewing (Gainesville:
    University Press of Florida, 2019), 226–41.
39. Report of Speech by Ernest Wallace, 23 December 1925, *MGP*, 10:351–52.

40. Robert A. Hill, "General Introduction" to Caribbean Series, *MGP*, 11:lxii; Brenda Gayle Plummer, "Garveyism in Haiti during the US Occupation," *Journal of Haitian Studies* 21, no. 2 (2015): 68–87; Frank A. Guridy, "'Enemies of the White Race': The Machadista State and the UNIA in Cuba," *Caribbean Studies* 31, no. 1 (2003): 107–37; Marc McLeod, "'Sin dejar de ser Cubanos': Cuban Blacks and the Challenges of Garveyism in Cuba," *Caribbean Studies* 31, no. 1 (2003): 75–105.

41. Ewing, *Age of Garvey*, 186–211; Michael O. West, "The Seeds are Sown: The Impact of Garveyism in Zimbabwe in the Interwar Years," *International Journal of African Historical Studies* 35, no. 2/3 (2002): 335–61.

42. Ewing, *Age of Garvey*, 212–37; C. L. R. James, "From Touissaint L'Ouverture to Fidel Castro," in *The Black Jacobins: Toussaint L'Ouverture and the San Domingo Revolution*, Revised, 2nd ed. (New York: Random House, 1963), 397.

43. Hill, "General Introduction" to Caribbean Series, *MGP*, 11:lxxxiv-lxxxv; Sullivan, "No Surrender," 71–73; Lewis, *Marcus Garvey*, 118; Claudrena Harold, *The Rise and Fall of the Garvey Movement in the Urban South, 1918–1942* (New York: Routledge, 2007), 30, 37. Reports from the UNIA's far-flung divisions, printed in the *Negro World*'s weekly "News and Views" feature, vividly attest to the wide range of local services provided by the organization.

44. Lara Putnam, *Radical Moves: Caribbean Migrants and the Politics of Race in the Jazz Age* (Chapel Hill: University of North Carolina Press, 2013), 16, 36; Frances Peace Sullivan, "'No Surrender': Migration, the Garvey Movement, and Community Building in Cuba," in *Global Garveyism*, 59–88.

45. Jacques Garvey, *Garvey and Garveyism*, 96–97.

46. For "internal borders," see Asia Leeds, "Toward the 'Higher Type of Womanhood': The Gendered Contours of Garveyism and the Making of Redemptive Geographies in Costa Rica, 1922–1941," *Palimpsest: A Journal on Women, Gender, and the Black International* 2, no. 1 (2013), 3.

47. Marcus Garvey argued that "aristocracy" was conferred not by wealth or education or titles but by "service and devotion to one's race, to one's country, to one's nation." Speech by Marcus Garvey in the *Negro World*, 13 March 1920, *MGP*, 2:256–57.

48. Leeds, "Toward the 'Higher Type of Womanhood'"; Anne Macpherson, "Colonial Matriarchs: Garveyism, Maternalism, and Belize's Black Cross Nurses, 1920–1952," *Gender and History* 15, no. 3 (2003): 507–27; Michele Mitchell, *Righteous Propagation: African Americans and the Politics of Racial Destiny after Reconstruction* (Chapel Hill: University of North Carolina Press, 2004); Barbara Bair, "True Women, Real Men: Gender, Ideology, and Social Roles in the Garvey Movement," in *Gender Domains: Rethinking Public and Private in Women's History*, eds. Dorothy O. Helly and Susan M. Reverby (Ithaca, NY: Cornell University Press, 1992): 154–66.

49. Honor Ford-Smith, "Women and the Garvey Movement in Jamaica," in *Garvey: His Work and Impact*, 73–82; Robert Trent Vinson, "'Hidden' in Plain Sight: Toward a History of Garveyite Women in South Africa and the Increased

Visibility of Africa in Global Garveyism," in *Global Garveyism*, 182–204. See also Rhoda Reddock, "The First Mrs. Garvey: Pan-Africanism and Feminism in the Early 20th Century British Colonial Caribbean," *Feminist Africa* 19 (1994): 58–77; Karen S. Adler, "'Always Leading Our Men in Service and Sacrifice': Amy Jacques Garvey, Feminist Black Nationalist," *Gender and Society* 6, no. 3 (1992): 346–75; Nicole Bourbonnais, "Our Joan of Arc: Women, Gender, and Authority in the Harmony Division of the UNIA," in *Global Garveyism*, 139–67; Keisha N. Blain, *Set the World on Fire: Black Nationalist Women and the Global Struggle for Freedom* (Philadelphia: University of Pennsylvania Press, 2018).

50. Ula Y. Taylor, "'Negro Women Are Great Thinkers as Well as Doers': Amy Jacques-Garvey and Community Feminism in the United States, 1924–1927," *Journal of Women's History* 12, no. 2 (2000): 104–26.

51. "Cubans Hear Great Talk on Independence," *Negro World*, June 17, 1922, 12.

52. Robert A. Hill, "From Marcus to Marley: Prophecy and Reggae Music," *Reggae and African Beat*, 4, no. 4 (August 1985), 15.

53. Hubert Harrison, "Two Negro Radicalisms," in *A Hubert Harrison Reader*, ed. Jeffrey B. Perry (Middletown, CT: Wesleyan University Press, 2001), 104.

54. Garveyism's religious revivalism drew on and galvanized traditions of Ethiopianism, which emerged in the eighteenth century and spread widely as a popular politics over the course of the nineteenth and early twentieth centuries. See Charles Reavis Price, "'Cleave to the Black': Expressions of Ethiopianism in Jamaica," *New West Indian Guide* 77, no. 1&2 (2003): 31–64; Robert A. Hill, *Dread History: Leonard P. Howell and Millennarian Visions in the Early Rastafarian Religion* (Kingston, Jamaica: Miguel Lorne, 2001), 16; Michael O. West, "Garveyism Root and Branch: From the Age of Revolution to the Onset of Black Power," in *Global Garveyism*, 30–33.

55. Robert Athlyi Rogers, *The Holy Piby* (Hogarth Blake, 2008), 15. For Garveyism's influence on popular religious revivals, see Jarod Roll, "Garveyism and the Eschatology of African Redemption in the Rural South, 1920–1936," *Religion and American Culture: A Journal of Interpretation* 20, no. 1 (2010): 27–56; Jacob S. Dorman, *Chosen People: The Rise of American Black Israelite Religions* (Oxford: Oxford University Press, 2013), 148–50; Ewing, *Age of Garvey*, chapter 6; Ewing, "Popular Pan-Africanism: Rumor, Identity, and Intellectual Production in the Age of Garvey," in *Global Garveyism*, 205–25. Marcus Garvey was notably critical of popular forms of religious expression. But as Lara Putnam observes: "Although Garvey himself rejected religions that howl, or create saints, or danced to frantic emotion, Garveyism fit easily into a spiritual landscape that had room for all of these. . . . Garvey's call to view God 'through the spectacle of Ethiopia' would lead in extraordinary directions." Putnam, *Radical Moves*, 80.

56. West, "Garveyism Root and Branch," 38; Ula Yvette Taylor, *The Promise of Patriarchy: Women and the Nation of Islam* (Chapel Hill: University of North Carolina Press, 2017), 2, 19.

57. Putnam, *Radical Moves*, 215–21; Hill, "Dread History," 16–45; West, "Garveyism Root and Branch," 38–47; Barry Chevannes, "Garvey Myths among the Jamaican People," in *Garvey: His Work and Impact*, 123–30. Editorial by Marcus Garvey, 22 May 1923, *MGP*, 5:313.

58. Ewing, *Age of Garvey*, 202–11; Y.Z. Mwasi, "My Essential and Paramount Reasons for Working Independently" (1933), National Archives of Malawi, Zomba, 84/BCAP/1/1 (a-d).

59. Bolland, *Politics of Labour*, 360.

60. Garvey is quoted in the first edition of *Abeng*: "Abeng Sounds a Call to Action," *Abeng*, 1, no. 1 (February 1969), 2. For Abeng and Black Power in the Caribbean, see Anthony Bogues, "The *Abeng* Newspaper and the Radical Politics of Postcolonial Blackness," in *Black Power in the Caribbean*, ed. Kate Quinn (Gainsville: University Press of Florida, 2014), 76–96; Rupert Lewis, "Learning to Blow the Abeng: A Critical Look at Anti-establishment Movements of the 1960s and 1970s," *Small Axe* 1 (February 1997): 5–17; Paul Hébert, "Abeng and Black Power in the West Indies," *Black Perspectives* (blog), African American Intellectual History Society, October 27, 2015. See also Rupert Lewis, "Jamaican Black Power in the 1960s," in *Black Power in the Caribbean*, 53–75.

61. Harry Mwaanga Nkumbula to William Sherrill, 26 July 1957, MSS 1066, Box 6, Universal Negro Improvement Association Papers, Manuscript, Archives and Rare Book Library, Emory University; Nnamdi Azikiwe, *My Odyssey: An Autobiography* (London: Hurst and Company, 1970), 66; Kwame Nkrumah, *Ghana: The Autobiography of Kwame Nkrumah* (Edinburgh: Thomas Nelson, 1957), 45; William Sherrill to Thomas Harvey, 8 March 1957; Sherrill to Harvey, 15 March 1957; T. D. T. Banda to Sherrill, 16 April 1957. All in Box 6: Correspondence, 1957, UNIA Papers, Emory University.

II

UNDERSTANDING THE LEGAL WRONG AND EFFORTS TO RIGHT IT

CHAPTER SEVEN

Travesty of Justice

*The Context of the Conviction and
How They Jailed a Rainbow*

Justin Hansford, Esq.

> It annoys me to be defeated; hence to me, to be once defeated is to
> find cause for an everlasting struggle to reach the top.
>
> —Marcus Garvey

THROUGHOUT MY YOUNGER years, I was captivated by the story of Marcus Garvey's politically motivated arrest and conviction in the summer of 1923. Not only did I greatly admire Garvey, but his conviction also represented one of the most poignant examples of the injustice that the law can exert on an individual's life trajectory and indeed the trajectory of thousands of people who follow that person if the individual is a political leader. I was morally outraged by it then, and I'm morally outraged by it now.

Garvey's conviction, and the way that it impacted the Black Liberation movement in the United States and around the world, forever changed the course of Black history. It eliminated a vision of racial justice for serious consideration during a time when Black people were fighting Jim Crow segregation and colonialism. It destroyed a robust economic justice vision for people of African descent that could have accrued benefits for decades. It altered the political landscape for the entire African diaspora throughout the twenty-first century.

This essay reviews Garvey's conviction of mail fraud in 1923. By analyzing the facts and the law involved in the case, as well as the circumstances surrounding the trial, I believe there is sufficient evidence to support the notion that Marcus Garvey was indeed wrongly convicted.

The ramifications of this wrongful conviction continue to reverberate today. A wound of indignity has been inflicted on Garvey's family, and throughout the twentieth century, Garvey's vision of racial justice never fully blossomed, as his movement's leader was silenced too early in his journey. Only by posthumously exonerating Garvey can we take an important step toward redress and repair, not only restoring Garvey's good name as an individual but also revitalizing the vision of Pan-African economic independence that Garvey shared and enhancing the depth and breadth of the self-concept and political possibility of the Black diaspora as a whole.

The Allegations of Fraud against the Blackstar Line

In February 1922, Garvey and the three other Black Star Line officers faced two indictments for mail fraud that together contained thirteen counts. The government eventually won a conviction against only Garvey, based on only one of the thirteen counts against him.

This count alleged that Garvey committed mail fraud by causing to be mailed a letter to Benny Dancy on December 20, 1920, which encouraged Dancy to buy stock in the Black Star Line (BSL) although, at the time, it had no ships, was near ruin, and would never obtain any more ships or return to solvency.[1] To find a violation of the mail fraud statute, the government would have to prove the following: 1) the existence of a scheme to defraud, and 2) the use of the US mail to effectuate or attempt to effectuate the scheme.[2]

Immediately after the indictment, the government seized all the books and records of both the Universal Negro Improvement Association (UNIA) and the BSL. The prosecutors then mailed questionnaires to all thirty-five thousand BSL stockholders in the hopes of accumulating evidence.[3] This only added to the fanfare of this trial, which was one of the first modern celebrity trials involving a Black activist.

Those Out to Get Garvey

To understand the stakes of the Marcus Garvey trial, one must understand that this case took place during a critical juncture in African American history. It was the height of Jim Crow segregation. State and federal government officials openly supported white supremacy, which was rife throughout American society.

In response to Jim Crow, various Black leaders proposed various solutions. In my past research,[4] I have arranged these groups into three camps. I have labeled the first camp the lobbyist reformers. Led by the National Association for the Advancement of Colored People (NAACP), which advocated for integration and federal government intervention, the most prominent figure in this camp was W. E. B. Du Bois. The second camp, I have labeled the Black Socialists, led by A. Phillip Randolph, founder of the Brotherhood of Sleeping Car Porters, who called for workers' rights and labor organizing. The third camp, I have labeled the communal self-helpers, initially led by Booker T. Washington, the founder of Tuskegee Normal and Industrial Institute (now Tuskegee University), and by the beginning of the 1920s, led by Marcus Garvey and the UNIA.

In the years before Garvey's indictment, the rivalry between these camps became so intense that it devolved into personal attacks, lawsuits, and ultimately a campaign by Garvey's opponents to rid Garvey of the political debate, the "Garvey Must Go!" campaign. The leaders of each of these racial justice campaigns often denigrated each other and saw their political visions as mutually exclusive and one being a threat to the other. There is a famous story of how Garvey and Du Bois once crossed paths in a hotel lobby one day during this period. As Garvey exited an elevator and Du Bois entered, "Garvey recognized Du Bois and 'his eyes flew wide open, stepping aside,' while Du Bois, ignoring

Garvey, 'looking straight forward, head uplifted, and nostrils quivering, marched into the elevator.'" In the Black press the next day, headlines read, "Du Bois and Garvey Meet! No Blood Is Shed!"[5]

Even if fisticuffs were avoided, the low point of the campaign was a letter sent to the US attorney general from various African American activists (including NAACP leadership, though not Du Bois himself) in 1922 calling for Garvey to be indicted on mail fraud charges. The letter urged the attorney general to "use his full influence completely to disband and extirpate this vicious movement" (referring to Marcus Garvey's UNIA) and implored the attorney general to "vigorously and speedily push the government's case against Marcus Garvey for using the mails to defraud."[6] By arguing that Garvey's central project, the BSL, was a Ponzi scheme or a fraud, the allegations struck at the heart of Garvey's credibility as a leader.

The ramifications of Black activists urging a Jim Crow-era government to intervene to "disband" a competing movement for racial justice are jarring. However, it was not as if a great deal of persuasion was necessary. In 1919, twenty-four-year-old J. Edgar Hoover was placed in charge of the General Intelligence Division of the Justice Department's Bureau of Investigation (later renamed the FBI) and immediately began his legendary campaign to rid the country of "Black Messiah" figures. Hoover spoke of Garvey in the following terms in that inaugural year in his position:

> [Garvey is] particularly active among the radical elements in New York City in agitating the Negro movement. Unfortunately, however, he has not as yet violated any federal law whereby he could be proceeded against on the grounds of being an undesirable alien, from the point of view of deportation. It occurs to me, however, from the attached clipping that there might be some proceeding against him for fraud in connection with his Black Star Line propaganda.[7]

By the time Garvey was finally brought to trial in May 1923, Judge Julian Mack was obtained to preside over the US District Court case.

The litigation began in an uproar as Garvey dismissed his attorneys when they encouraged him to cop a plea. Garvey felt the lawyers were setting him up for a trap. However, as a layperson, Garvey was sorely outmatched in trial practice, pitted against the experienced federal prosecutor. Normally, a judge would note this concern for the sake of the fairness of the outcome and advise against self-representation. However, Judge Mack failed to effectively intervene, and subsequent historical analysis suggests possible motivations as to why.

Judge Julian Mack's Personal Reasons to Convict Garvey Resulted in Two Courtroom Violations

Judge Mack was known for his enthusiastic dedication to political causes. Benjamin Cohen, the well-known jurist, once noted concerning Judge Mack, "He did not merely lend his name to movements, he was active, a doer . . . [he would help] not half-heartedly, but wholeheartedly."[8] Additionally, Judge Learned Hand, another renowned judge, was dismayed by the public interest activism of his colleague Judge Mack. Judge Hand felt that this activism sometimes put Judge Mack's neutrality into question.[9]

Particularly relevant to this case is the fact that Judge Mack ideologically sympathized with the NAACP; maintained a membership in the organization; and made financial contributions to it.[10] This point is key, because the NAACP was Garvey's primary archnemesis throughout his career.

The NAACP also may have taken action to capitalize on Judge Mack's presence. On the day before the trial was set to begin, Judge Mack received a mysterious correspondence from James Weldon Johnson, secretary of the NAACP, in relation to the Garvey case.[11] Regardless of the contents of that correspondence, the mere existence of such contacts between the NAACP and Judge Mack raises concerns about the objectivity of the proceedings.

It appears that Judge Mack's contacts led to at least two separate acts inside the courtroom that constituted severe violations of Marcus Garvey's right to a fair trial, which by themselves could stand as a sufficient basis for exonerating Garvey of the conviction he received in this biased court. Those violations are as follows.

Violation 1

Judge Mack Wrongfully Failed to Recuse Himself

At trial, Garvey presented a petition for Judge Mack to recuse himself from the case. Only three years before this trial, the Supreme Court handed down a landmark decision on judicial disqualification, Berger v. United States. In Berger, the trial judge publicly revealed that he had a personal bias against people of German ancestry. The defendants, who were of German descent, filed an affidavit alleging personal bias and prejudice, and the judge was indeed found biased. The court in Berger articulated that for judicial bias to be sufficient for recusal, the bias "must be based upon something other than the rulings in the case."[12] This extrajudicial requirement for recusal thereafter became one of the bedrock notions of judicial disqualification. The Berger court further enunciated the recusal standard as requiring the recusal petition to state reasons that are "not frivolous or fanciful, but substantial and formidable."[13]

Garvey's motion for recusal was filed based on Judge Mack's "membership in and affiliation with the National Association for the Advancement of Colored People."[14] Although the NAACP was not technically a party to the case, it was one of the leading entities that demanded the investigation and loudly proclaimed the allegations that spurred the government to file charges. Additionally, Garvey included in his petition the full letter written to the attorney general advocating for his indictment in which four of the eight signatories currently held office in the NAACP: Harry Pace, John Nail, Robert Bagnall, and William Pickens. Garvey also asserted that Judge Mack financially contributed to the NAACP and regularly subscribed to *The Crisis* magazine, which as of that date had published five incendiary articles about Garvey's role in the BSL. Garvey argued that exposure to such propaganda against him had caused the judge to be "unconsciously swayed to the side of the

Government against this petitioner," prejudicing him in "the very issues of which will come before your honor in this trial."

As Garvey's allegations of bias focused on Judge Mack's membership in and related activities supporting the NAACP, they were founded on something other than the rulings in the case and thus satisfied the Berger extrajudicial requirement. Furthermore, Garvey's petition for recusal met the Berger "substantial" requirement because of Judge Mack's heavy involvement in the NAACP, as he even participated in the organization's founding meetings.

In denying the petition for recusal, Judge Mack admitted that he contributed to the NAACP and read its magazine but refused to confirm his membership within the NAACP. He disclosed that he read the NAACP's journal, *The Crisis* magazine, asserting that he had only "perhaps glanced at the headlines."

Violation 2

Judge Mack Ignored Perjury by the Key Prosecution Witness

Judge Mack's failure to address perjured testimony by Schuyler Cargill, the key prosecution witness (who himself admitted that his testimony was perjury!), provides another indication of bias in this case. The sole count on which the government convicted Garvey—the allegation that Garvey caused to be mailed a letter soliciting Benny Dancy's purchase of BSL shares of stock when the organization was near insolvency—depended on Cargill's testimony.

Under cross-examination, Schuyler Cargill, a nineteen-year-old BSL office assistant, claimed to be the employee who had mailed the fraudulent advertisement to Benny Dancy.[15] Cargill was the only witness who testified that he was an actual participant in the sending of false advertisements by US mail. Often, he contradicted himself during his testimony. Later in his cross-examination, he admitted that the prosecutor, Maxwell Mattuck, had told him to lie on the stand. Specifically, Mattuck instructed Cargill to say that he had worked for the BSL in 1919 and 1920. However, when the cross-examination revealed that

Cargill did not even know who the supervisor of the mailing division
during those times was, he admitted reluctantly that the prosecutor had
told him to mention those dates.

At the time of Garvey's trial, the perjury rule authorized courts to
grant a new trial if one could prove that a witness willfully and deliberately had testified falsely.[16]

Judge Mack failed to strike this testimony, instruct the jury to disregard it, or grant a new trial. Judge Mack also altogether ignored both
the perjury and the subornation of perjury that Cargill admitted to on
the witness stand, and neither was pursued nor corrected.

Understanding the Merits of the Garvey Mail Fraud Case

Legal Issue 1

Garvey had no intent to defraud, and
intent was a key element of the crime

Remember, to be found guilty, the government would have to prove that
Garvey operated the BSL with fraudulent intent, that the mailing of
the advertisement to Benny Dancy was done with the intent to defraud
Dancy. But with no direct evidence of fraudulent intent, the prosecution proceeded to paint a generally negative picture of Garvey and his
officers, attempting to show that they were not serious businesspeople
and establish an aura of mistrust surrounding their activities. Indeed,
the BSL officers engaged in unprofessional business practices that gave
the government grounds on which they could arouse suspicion of the
officer's judgment. BSL accountants lost one of the accounting ledgers;
UNIA newspaper or restaurant business funds were sometimes used
to pay back BSL debts;[17] and the BSL purchased ships without expert
consultation or sufficient inspection, leading to huge losses. However,
regardless of the impropriety of these acts, none of them could be understood to fulfill the legal definition of fraud pursuant to statute.

After confiscating the organization's records, the government found that Garvey took no money for his own personal use—consequently, it was not even alleged in the indictment. If Garvey received no personal enrichment from the sale of the stock, what motive did he have to commit fraud? How likely was he to have intended for the BSL to fail? Although personal enrichment was not an element of the mail fraud statute, it is unlikely that the drafters contemplated that a fraud scheme in which someone would run an expensive, time-consuming operation such as a shipping company for no personal benefit would fall under the statute's purview.

Indeed, Garvey had many financial incentives for making it a success. He was supposed to receive a salary of US$10,000 a year from the BSL, but it never materialized once the company went into financial decline. The board of directors determined whether Garvey would receive the salary. The board's decision, in turn, depended on the organization's financial strength.[18] Also, Garvey owned two hundred shares of stock, which he purchased with his personal money—meaning that when the BSL went under, Garvey stood to lose much of his own money as well. The premise of Garvey's conviction was that he intended to run the BSL in a way that would cause it to never gain in value, yet in spite of this sell stock at an inflated price. However, because Garvey had so much of his personal financial fate invested in the project, by purposefully ruining the project, Garvey would have lost thousands of dollars himself and gained nothing.

In addition to his financial stake, Garvey's reputation as a Black leader turned on the success or failure of the BSL. After a lifetime of working to reach the level of prominence he had attained, for Garvey to purposefully seek failure would have constituted the pursuit of his own demise. After his release from prison, Garvey spent the rest of his life fighting for Black people's rights. It is unreasonable to assume that Garvey would have attempted to sabotage his career and waste the money of the Black masses, while standing to gain no personal financial benefit, when his commitment to racial leadership never waned, even after his conviction and deportation.

Legal Issue 2

Garvey could not have known that his advertisement was misleading at the time it was sent

There is no evidence that Garvey knew that the advertisements that the prosecutor identified as fraudulent would mislead people or that the statements made in it would turn out to be untrue. This is because when Garvey expressed assurance in his own future success, he had little control over or knowledge of the two factors that would do the most to ensure his venture's economic failure—the vagaries of the shipping market and treachery from inside the organization.

The Market Downturn

During World War I (1914–18), rates for ocean transportation rose as high as 1,250 percent, and shipping companies made huge profits.[19] It appeared to be the perfect time to get into that business. When the war ended, the military powers had surplus ships that they were trying to unload on the public cheaply. One shipping executive testified in front of the Senate that "anybody experienced or inexperienced in the shipping trade could make money." It was not unreasonable for Garvey to believe that Blacks could make these profits as well as anyone else. Indeed, in a little over a year from its inception, the BSL had acquired two ships and was up and running. Thus, the expression of confidence in the creation of a Black steamship company was not an unrealistic entrepreneurial vision, and certainly it was not a fraudulent act.[20]

. However, by May 1919, Garvey could not have foreseen the industry downturn. By 1922, the US Shipping Board would announce a loss of US$51 billion, and $44 billion the following year. In fact, President Warren Harding introduced the Ship Subsidy Bill in February 1922, proposing that Congress subsidize the US Shipping Board to reduce government operating costs. Opening a shipping company during this time was like opening a mortgage company on the cusp of the US housing crisis in 2008. Although it may have seemed like a great idea only three years prior, by the time Garvey filed all his papers and opened for business, the industry had collapsed, and he never even had a sporting chance.

Many other shipping lines also failed during these years. These other companies still ran advertisements throughout their lean years without facing suit for fraud based on their overconfident advertisements. This makes sense because the market fluctuations that determined their fate were not foreseeable. Only Garvey was indicted for continuing to engage in advertising during the market downturn. Even if the commercials were overly optimistic or unwise, such dogged optimism did not constitute a crime of fraud punishable by five years of imprisonment.

Treason from Within

In addition to market fluctuations, the BSL also fell victim to treason from within. Within three months of incorporating the BSL, Garvey had amassed enough money to buy the company's first ship, the *Yarmouth*.[21] Garvey paid US$165,000 for this ship on September 17, 1919, through a deal arranged by Joshua Cockburn, one of the few Black men qualified to be a ship captain at the time. Garvey did not know that Cockburn received a kickback of "about US$1,600" secretly paid to him from the seller of the ship for making this deal, and Garvey did not know that he had paid US$165,000 for a ship that one of the other officers judged to be worth "not a penny more than US$25,000."[22] The *Yarmouth* proved to be a financial disaster. It suffered constant malfunctions that called for expensive repairs and was finally sold in November 1921 for US$1,625.[23]

Cockburn was not the only officer who cheated the BSL. Elie Garcia, the secretary, was also convicted of larceny for stealing from UNIA. Orlando Thompson, the BSL vice president, took actions that did even more damage than those of Cockburn and Garcia. The BSL had been working on a deal for a new ship for quite some time when, at the company's annual convention in January 1921, Thompson announced the near completion of negotiations to purchase the SS *Tennyson*. This was a British vessel that Garvey planned to rename in honor of the Black poet Phillis Wheatley and use to make a transatlantic run to Africa. Based on Thompson's assurances that the ship was fit to make such a trip, Garvey traveled to the Caribbean and Central America in early February 1921 to raise funds for the final purchase. Garvey entered as an exhibit at trial a letter that he received in June 1921 while he was abroad (which Orlando Thompson admitted to writing) that informed Garvey that the *Phyllis Wheatley* had already been purchased.[24]

Unfortunately, Thompson had lied to Garvey. In truth, negotiations for the sale had broken down that March. At that time, Thompson hired Anthony Silverstone, a white operator of "a questionable one-man ship exchange" to complete the purchase on the BSL's behalf, thereby avoiding the racial prejudice that Thompson believed was hampering the deal.[25] Thompson gave Silverstone more than US$20,000 in BSL deposit money, but Silverstone deposited only US$12,500 with the shipping board, absconding with the rest. Once these facts came to light, a warrant was issued for Thompson's arrest; yet Thompson never faced full prosecution.

Meanwhile, the State Department had denied Garvey reentry into the US "in view of the activities of Garvey in political and race agitation." He was not able to reenter the country until August, and upon his arrival, Garvey immediately revoked Silverstone's power of attorney. However, by that time, most of the damage had been done.

Garvey was ultimately convicted of mail fraud for sending an advertisement to Benny Dancy in December 1920 allegedly inviting him to buy stock and urging him to "ride back to Africa" on the *Phyllis Wheatley*, a ship that the advertisement held would soon be purchased. The prosecution argued that, because the letter to Dancy contained an exhortation to buy more stock in light of the future existence of the *Phyllis Wheatley*, the letter was fraudulent.[26] The prosecution declared:

> What could be more fraudulent than this advertisement which appeared in Garvey's paper, the "Negro World" on March

26th 1921?" "BLACK STAR LINE. Passengers and freight
for Monrovia, Africa. By SIS PHYLLIS WHEATLEY. Sailing
on or about April 25th Book your baggage now."

As indicated earlier, if Garvey did personally approve of these advertisements, he did so from overseas, and he did so based on Thompson's
assurances and based on the belief that the BSL had already paid the full
deposit sum to the buying agent. If not for the government's harassment
and Thompson's deception, Garvey would have been able to return to
the US and stop the misleading advertisements from being issued.

In the end, most of the money was returned to those who bought
passages or stock in the *Phyllis Wheatley*. Those who did not receive
refunds did not ask for them because they wanted the money to support
the BSL in case the venture would materialize sometime in the future.[27]
However, none of Garvey's supporters could undo the damage that had
already been done by the BSL officers.

Unfortunately, this counternarrative was never told effectively in
the courtroom, so the declining market and the thievery from within
the organization were nonfactors in the trial.

Legal Issue 3

The Appeal Was Tainted with Racial Bias

Garvey's conviction was upheld on appeal, but a close reading of the judicial opinion demonstrates tinges of bias. It begins by mocking Garvey
and making light of his lifetime of activism, asserting, "It may be true
that Garvey fancied himself a Moses, if not a Messiah; that he deemed
himself a man with a message to deliver, and believed he needed ships
for the deliverance of his people."[28] The court takes Garvey's program
of liberation and redefines it as nothing but the unrealistic daydream
of a fool.

In addition to presenting Garvey as a scam artist at worst and a
delusional buffoon at best and presenting the BSL as a worthless scheme,
the opinion manages to denigrate Garvey's followers as well—those

whom the court is purportedly attempting to protect from victimization. It does so by explicitly reinforcing the basest stereotypes of Blacks as overly emotional and ignorant. Benny Dancy, a Garvey supporter who apparently purchased fifty-three shares of stock, is the putative victim of the crime. The entire case depended on his testimony. However, he is described in the opinion as "a man evidently both emotional and ignorant," and a misunderstanding between Dancy and Garvey during cross-examination is quoted word for word in another attempt at mockingly judging his "caliber."

Dancy is presented as a synecdoche of all Garvey's followers, who in general are characterized as children who are too ignorant and emotional to be trusted. However, in the case of Dancy, it is illogical for the court to make this argument. Remember, Dancy was the purported victim of the crime and the only witness who actually saw the supposedly fraudulent advertisement, and so the whole case turned on the testimony of this "emotional and ignorant" witness.

After disposing of Dancy in a conclusory fashion, the court declares:

> exhibited by practically uncontradicted evidence ... stripped of
> its appeal to the ambitions, emotions, or race consciousness of
> men of colour, [the scheme] was a simple and familiar device
> of which the object (as of so many others) was to ascertain
> how it could best unload upon the public its capital stock at
> the largest possible price.

In subsequent writings, Garvey made two arguments in rebuttal to this holding. First, Garvey reminds readers the BSL never put its stock up for public offering. Instead, the BSL offered its stock only to its constituency and members of its organization and refused to increase profit by offering stock to the broader public. Secondly, the court failed to explain why it decided to "strip" the project of its motivating appeal to the emotions and race consciousness of people of color. As Garvey argued, "Let us strip the Christian religion of its moral, ethical appeals and emotions and we have robbery, pocketpicketing and virtual hold-ups in the name of Christ every Sunday by way of appeals for financial support."[29]

What impact can a circuit court opinion and a Westlaw head note have on the legacy of one of the most prodigious activists for racial justice in the history of our nation? We must remember that public opinion, if repeated often enough, becomes historical narrative. And many supposedly "objective" scholars, and even many pro-Garvey scholars, have been guilty of unquestioningly internalizing the perspective of the court and accepting the veracity of the narrative. Many are quick to point to Garvey's "incompetence" at business matters as an explanation of what went wrong with the BSL. However, both the counternarrative of the history of the BSL and a close reading of the appellate opinion should help bring to light the true nature of the coordinated effort to manipulate and sully the story of Garvey and the BSL.

The Aftermath

For many years, this was thought to be the end of the story. However, when Attorney General John Sargent was appointed in 1925, he made it known that he did not approve of Hoover's overzealous investigative tactics.[30] Consequently, when letters of protest from angry Garvey supporters flooded the attorney general's office after Garvey's conviction, Sargent reconsidered the case based on the facts.[31] Sargent soon thereafter informed President Calvin Coolidge that "an enormous petition" signed by "over [70,000] Negroes" was presented to the Department of Justice on Garvey's behalf.[32] Garvey's purported victims argued that Garvey had not defrauded them and that his conviction was a miscarriage of justice.[33]

Eventually, Sargent recommended the commutation of Marcus Garvey's prison term. In response, President Coolidge commuted Garvey's sentence in 1927, and Garvey was immediately deported as an undesirable alien under the applicable law of the time.

In addition to the president's commutation of Garvey's sentence and implicit disagreement with the judiciary, members of the legislative branch have also clamored for a posthumous pardon of the charges against Garvey. Former congressman Charles Rangel of Harlem has led the call for Garvey's pardon. In 1987, he held a hearing that concluded that Garvey's conviction was "unjust and unwarranted," a conclusion supported by all the mainstream historians who have studied Garvey and the circumstances surrounding the mail fraud trial. Since that hearing, members of Congress have consistently introduced legislation asking the president to grant Garvey a posthumous pardon. Such legislation is before Congress even today, with multiple cosponsors.

Conclusion

After his deportation in 1927, Garvey would never again set foot on American soil. In his absence from the US, the UNIA—formerly an organization of millions—had soon lost its driving force. After several failed attempts to reignite the UNIA from Jamaica, Garvey went to England in 1935 to reclaim his lost magic. Garvey remained productive during this period, publishing *Black Man* magazine for almost five years and, in 1938, founding a short-lived institution called The School of African Philosophy in the hopes of teaching his organizing strategies to future racial justice advocates. However, in London, Garvey's work suffered from his distance from the center of the action in Harlem, and he often faced severe bouts of pneumonia and bronchitis due to the damp chill of the icy London winters. In January 1940, Garvey suffered a stroke that left him paralyzed down the right side of his body and impaired his ability to write or give public speeches.

By May of that year, Garvey had been moving steadily along the road to recovery. However, on May 18, incorrect reports of Garvey's death had spread throughout the media. The condolences rolled in and hundreds of mainstream papers had printed obituaries of Garvey, many quite unflattering. Garvey became engrossed in the reading of his own narrative as retold by friend and foe alike; pictures of him with deep black borders, cursory summations of his life's work and results—all these fed stories that greatly disturbed Garvey. It is widely held that later that month, Garvey read an obituary of himself in the *Chicago*

Defender, a Black-owned newspaper, that held that he had died "broke, alone, and unpopular." It was while reading this obituary that Garvey let out a loud moan and suffered another stroke, this one being fatal.

Marcus Garvey's mail fraud conviction did not define him. He will ultimately be judged on the monumental contributions he made to the struggle for Pan-African freedom. However, the unjust conviction of mail fraud that did much to interfere with his program should be more completely understood, and Marcus Garvey should be exonerated.

Justin Hansford is a professor of law at Howard University School of Law. He is also the executive director of the Thurgood Marshall Civil Rights Center and in December 2021 was elected by the United Nations General Assembly as an inaugural member of the UN Permanent Forum on People of African Descent. Special thanks to Jy'Mir Starks, a junior at Howard University, for research assistance with this essay.

Notes

1. Colin Grant, *Negro with a Hat* (New York: Oxford University Press, 2008), 326.
2. "There is a distinction between the [old and the new provisions], and the elements of an offense under [the 1909 amendment] are (a) a scheme devised or intended to be devised to defraud, or for obtaining money or property by means of false pretenses, and, (b) for the purpose of executing such scheme or attempting to do so, the placing of any letter in any post office of the United States to be sent or delivered by the post office establishment." See United States v. Young, 232 U.S. 155, 161 (1914).
3. Amy Jacques Garvey, ed., *The Philosophy and Opinions of Marcus Garvey*. 2 vols.(New York: Universal Publishing House, 1923 and 1925; Dover: The Majority Press, 1986), 145.
4. Justin Hansford, "Jailing a Rainbow: The Marcus Garvey Case," *Georgetown Journal of Law and Modern Critical Race Perspectives* 2 (2009): 325.
5. Grant, *Negro with a Hat*, 298.
6. See Letter from Harry H. Pace et al., to Harry M. Daugherty, United States Attorney-General, available at http://www.pbs.org/wgbh/amex/garvey/filmmore/ps_go.html.
7. Memorandum from J. Edgar Hoover to Special Agent Ridgely (October 11, 1919), available at http://www.pbs.org/wgbh/amex/garvey/filmmore/ps_fbi.html.
8. Harry Barnard, *The Forging of an American Jew: The Life and Times of Judge Julian Mack* (New York: Heryzl Press, 1974), 121.
9. Barnard, *The Forging of an American Jew*, 143.
10. Barnard, *The Forging of an American Jew*, 77, 113.

11. Robert Hill, ed., *The Marcus Garvey and Universal Negro Improvement Association Papers (MGP)*, vol. 5 (Los Angeles: University of California Press, 1987), 286.
12. See Berger v. United States 255 US 22, 31 (1921).
13. Berger vs. United States.
14. Jacques Garvey, *Philosophy and Opinions*, 301–02.
15. Jacques Garvey, *Philosophy and Opinions*, 358, n. 28.
16. See Smith v. Mitchell, 221 P. 964, 967 (Cal. Ct. App. 1923); see also Randall v. Packard, 36 N.E. 823, 825 (N.Y. 1894). "New trials have been granted also when . . . The witnesses for the prevailing party are manifestly shewn to have committed perjury." Although there was no Supreme Court case law or federal statute specifically outlining a rule for a new trial as a remedy for subornation of perjury at the time, it was known that perjury could be a sufficient basis for ordering a new trial, as shown by this argument by Roscoe Pound, one of the preeminent legal scholars of the era. See Roscoe Pound, *Readings on the History and System of the Common Law* (Lincoln: Jacob North, 1904), 326.
17. Grant, *Negro with a Hat*, 168.
18. Statement by Elie Garcia (13 Jan., 1922), in Robert Hill, ed., *The Marcus Garvey and Universal Negro Improvement Association Papers*. Vol. V, 371.
19. See Judith Stein, *The World of Marcus Garvey: Race and Class in Modern Society* (Baton Rouge: Louisiana State University Press, 1986), 70.
20. The Second Circuit Court of Appeals, in its opinion on Garvey's case, seems to disagree with this first point, on the racist grounds that it was unrealistic for a Black person to think they could successfully own and operate a Black shipping company. See Garvey v. United States, 4 F.2d 974 (2d Cir. 1925).
21. Tony Martin, *Race First: The Ideological and Organizational Struggles of Marcus Garvey and the Universal Negro Improvement* (Westport, CT: Greenwood Press, 1976), 153.
22. Cockburn admitted this during cross-examination. See Hill, *MGP*, vol. 5, 329, n.5, 153.2a Brief for the United States, Garvey vs. United States, 4F.2d 974, 2d Cir. 1925, (No.66), in Hill, *The Marcus Garvey and Universal Negro Improvement Association Papers*, vol. VI, 49, 54.
23. Brief for the United States, Garvey vs. United States, 4F.2d 974, 2d cir. 1925, (No. 66), in Hill ed., *The Marcus Garvey and Universal Negro Improvement Association Papers Vol. VI*, 49, 54.
24. Speech by Marcus Garvey (June 17, 1923) in the *Negro World*, June 23, 1923; Reprint, Hill, *The Marcus Garvey and Universal Negro Improvement Association Papers*, vol. V, 359.
25. Cronon, E. David, *Black Moses: The Story of Marcus Garvey and the Universal Negro Improvement Association* (Madison: University of Wisconsin Press, 1960), 95.
26. Brief for The United States, Garvey v. United States, 4 F.2d 974 (2d Cir. 1925) (No. 66), in *The Marcus Garvey and universal Negro Improvement Association Papers Vol. VI*, 55–7, 60–2.

27. Report by Special Agent Mortimer J. Davis (14 Jan., 1922), in Hill ed., *The Marcus Garvey and Universal Negro Association Papers, Vol. IV*, 350.

28. Garvey v. United States, 4 F.2d 974 (2d Cir. 1925).

29. Jacques Garvey, *Philosophy and Opinions*, 179.

30. See John Garibaldi Sargent, http://law.jrank.org/pages/10006/Sargent-John-Garibaldi.html (accessed April 3, 2024).

31. Hill ed., *The Marcus Garvey and Universal Negro Imrpovement Association Papers Vol. IV*, 390.

32. Letter from John Sargent, Attorney General, to Calvin Coolidge, President of the United states (27 Jan., 1926) in *The Marcus Garvey and Universal Negro Improvement Association Vol. VI*, 314.

33. Martin, *Race First*, 200.

CHAPTER EIGHT

Wrongful Conviction, Grave Injustice

Anthony Pierce, Esq.

> The fall will come. A fall that will cause the universal wreck of the civilization that we now see, and in this new civilization that we now see, and in this new civilization the Negro is called upon to play his part. He is called upon to evolve a National Ideal, based upon freedom, human liberty and true democracy.
>
> —Marcus Garvey

IN 1923, MARCUS Mosiah Garvey's wrongful federal conviction for use of the mails in furtherance of a scheme to defraud effectively ended a global movement that fervently pushed for the advancement of economic and human rights for people of African descent. As the leader of the Universal Negro Improvement Association (UNIA), Garvey was one of the most prominent leaders of the civil rights movement in the first half of the twentieth century. Born in Jamaica, Garvey first came to the United States in 1916 to meet Booker T. Washington, after having been inspired by his autobiography, *Up from Slavery*. By 1921, Garvey had built the largest Black organization in history, the UNIA, with a membership comprising nine hundred branches and nearly six million people and with chapters in forty countries and forty-one states.[1] He was an advocate for the social, political, and economic independence of people of African descent across the world.

A congressional inquiry and review of the historical record has led to resounding agreement that Garvey was wrongfully convicted of using the mails to further a scheme to defraud in the United States District Court for the Southern District of New York. That conviction led to Garvey's deportation, effectively ended the movement that he created, precipitated his own personal demise, and has harmed his family, community, and devotees for over ninety years.

In fact, Garvey was the target of a concerted government effort to obliterate the popular Garveyism movement based on contemporary fears of a resurgent Black community. Garvey faced intense, covert opposition from no less than the director of the FBI and the US Justice Department, among many others. After Garvey proceeded without the benefit of counsel, his criminal trial was replete with errors and prosecutorial misconduct, including the subordination of perjury by a key government witness. From the moment of his indictment and until his death, Garvey maintained his innocence. In his closing statement at trial, Garvey declared: "I want no mercy, only justice—justice—justice. I would not betray my struggling race. If I did I should be thrown into the nethermost parts of hell."[2] Supported by his many thousands of Garveyites, during his lifetime, Garvey fought to seek pardon, clemency, and full relief from his unjust conviction—an effort that continues even today.

Garvey Amassed Followers—But Not All of Them Are Supporters

Starting out as a street corner orator in Harlem, Garvey founded a movement that instilled racial pride and "focused on the need to develop and influence the inclusion of African Americans into the economic spectrum of American life."[3] At the heart of Garvey's teachings were the tenets of economic development and self-sufficiency in the Black community.

He championed a variety of platforms to spread his message, including the *Negro World*, a weekly publication he founded in 1918, which became the most widely circulated Black newspaper of its time. The Negro Factories Corporation, the UNIA's financial empowerment and employment division, put hundreds of Black men and women to work. Garvey also organized numerous convention-style meetings of supporters.

Garvey's teachings challenged conventional attitudes that Black Americans were inferior citizens. As Garvey explained, "We are organized for the absolute purpose of bettering our condition, industrially, commercially, socially, religiously and politically. We are organized not to hate other men, but to lift ourselves, and to demand respect of all humanity."[4] He exhorted his followers: "Up you mighty race, you can accomplish what you will."[5]

The US federal government, however, viewed his teachings as a threat to the existing social order. A man who delighted in public speaking and could ignite the passions of thousands of everyday Black Americans with only his words, Garvey's ability to build movements posed a risk that the federal government would not ignore.

Garvey's message also sparked controversy within the Black community, where other large-scale movements were forming, with competing methods of advancing the rights of Black people. Rival movement leaders A. Phillip Randolph and Chandler Owen, along with Reverend Robert Bagnall, the National Association for the Advancement of Colored People's (NAACP's) director of branches, and Professor William Pickens, the NAACP's field secretary, formed The Friends of Negro Freedom, an organization that lasted from 1920 to 1932.[6] This organization, assisted by other Black leaders of the NAACP and the African Blood Brotherhood, was the driving force behind a campaign to discredit and ultimately imprison Garvey, known as the "Garvey Must Go!" campaign.[7] The members of the campaign were motivated by a combination of ideological, financial, and personal factors.[8] For instance, Cyril Briggs, a native of St. Kitts who embraced communism and later founded the African Blood Brotherhood, attempted a coup of the UNIA at an international convention and had Garvey arrested and tried for libel when Garvey called Briggs "[a] [w]hite [m]an ... [who] claims to be a Negro."[9] At this time, "Garvey was receiving millions of dollars in contributions to Black Star Line" and therefore "killing the ...

contribution market" for other activists.[10] Briggs went on to publish an issue of his magazine, *The Crusader*, with ten editorials criticizing Garvey.[11]

The "Garvey Must Go!" campaign launched a media attack to dictate the public narrative about Garvey and influence state actors to take action against him. In August 1922, the leaders of the rival movements behind the "Garvey Must Go!" campaign held a series of large public events denouncing Garvey, and over the years, each published inflammatory rhetoric about Garvey and his movement in their respective newspapers.[12] The campaign's self-described Committee of Eight, led by Pickens, also corresponded with the federal government, encouraging the US attorney general to engage in surveillance of Garvey and to "use his full influence completely to disband and extirpate [Garvey's] vicious movement" by aggressively pursuing charges against him.[13]

The Federal Government Targets Garvey

Garvey attracted the attention of federal investigators not long after his arrival in America. By 1918, while the United States and other world powers were embroiled in the horrors of World War I, the Military Intelligence Division of the United States Army began receiving reports regarding Garvey's activities in New York. The first report stated simply that "there was a man by the name of Garvey (colored) who preaches every night against the white people, generally from 134th to 137th Street and Lenox Avenue."[14] On September 18, 1918, the Bureau of Investigation (renamed the Federal Bureau of Investigation [FBI] in 1935) reported that a "confidential employee" had been inserted into Garvey's street meetings, who later submitted a report and a copy of the *Negro World*.[15] This development was followed by reports from the Bureau of Investigation about Garvey's meetings and contents of the *Negro World* and a warning that it was "imperative that Mr. Garvey's activities should be closely watched until the terms of peace are signed."[16]

In 1919, US Attorney General Mitchell Palmer placed J. Edgar Hoover as head of the General Intelligence Division of the Justice Department's Bureau of Investigation, responsible for gathering evidence against radicals and immigrants Palmer feared were promoting communism.[17] It was in this fearful atmosphere that the General Intelligence Division began taking measures to arrest and deport Garvey. In 1919, Hoover wrote in a memorandum that Garvey was "particularly active among the radical elements in New York City in agitating the Negro movement. Unfortunately, however, he has not as yet violated any federal law whereby he could be proceeded against on the grounds of being an undesirable alien, from the point of view of deportation. It occurs to me, however, from the attached clipping that there might be some proceeding against him for fraud in connection with his Black Star Line propaganda."[18]

For years before Garvey's eventual arrest for mail fraud in connection with the Black Star Line, Hoover pursued and targeted Garvey. Indeed, Hoover employed many invasive investigatory tactics against Garvey, who became an early target of Hoover's now-infamous surveillance programs later used against another prominent civil rights activist, Martin Luther King Jr. For example, as early as June 1920, Hoover attempted to prosecute Garvey under the Mann Act, a federal law enacted to combat human trafficking and prostitution of women, especially as it involved transportation across state lines. Hoover sought to bring a case under the Mann Act against Garvey for traveling with Amy Jacques, Garvey's then-secretary and future wife.[19] In an effort to gather evidence against Garvey for Mann Act violations, Hoover posted observers to surveil Garvey's hotel rooms in an attempt to catch Garvey in immoral acts.[20] Not unsurprisingly, the government was never able to develop sufficient evidence against Garvey to bring trafficking or prostitution charges.[21]

Nonetheless, by early 1920, multiple federal agents had infiltrated Garvey's organization or befriended him. Herbert Boulin, who went by the code name P-138, used his status as a fellow Jamaican to gain Garvey's trust, all the while reporting on his activities to the Bureau

of Investigation. Boulin reported skepticism about the viability of
the Black Star Line and fed the bureau rumors from the streets of
Harlem about Garvey and whether the Black Star Line could truly be
successful.[22]

In early 1921, Hoover learned that Garvey intended to leave the
country. He wrote to an aide:

> [I]t is my desire, should Garvey leave this country, that he
> be denied entry in the future, and it is suggested that some
> arrangement be made with the State Department on this
> matter.[23]

Despite informing the commissioner of immigration, consuls in the
Caribbean, and officials at various entry ports that Garvey should be
denied reentry, Hoover's efforts failed, and Garvey ultimately returned
after several months of being denied readmission.

Thereafter, federal agents changed tactics. R. P. Stewart, an assistant
to the attorney general, wrote in a letter to the secretary of labor:

> In the event your Department determines that there is no
> action it can take looking to the deportation of Garvey, it
> is suggested that you refer all the papers to the Postmaster
> General in order that an investigation may be conducted for
> the purpose of determining whether Garvey has been guilty of
> using the mails in furtherance of a scheme to defraud.[24]

Thus began the government's efforts to develop a mail fraud case
against Garvey.

The Indictment

In February 1922, Garvey and three other Black Star Line officers
were indicted for mail fraud and charged with "[u]sing the mails in

furtherance of a scheme to defraud and conspiring so to do."[25] Garvey
was accused of defrauding investors when an employee of the Black
Star Line mailed out thousands of brochures picturing a ship that was
purported to be the SS *Phyllis Wheatley*, a ship that the Black Star Line
sought to buy but was never able to purchase. Ultimately, the government charged Garvey with defrauding one man of US$25.[26]

Examining the context makes clear that the charges against
Garvey were unwarranted. The shipping industry was bustling at the
end of World War I due to the surplus of ships available for purchase
at depressed prices from the military. However, the boom was short-
lived, and by the time the Black Star Line was incorporated in 1919, the
shipping industry was on the verge of collapse. The US Shipping Board
announced a loss of US$51 billion in 1922 and another $44 billion loss
in 1923.[27] Shortly thereafter, other shipping companies, including the
Black Star Line, failed. During that time, the Black Star Line and its
competitors continued to advertise shipping voyages until the day the
companies ceased to do business. However, only Garvey was charged
with engaging in misrepresentation for undertaking the same actions
as his competitors by endeavoring to keep his operation afloat during
the industry's depression.

These industry-wide challenges were only compounded by Garvey's
status as a Black man. From its inception, the Black Star Line encountered significant obstacles because of its founders' race. For example,
when purchasing vessels for voyage, the Black Star Line encountered
inflated prices for ships at rates that exceeded their actual value, as well
as higher deposits and bond requirements. The Black Star Line also
struggled to find qualified captains and first mates to crew its ships
given the sparse opportunities for promotions available for Black sailors
at that time. The challenges facing the Black Star Line were simply too
great for the company to survive.

Following the indictment, the government seized the books and
records of both the Black Star Line and the UNIA, and prosecutors
solicited evidence by mailing questionnaires to all thirty-five thousand

Black Star Line stockholders.[28] Although Garvey was charged with defrauding investors, Black Star Line stockholders were almost always Garveyites who believed in Garvey and his goals:

> Everyone connected with the Black Star Line understood its higher purpose—including both employees and stockholders. Often employees would work without asking for payment, simply because they knew that the Black Star Line was part of a greater plan to uplift the Black Diaspora. The stockholders generally contributed in the hopes that they could see the project come into fruition, not to reap financial profit for themselves. In the beginning, Garvey solicited funds as donations and turned to selling stocks later when the District Attorney urged him to incorporate the business. Garvey then appealed to the same people (UNIA members) for stocks as he did for donations. Consequently, it seems that even the sales of stock were more like philanthropic contributions than profit driven investments. As one investor said, "Colored people do not always think in dimes and dollars . . . . If Garvey fails and we all loose [sic] our money it is our business."[29]

Garvey and his codefendants were reindicted in January of 1923.[30] The indictments alleged multiple counts of mail fraud, charging that Garvey had solicited Black Star Line stock purchases using a brochure sent through the US mail that featured a ship that the Black Star Line had not yet purchased.[31] Unlike the first indictment, the second indictment did not include a charge for conspiracy, reflecting a shift in priorities to focus more heavily on Garvey instead of his three codefendants.[32]

The Prosecution—Trial Improperly Proceeded before Judge Julian Mack Despite Evidence of Bias

From the outset, the trial proceedings failed to meet constitutional standards. The trial lacked an impartial judge. Garvey proceeded pro se without a legal adviser. Perjured testimony was offered at trial. Garvey's conviction—a reflection of a bygone era—represents a significant miscarriage of justice.

Prior to trial, Garvey petitioned for Judge Julian Mack's recusal due to Judge Mack's affiliation with the NAACP, the organization from which most members of the "Garvey Must Go!" campaign hailed.[33] Garvey's affidavit in support of the recusal petition alleged that

1. Judge Mack was a member of the NAACP;
2. four of the eight signatories of a letter written to the attorney general advocating for Garvey's indictment were NAACP members;
3. Judge Mack financially contributed to the NAACP; and
4. Judge Mack "regularly subscribed to *The Crisis* magazine which, . . . had published five incendiary articles about Garvey's role in the Black Star Line."[34]

During the time of Garvey's trial, US Supreme Court precedent required that another judge be designated to hear a recusal request, so that the judge assigned to the case was "relieved from the delicate and trying duty of deciding upon the question of his own disqualification."[35] In applicable precedent, the court unambiguously called for "an immediate cessation of action by the judge whose bias or prejudice is averred, and in his stead, the designation of another judge."[36]

Despite this mandate, Judge Mack personally reviewed and promptly rejected Garvey's petition questioning his impartiality. Judge Mack admitted that he contributed financially to the NAACP and viewed its magazine's headlines but refused to acknowledge membership in the organization.[37] Judge Mack then concluded that there were no direct or indirect statements in Garvey's affidavit alleging judicial bias and denied the request.[38] This improper determination of Judge Mack's fitness to hear the case was the first of many errors that undermined Garvey's right to a fair trial.

150 Justice for Marcus Garvey

The Prosecution—Judge Mack Allowed Garvey to Undertake an Invalid Waiver of His Right to Counsel

The trial began on May 18, 1923, with Garvey represented by attorney Cornelius McDougald. However, on May 22, McDougald announced that Garvey no longer wished to retain him as counsel and that Garvey sought to continue pro se.[39]

Waiver of the right to assistance of counsel at a criminal trial must be made intelligently and knowingly before the trial court.[40] However, Judge Mack did not test Garvey's awareness of the consequences of forgoing counsel before allowing him to waive the right. Today, before allowing such an event to occur, the court would engage in a colloquy with the defendant to ensure understanding of the decision and its consequences. Yet when Garvey's attorney informed the court that Garvey wished to relieve his attorney and continue the trial representing himself, Judge Mack immediately accepted the withdrawal, tersely stating, "Very well."[41]

Judge Mack's only comment on the issue—addressed mostly to counsel and not Garvey—occurred when a codefendant's attorney asked whether he could continue to help Garvey with his defense.[42] Judge Mack responded that Garvey "may either conduct the case in person or by counsel; he cannot do both . . . so far as the Court is concerned the defendant has a perfect right to do exactly as he chooses, and it is his privilege to exercise his own judgment and not my judgment."[43] The government attorney prosecuting the case, Assistant US Attorney (AUSA) Maxwell Mattuck, eagerly followed up on Judge Mack's comments, urging, "Mr. Garvey understands that. You understand that? . . . If you are conducting your own defense you will have to conduct it all the way through?"[44]

This third-party remark from opposing counsel could not equate to the required vetting by the court and did not at all address the rights at stake. Judge Mack engaged in no questioning to ensure that the waiver was made intelligently and knowingly with full awareness of the consequences. As a result of this invalid waiver of counsel, Garvey suffered multiple reversible errors at trial that a competent attorney could have prevented.

The Prosecution—Prosecutorial and Judicial Misconduct Culminated with the Suborning of Perjury

The trial proceedings included multiple instances of prosecutorial and judicial misconduct aimed at disparaging Garvey. Both Mattuck and Judge Mack made statements throughout the trial that resulted in errors that should have resulted in reversal of the verdict.

For example, Mattuck interrupted Garvey and belittled him in front of the jury, often emphasizing Garvey's unfamiliarity with the law and improperly critiquing Garvey's lines of questioning.[45] In these interruptions, Mattuck made direct orders to Garvey, undermining Garvey's credibility with the jury, yet provoking little intervention from the court.[46] Grievously, Judge Mack frequently joined in the ridicule in the presence of the jury by remarking that he had to conduct a law school, or that he refused to continue to conduct a law school, for Garvey's benefit as he defended himself pro se.[47] Judge Mack heaped scorn upon Garvey, sustaining objections to Garvey's lines of questioning when no objection had been made, taking over examination of witnesses and then preventing Garvey from asking further questions, and answering questions for witnesses when Garvey sought their sworn testimony.[48]

In fact, judicial conduct of this nature has since been held to violate the right to fair trial in Offutt v. United States[49], a case decided after the conclusion of Garvey's criminal trial. For example, upon reviewing the trial record, the District of Columbia Court of Appeals found that the record revealed issues "of degrading and belittling remarks directed at defense counsel by the judge, restrictions upon cross-examination, the judge's assumption of the function of an advocate, lack of impartiality, and prejudicial remarks by the prosecutor."[50] On further review of the Offutt case, the US Supreme Court reversed the petitioner's conviction, stating:

Our concern is with the fair administration of justice. The record discloses not a rare flareup, not a show of evanescent irritation—a modicum of quick temper that must be allowed even judges. The record is persuasive that instead of representing the impersonal authority of law, the trial judge permitted himself to become personally embroiled with the petitioner. There was an intermittently continuous wrangle on an unedifying level between the two. For one reason or another the judge failed to impose his moral authority upon the proceedings. His behavior precluded that atmosphere of austerity which should especially dominate a criminal trial and which is indispensable for an appropriate sense of responsibility on the part of court, counsel and jury. Such an atmosphere will also make for dispatch insofar as is consonant with a fair trial.[51]

Even during Garvey's lifetime, the US Supreme Court held as to the prosecutor's conduct that "the United States Attorney is the representative not of an ordinary party to a controversy, but of a sovereignty whose obligation to govern impartially is as compelling as its obligation to govern at all; and whose interest, therefore, in a criminal prosecution is not that it shall win a case, but that justice shall be done."[52] Set against this principle, the statements made by Mattuck and Judge Mack throughout Garvey's trial were "thoroughly indecorous and improper," particularly in the presence of the jury.[53]

In other instances, Mattuck evidenced efforts to guide the testimony of witnesses who were perceived as giving harmful testimony.[54] Among these occurrences, while a defense witness testified on direct examination that there appeared to be a "premeditated plan" to sabotage a Black Star Line vessel and that there was dissension among the UNIA ranks that created animus toward Garvey, Mattuck then instructed the witness that she could answer with only a "yes or no" response.[55] Mattuck also requested, and Judge Mack granted, that this testimony be stricken from the record without offering any basis for the objection.[56]

However, most egregious was Mattuck's procurement of perjury by Schuyler Cargill, a key prosecution witness. Throughout his testimony,

Cargill, a nineteen-year-old Black boy who still lived at home with his parents, was noticeably uncomfortable on the stand. Cargill testified that he was approached to be a witness in the case by a white man at the post office and that he came to court to testify following his parents' advice.[57] He spoke so quietly that he had to be told numerous times to speak up, and at one point, he had to be reassured that no one was "mad" at him as he struggled through the questioning.[58]

Cargill testified that he worked at the Black Star Line as an office boy from 1919 to 1921 and that he mailed the offending brochure, making his testimony the only testimony that concerned the mailing for which Garvey was convicted. During cross-examination, Garvey raised the question of whether Cargill was even employed at the Black Star Line at the time the letter was allegedly sent, noting that the man that Cargill claimed had hired him did not work at the Black Star Line when Cargill said he began working there.[59] Cargill was also unable to remember the name of the office timekeeper, with whom he would have had to speak with every day for two years to have his time card punched as he clocked in and out of work.[60] In light of these troubling admissions, Judge Mack began putting questions to the witness. Under questioning by the court, Cargill admitted under oath that Mattuck had instructed him about what dates he should mention concerning when he was employed with the Black Star Line.[61] Next, Cargill was confronted with the fact that he repeatedly gave the wrong location for the post office station where he claimed that he mailed the brochures.[62] Upon further cross-examination, Cargill stated that an inspector for the case had told him what he must say as to the location where the brochures were put into the mail.[63] Despite Cargill's stark admission on the stand that a government investigator orchestrated his testimony, after immediate redirect by Mattuck, Cargill testified simply that he had "made a mistake" when he stated that the government told him what to say.[64]

Notwithstanding the vigorous objections throughout Cargill's testimony from both Garvey and counsel for the codefendants, Judge Mack only once struck remarks, but it was never made clear to the jury that it should disregard any portion of Cargill's testimony.[65] The testimony was allowed to remain as part of the record even though the law authorized courts to grant a new trial if one could show that a witness willfully and deliberately testified falsely.[66]

In the aggregate, these improper statements from and conduct by the prosecutor, with tacit approval and even participation by the presiding judge, undermined Garvey's right to a fair trial.[67]

Garvey's Conviction and Commutation

Of the four codefendants on trial, only Garvey was found guilty. He was sentenced to the maximum penalty for mail fraud—five years in prison. Garvey's conviction was upheld on appeal, and he began serving his five-year sentence in February 1925.[68]

Calls for Garvey's release were instant. Notably, nine of the twelve jurors who voted to convict Garvey later signed an affidavit recommending commutation of his sentence.[69] Garvey's personal secretary and second wife, Amy Jacques Garvey, raised tens of thousands of dollars from Garveyites for Garvey's defense. Millions of supporters sent letters and signed petitions calling for Garvey's release.[70] In addition, representatives of the UNIA established official efforts to clear Garvey's name through an April 1925 petition for pardon submitted on Garvey's behalf and signed by "tens of thousands of American citizens."[71]

Recognizing that even an incarcerated Garvey remained a powerful symbol within the Black community and realizing that his sentencing had only further agitated his supporters—who saw the prosecution as unjust and politically motivated—federal agents recommended that Garvey be released and subsequently deported. As US Attorney General John Sargent wrote in his November 12, 1927, letter to President Calvin Coolidge recommending immediate commutation of Garvey's sentence,

> The situation as presented in the Garvey case is most unusual.
> Notwithstanding the fact that the prosecution was designed
> for the protection of colored people, whom it was charged

Garvey had been defrauding by means of exaggerated and incorrect statements circulated through the mail, none of these people apparently believe that they have been defrauded, manifestly retain their entire confidence in Garvey, and instead of the prosecution and imprisonment of the applicant being an example and warning against a violation of law, it really stands and is regarded by them as a class as an act of oppression of the race in their efforts in the direction of race progress and of discrimination against Garvey as a negro.

This is by no means a healthy condition of affairs . . . In view of subsequent representations made in behalf of Garvey, I am inclined to think that the facts as reported to the Department are perhaps somewhat severely stated and are susceptible of modification and explanation in many respects.[72]

On Attorney General Sargent's recommendation, Garvey's sentence was commuted by order of President Calvin Coolidge on November 18, 1927, and Garvey was deported from the United States, never to return.

Anthony Pierce is the partner in charge of Akin Gump's Washington, DC, office. He draws on more than three decades of trial and litigation experience.

Notes

1. Justin Hansford, Notes, "Jailing a Rainbow: The Marcus Garvey Case," *Georgetown Journal of Law and Modern Critical Race Perspectives* 2 (2009), 325, 336 (with Samantha Godwin, "Reactions," *Georgetown Journal of Law and Modern Critical Race Perspectives* [2009], 373).
2. Transcript of *American Experience*, "Marcus Garvey: Look for Me in the Whirlwind," directed by Stanley Nelson, aired February 12, 2001, on PBS, https://www.pbs.org/wgbh/americanexperience/films/garvey/#transcript.
3. Mail Fraud Charges against Marcus Garvey: Hearing Before the Subcomm. On Crim. Just. Of the H. Comm. On the Judiciary, 100th Cong. 8 (1988) (prepared statement of Rep. Charles B. Rangel.
4. Amy Jacques Garvey, ed., *The Philosophy and Opinions of Marcus Garvey, Journal of Pan African Studies ebook*, 2009, 46.

5. Hansford, "Jailing a Rainbow," 335 (citing Richard Delgado, "Storytelling for Oppositionists and Others: A Plea for Narrative," *Michigan Law Review* 87 [1989]: 2411).

6. Hansford, "Jailing a Rainbow," 340 (citation and internal quotations omitted).

7. Hansford, "Jailing a Rainbow," 340.

8. Hansford, "Jailing a Rainbow," 340–42.

9. Tony Martin, *Race First: The Ideological and Organizational Struggles of Marcus Garvey and the Universal Negro Improvement* (Westport, CT: Greenwood Press, 1976), 240 (quotations omitted).

10. Hansford, "Jailing a Rainbow," 341 (citing Judith Stein, *The World of Marcus Garvey: Race and Class in Modern Society* [Baton Rouge: Louisiana State University Press 1986], 71); Interview by Charles Mowbray White with Chandler Owen and A. Philip Randolph, editors and publishers of *The Messenger* (Negro) and leaders of the Negro Socialist Party of the Bronx and Harlem, in Manhattan, NY (August 20, 1920), in Robert A. Hill, ed., *The Marcus Garvey and Universal Negro Improvement Association Papers* (*MGP*), vol. 2 (Berkeley: University of California Press, 1983), 609.

11. Hansford, "Jailing a Rainbow," 342 (citing Tony Martin, *Race First*, 240).

12. "Marcus Garvey Must Go!" campaign poster (August 1922), in Hill, *MGP*, vol. 9, 553; Hansford, "Jailing a Rainbow," 342–43.

13. Hill, *MGP*, vol. 9, 556, n.2 (quotation marks omitted) (citing Letter from William Pickens, et al. to US Att. Gen. Harry M. Daugherty [January 15, 1923]).

14. Emory J. Tolbert, "Federal Surveillance of Marcus Garvey and the UNIA," *Journal of Ethnic Studies* 14 (1987), 25, 28 (quotation marks omitted) (citing National Archives, RG 165, 10218-116-29-124, records of the War Department, General and Special Staffs, Office of the Chief of Staff).

15. Tolbert, "Federal Surveillance," 28 (quotation marks omitted) (citing National Archives, RG 65, File OG 258421, Report by S.B. Pfeifer).

16. Tolbert, "Federal Surveillance," 28–29 (quotation marks omitted) (citing National Archives, RG 165, 10218–261 (23) 2–1/273).

17. Hansford, "Jailing a Rainbow," 344 (citing *American Experience*, "People & Events: J. Edgar Hoover," http://www.shoppbs.pbs.org/wgbh/amex/garvey/peopleevents/p_hoover.html (accessed May 12, 2022).

18. Online Memorandum from J. Edgar Hoover to Special Agent Ridgley (October 11, 1919), *American Experience*, http://www.shoppbs.pbs.org/wgbh/amex/garvey/filmmore/ps_fbi.html (accessed May 12, 2022).

19. Hill, *MGP*, vol. 2, 345; Hansford, "Jailing a Rainbow," 345; Report by Bureau Agent F. B. Faulhaber, dated August 31, 1921, in Hill, *MGP*, vol. 3, 723–25.

20. Hansford, "Jailing a Rainbow," 345.

21. Tolbert, "Federal Surveillance," 32–33; Hill, *MGP*, vol. 2, 345.

22. Tolbert, "Federal Surveillance," 36.

23. Tolbert, "Federal Surveillance," 33 (citing National Archives, RG 65, BS 198940, J. Edgar Hoover to Mr. Bailey, February 11, 1921).

24. Tolbert, "Federal Surveillance," 41 (citing National Archives, RG 60, 198940–4).
25. Transcript of Record, 15, 1052, Garvey v. United States, 4 F.2d 974 (2d Cir. 1925) (No. 66).
26. *American Experience*, "Marcus Garvey."; Hannah-Grace Fitzpatrick, "Marcus Garvey," University of Liverpool, https:// www.liverpool.ac.uk/black-atlantic/ information/peopled-j/marcus_garvey2 (accessed May 12, 2022).
27. Hansford, "Jailing a Rainbow," 359 (citation omitted).
28. Hansford, "Jailing a Rainbow," 350 (citing John Henrik Clarke, ed., *Marcus Garvey and the Vision of Africa* [Trenton, NJ: Africa, 1974], 73, 145–46).
29. Hansford, "Jailing a Rainbow," 337 (citations and quotation marks omitted).
30. Mail Fraud Charges against Marcus Garvey, 73 (testimony of Robert A. Hill).
31. Mail Fraud Charges against Marcus Garvey, 101–02 (testimony of Tony Martin); Hansford, "Jailing a Rainbow," 356.
32. Mail Fraud Charges against Marcus Garvey, 73 (testimony of Robert A. Hill).
33. Transcript of Record, 36–53; see also Mail Fraud Charges against Marcus Garvey, 103–04 (testimony of Tony Martin).
34. Hansford, "Jailing a Rainbow," 352 (citations omitted); Transcript of Record, 36–53.
35. Berger v. United States, 255 U.S. 22, 32 (1921) (citation and quotation marks omitted).
36. Berger v. United States, 33.
37. Mail Fraud Charges against Marcus Garvey, 94 (prepared statement of Tony Martin).
38. Mail Fraud Charges against Marcus Garvey, 94 (prepared statement of Tony Martin).
39. Transcript of Record, 184–85; see also Mail Fraud Charges against Marcus Garvey, 74 (testimony of Robert A. Hill).
40. Johnson v. Zerbst, 304 U.S. 458, 465 (1938) ("[D]uty imposes the serious and weighty responsibility upon the trial judge of determining whether there is an intelligent and competent waiver by the accused. While an accused may waive the right to counsel, whether there is a proper waiver should be clearly determined by the trial court, and it would be fitting and appropriate for that determination to appear upon the record."); see also Faretta v. California, 422 U.S. 806 (1975); United States v. Roy, 444 F. Appendix 480, 484 (2d Cir. 2011) (citation omitted) ("'[T]he district court should engage the defendant in an on-the-record discussion to ensure that [he] fully understands the ramifications of [his] decision.'").
41. Transcript of Record, 184–85.
42. Transcript of Record, 185–86.
43. Transcript of Record, 185.
44. Transcript of Record, 186.
45. See, for example, Transcript of Record, 1091 ("Ask about one circumstance at a time."), 1114, 1119, 1216, 1257 ("You cannot argue with your own witness" and "Don't lead.").

46. Transcript of Record, 1091, 1257.
47. See, for example, Transcript of Record, 1026 ("to divide the cross-examination into two parts is utterly unnecessary. Another law school lecture but it will be the last I hope."); 1111 ("There was a great deal that was brought out by Mr. Garvey's cross-examination that was utterly irrelevant to this case. Every lawyer in the room, of course, knows that."); 1117 ("I said a layman has a right to conduct his own case, but I cannot change the rules of law because he conducts it."); 1220 ("Now, I have got to make another law school lecture."); 1288 ("The patience of the Court will be about reaching the limit if this sort of thing keeps on. The result will be serious in the continuation of the examination if that limit is reached. There are limits, even if the defendant conducts his own defense. I am trying to extend those limits to the utmost, but a persistent violation of the instructions of the Court will lead to a stoppage of the examination by the defendant himself. Now, let's get on."); 1525 ("The sessions of the Law School will begin later. In the meantime if you want legal advice consult your lawyer or consult a lawyer.").
48. Transcript of Record, 1317 ("Mr. Garvey [questioning witness]: Do you know what Mr. Tobias' office is? The Court: What difference does that make? . . . The witness has said at the time she worked for the 'Negro World' she was on the pay roll of the Black Star Line. That does not make any difference what Mr. Tobias was."); 1323 ("The Court [to Mr. Garvey attempting to question witness]: Pardon me, I do not need any help when I am examining the witness. When I get done you can ask any additional questions you wish, and if I need any help I will call for assistance."); 1329 ("The Court [to Mr. Garvey]: No, no, no. In the first place that is leading, and in the second place you have gone all over it before. Mr. Garvey: You take it for granted that I want the truth of the situation. The Court: You have gone all over that."); 1330 ("Mr. Garvey [questioning witness]: Was [Mr. Tobias] treasurer of any other than the Black Star Line? The Court: Sustained. You have asked her that and she has answered.").
49. Offutt v. United States, 348 U.S. 11 (1954).
50. Peckham v. United States, 210 F.2d 693, 702 (D.C. Cir. 1953).
51. Offutt, 348 U.S. at 17.
52. Berger v. United States, 295 U.S. 78, 88 (1935).
53. Berger v. United States, 84.
54. Transcript of Record, 1327–28 (Mattuck eliciting an objection for stating, "Now, I want to get you straightened out on this . . ." after witness gave conflicting testimony about her payment by the Black Star Line as compared to the *Negro World* newspaper and UNIA).
55. Transcript of Record, 1097–103.
56. Transcript of Record, 1101.
57. Transcript of Record, 683, 694, 702–03; Hansford, "Jailing a Rainbow," 353–54.
58. Transcript of Record, 685, 688, 692, 697, 702.
59. Transcript of Record, 687–88.
60. Transcript of Record, 685, 689.

61. Transcript of Record, 688–89.
62. Transcript of Record, 697–98.
63. Transcript of Record, 697–98.
64. Transcript of Record, 697–98.
65. Transcript of Record, 683–704.
66. See Smith v. Mitchell, 221 P. 964, 967 (Cal. Dist. Ct. App. 1923) (granting new trial where "uncontradicted evidence" revealed that witness had been induced to give perjured testimony in matters material to the case).
67. See Berger v. United States, 295 U.S. 78; Offutt v. United States, 348 U.S. 11.
68. *American Experience*, "Marcus Garvey."
69. H.R. Con. Res. 44, 111th Cong. (2009).
70. *American Experience*, "Marcus Garvey."
71. Letter from UNIA Assistant President-General William Sherrill to U.S. President Calvin Coolidge (April 28, 1925), in Hill, *MGP*, vol. 4 (Berkeley: University of California Press, 1989), 144 Hill, *MGP*, vol. 4, 314 (Letter from Attorney General John Sargent to President Calvin Coolidge (January 27, 1926), "[A]n enormous petition [was] signed, so I understand it is claimed, by over seventy-thousand Negroes . . . and since that time additional petitions and considerable correspondence have been received.").
72. Hill, *MGP*, vol. 4, 607–08 (Letter from Attorney General John Sargent to President Calvin Coolidge, November 12, 1927).

CHAPTER NINE

Howard University—A Century in Defense of Marcus Garvey

Mwariama Kamau

> Great principles and great ideals know no nationality.
> I know no national boundary where the Negro is concerned.
> The whole world is my province until Africa is free.
>
> —Marcus Garvey

THE MOST HONORABLE Marcus Garvey's conviction in 1923 for a trumped-up charge of mail fraud ignited a serious backlash from a number of Howard University (HU)-affiliated personalities. In fact, ever since his arrest a hundred years ago for the conspiracy to commit mail fraud, a significant contingent of HU students, faculty, and alumni rallied to his defense in the media and lobbied the White House for his release. This overlooked account of the Howard University community's steadfast support for the legal and political exoneration of the Right Excellent Marcus Garvey over the last hundred years lends itself to a dynamically new understanding of the Garvey movement's relationship with Negro intelligentsia, particularly at the capstone of Negro education.

In 1922, when Mr. Garvey was first arrested, members of the HU community were among his strongest defenders. When the Friends of Negro Freedom, a rival organization to Mr. Garvey's Universal Negro Improvement Association (UNIA), sent a provocative questionnaire to twenty-five prominent Negroes, asking if Mr. Garvey should be deported for causing mischief, four of the recipients with ties to Howard

University (Carter G. Woodson, Kelly Miller, Emmett Scott, and Carl Murphy) all decidedly replied no, and several expressed offense with the survey. In fact, Professor Kelly Miller was "surprised that the suggestion of deportation came from another Negro." Professor Miller went on to say, "I do not believe in the imprisonment, expulsion or suppression of ideas . . . If Garvey's doctrines are false, combat them with truth."[1] Paradoxically, the ringleader of the campaign, A. Philip Randolph, editor of *The Messenger*, contradicted his own magazine's mission statement that detested the act of deportation for the "expression of political or class war opinions."[2]

During this period, Mr. Garvey and his association could boast having a considerable number of Howard alumni among UNIA and African Communities League (ACL) high officials and editorial staff of the *Negro World*. John Edward Bruce was a contributing editor of the *Negro World*; Timothy Thomas Fortune served as assistant managing editor; and Charles Augustin Petioni served as the newspaper's Howard University correspondent. Robert Lincoln Poston served as secretary-general of the association; jazz singer Revella Hughes was the UNIA choir director and Dr. Lionel Antonio Francis served as president of the Philadelphia division. The Howard-trained Jimmy McLendon briefly served as Mr. Garvey's attorney in 1922; and First Lieutenant Clarence Benjamin Curley, the Howard Law School graduate turned professor in the School of Commerce, was a board director of the Black Star Line, as well as accountant and secretary.

In January 1923, Dr. W. E. B. Du Bois and eight prominent Negroes wrote the State Department and US Attorney General John Sargent, respectively, in an effort to discredit Mr. Garvey as an undesirable alien and to vilify the UNIA.[3] Mr. Garvey refuted the false allegations and challenged Dr. Du Bois to a debate for the dozenth time.[4] Upon receiving no response, Mr. Garvey exclaimed, "My enemies and those opposed to the liberation of the Negro to nationhood are so incompetent and incapable of meeting argument for argument and tolerance with tolerance that they have cowardly sought the power of government to combat and destroy me."[5] Professor Miller likewise reminded his peers seeking Mr. Garvey's arrest, "You cannot imprison ideas. It is better to let the false battle with the true and rely upon the survival of the fittest."[6] He later added that it bodes nothing for "the Negro protagonist in the intellectual arena . . . to ridicule Garvey's practical absurdities or to denounce his irregular methods." One "must be able to sustain his own thesis on the platform of public debate and disquisitional skill."[7]

By June 1923, Marcus Garvey was convicted of conspiracy to commit mail fraud, sentenced to five years in jail by Judge Julian Mack, taken into custody, and ultimately given an inordinately high appeal bond, due to false rumors by the prosecutor that Mr. Garvey was "a menace to the community and a dangerous person."[8] Immediately, the Marcus Garvey Committee on Justice (MGCJ) was formed, chaired by HU graduate David Elliot Tobias, who boldly proclaimed:

> We are going to ram it into the realm of practical politics and ram it for all it is worth. And we will. This case cannot be discussed with a sneer and it will not be allowed to rest in the grave dug for it by the able conspirators who assisted the court to render an unfair decision that smells rank to Heaven . . . Whatever happens, the vindication of Marcus Garvey is opined and the damnation of the plotters who imagined they have despoiled him is a foregone conclusion."[9]

The MGCJ also included two other Howardites, UNIA Secretary-General Robert Lincoln Poston and Washington Division No. 183 President Attorney Joseph Henderson Stewart. On July 6, 1923, the MGCJ delivered a petition with a hundred pages of signatures to the Justice Department and White House, demanding they investigate the trial of Marcus Garvey.[10] The petition heading read, in part, "Let Justice Be Done, Though The Heavens Fall . . . Convicted Through Prejudice On The Prosecution Of Mr. Maxwell S. Mattuck, Assistant District Attorney Of The Southern District Of New York, And Tried Before His Honor Judge Julian Mack, And Denied Bail On Appeal

Through Further Persecution Of Said Assistant District Attorney."[11] The petition drew the president's attention to their contention that

> Marcus Garvey... through the machinations of political and
> organization enemies within and without the race, was indicted
> under Section 215 of the Postal Laws, namely, conspiracy to
> use the mails to defraud. This we commonly, jointly, separately
> and distinctly believe to be a frame-up charge against the said
> Marcus Garvey by his enemies.

Later that evening, President Stewart hosted a local mass meeting for the delegation to circulate a petition urging a new trial and to raise resources for the Marcus Garvey Defense and Appeal Fund.[12] Three weeks later, the committee returned to the White House with 140 additional pages of signatures, renewing the charges of unfairness previously laid before the president, demanding a Justice Department inquiry.[13]

Following the death of US President Harding a month later, President Stewart followed up by sending a local convention resolution to President Coolidge, expressing similar sentiment. However, the resolution inferred that "many Negro leaders in the United States have become full of envy and jealousy because of the success of the leadership of Marcus Garvey among Negroes, and it is believed that they got together and did all they could to put Marcus Garvey behind bars."[14]After three months, the committee successfully secured the release of Mr. Garvey on bail pending appeal with assistance from UNIA's director of publicity, Henry [Harry] Vinton Plummer Jr.[15]

In January 1924, shortly after many of the UNIA's rival organizations formed a group called the Negro Sanhedrin, Mr. Garvey spoke at Howard University about the failings of the US criminal justice system. He declared, "There is no law but strength; no justice but power."[16] He later took the liberty to warn his followers about the old crop of leaders "steeped in hypocrisy, fraud, deception and selfishness" and cautioned them to rise "to the point where they can discriminate between

appointed leadership and elected leadership."[17] He further likened
the persecution and antagonism meted out against his message and
movement by members of the Negro Sanhedrin to the hostilities Jesus
suffered from the Jewish Sanhedrin in his day. Surprisingly, Professor
Miller, head of the Negro Sanhedrin concurred, explaining,

> The trick is as old as human cunning. Always put the trou-
> blesome reformer on the wrong side of the law and send him
> to the penitentiary or to the gallows. It is the same type of
> tactics resorted to in case of Jesus, Socrates, John Brown and
> Gandhi . . . And yet it is doubtful if the proposals of Garvey are
> any more absurd than the plans of John Brown or the preach-
> ments of Gandhi. The pretensions of Jesus, to the orthodox
> mind of his day, were the acme of absurdity.[18]

Professor Miller was well aware that the "technicality of the law is the
easiest way to get rid of troublesome Negroes. Just watch them closely
and at some turn of the road they will violate established regulations,
then crucify them with the law's rigid feature." He concluded with the
realization that "it is not Marcus Garvey, per se, who is sent to prison
but Marcus Garvey who had the effrontery to promote and proclaim
ideas which do not suit the white man's preconceived notion of things.
Any Negro who dares like audacity may expect a like fate."[19]

This lamentable spectacle compelled Professor Miller to declare,
"A race clamorous for free speech is very prone to deny the privilege
to each other when it runs counter to pet predilections and cherished
opinions." He observed how "they who had been persecuted quickly
turned persecutors and demanded that Mr. Garvey should be banished
from the country," rather than challenge his "pernicious doctrine" by
"argument, reason and persuasion."[20] Mr. Garvey's second wife, Mrs.
Amy Jacques Garvey, shared a similar opinion of the hypocrisy of some
leaders who ran to the attorney general under the pretense of securing
justice, all the while knowing he was "notorious for his crooked, shady
political dealings."[21]

Following the Fourth International Convention of the Negro
Peoples of the World, sponsored by the UNIA in August 1924, President Stewart was a member of the convention delegation dispatched
to present President Coolidge with a petition signed by four million
Negroes that read in part,

> We also beg to draw to Your Excellency's attention that
> the leader of the Movement, Honorable Marcus Garvey, its
> President-General, has been wickedly persecuted by Agencies
> under the control of your Government, used as they have been
> by jealous rivals of our own race, and that any effort on your
> part in preventing any agencies of the Government under
> your control being further used to unfairly handicap us in
> this endeavor of ours to solve the race problem, will be highly
> appreciated.[22]

Cubs in the Bushes

Several months later, on February 5, 1925, Mr. Garvey lost his appeal,
was apprehended, and incarcerated at the Atlanta Penitentiary. The
Universal Negro Political Union (UNPU), the Garvey movement's
political wing, immediately launched an international campaign for
his release, soliciting the support of a number of national personalities, including the former dean of Howard University's School of Law,
Professor William H. H. Hart. By March of 1925, Professor Hart—
with the support of the new president of the Washington Division of
the UNIA, HU-trained attorney Perri Frisby—held a series of mass
meetings, hosted by the UNPU National Political Director General
Aaron Prioleau, to raise public awareness and funds for Mr. Garvey's
legal defense. Professor Hart told the audiences that "Garvey had
been wrongly incarcerated, and, with proper legal procedure, could
be released from prison within a fortnight . . . Garvey had been committed to prison on the inference that an empty envelope sent to
one Dancy in Brooklyn contained a letter, which was an improper

solicitation for money."[23] Later that year, Frisby sent a mass meeting resolution to President Coolidge, expressing the grievance of the membership "over the imprisonment of Marcus Garvey." The resolution urged President Calvin Coolidge to use his good office and the power given him by constitution to release Mr. Garvey during the Christmas holiday, 1925.[24]

Howard professor James Cobb and former UNIA member and attorney Robert L. Vann approached Mrs. Amy Jacques Garvey in 1925 and "suggested rather confidently that for a fee of $5,000, they could obtain a presidential pardon for Marcus Garvey. It is probable that this was a scheme which originated with the trio Emmet Jay Scott, Cobb, and Vann, and that all three men were depending on their relationship with Coolidge to obtain the pardon for Garvey."[25] Mrs. Garvey declined the offer and instead "sought her husband's advice, lobbied in Washington, D.C. and arranged for committees to meet with the attorney general and President Coolidge. Ultimately, however, she was advised to have her husband set his own grounds for a pardon. Therefore, she never retained Cobb and Vann."[26]

Within the next two years, the movement for Garvey's release continued robustly, ultimately garnering sympathy from many former traducers, who began casting doubt over the merit of his incarceration. Howard University's first Black president, Mordecai Wyatt Johnson, supported Mr. Garvey's release and Howard graduate turned Howard professor Edward Franklin Frazier helped shape a more sympathetic public opinion of the UNIA leader when he published in *The Nation* one of the first important sociological studies of the Garvey movement's mass appeal, offering a comparative analysis of the UNIA and its leading rivals.[27] He additionally averred:

The Garvey Movement is a crowd movement essentially different from any other social phenomenon among Negroes.

Most discussions of the Garvey Movement have been concerned with the feasibility of his schemes and the legal aspects of the charge which brought him finally to the Atlanta Federal Prison.

It is uncritical to regard Garvey as a common swindler who has sought simply to enrich himself... He has the distinction of initiating the first real mass movement among American Negroes.[28]

By April 1927, news of Mr. Garvey's declining health motivated some of his political detractors to question the usefulness of his continued incarceration. Howard alum Joseph Dandridge Bibb, editor of *the Chicago Whip*, and future HU trustee Plummer Bernard Young, editor of *the New Journal and Guide*, both published editorials calling for executive clemency. Dean Kelly Miller published an article in the *Contemporary Review* entitled "After Marcus Garvey, What of the Negro?" where he sympathetically touted Mr. Garvey's "unfathomable faith in his people." Although he depicted Mr. Garvey as a wide-eyed, reactionary idealist from Jamaica whose "intellectual and moral faculties, though untutored, were wildly active," he admitted that Mr. Garvey's vision, "the federation of the Black members of the human family into a world empire under self-dominion was a bold dream which no mortal had ever dared to dream before" and "worth 1,000 years of the united endeavor of mankind" to fulfill. He then exposed the political imperative behind Mr. Garvey's legal punishment, not for his behavior, but for his beliefs:

> Negro newspapers and magazines were filled with criticisms and denunciations of this new and dangerous doctrine. The Garvey Movement became the Garvey Menace. This interloper was denounced as a trouble-maker, dangerous to whites and Blacks alike. His motive and his honesty were impugned. It was strongly urged that he should be deported as a foreigner stirring up strife among native born Americans. His business transactions became involved in legal tangles.

During the trial, Garvey fought like a lion at bay. He and his disciples believed that he was persecuted for righteousness sake and that the technicality of the law was invoked as a pretext to defeat his racial objective.

No personal wrong doing was attributed to him by way of improper personal profit ... This is the price which the reformer must reckon to pay when his propaganda is at vital variance with established public policy.[29]

Later that year, the National Association for the Advancement of Colored People (NAACP) hosted the Fourth Pan-African Congress (PAC) as enthusiasm about Africa began to wane among African Americans in Mr. Garvey's absence. In fact, interest in Africa had become so weak that even Dr. Du Bois admitted the congress was but "a rather empty gesture to keep the idea alive."[30] In an obvious effort to attract Garveyites to the event, the PAC was hosted in New York during the month of August, the same time and place the UNIA would typically hold their international conventions. At the outset of the congress, Professor Miller published an additional article, entitled "Why Marcus Garvey Should Be Pardoned," stating, "Many of the Negro Intelligentsia furnished information to the government leading to his conviction."[31] He then argued "to help send Garvey to prison ostensibly on a technical legal charge, but really because his propaganda differed from theirs is of the same order of meanness as if I should spy out some violation of traffic regulations and have my opponent put in jail because he does not agree with me on the Eighteenth Amendment." The article then suggested, "The Negro race should join one united petition for the pardon of Marcus Garvey. Our newspapers should open their columns for signature to the monster petition. Those who had any complicit part in his imprisonment should be the most zealous in seeking his release." In conclusion, he solemnly declared, "Before this reaches the light of print, the Fourth Pan African Congress under sponsorship of Mrs. Hunton and inspiration of Du Bois will be under way. I trust that the first act of this Congress will be to send a request to President Coolidge for the pardon of Garvey."

This writing set the tone for a congress that was much more sympathetic to Mr. Garvey than any previous. Surprisingly, the congress—well attended by a number of Howard University professors, including Professor Hansberry, Professor Charles Wesley, and former professors George Cook and Rayford Logan—erupted in applause at the mention of Marcus Garvey, sang praises for his unmatched leadership abilities, and at least attempted to pass a resolution demanding executive clemency.[32] Shockingly, even Dr. Du Bois gleefully proclaimed Mr. Garvey's popular slogan, "Africa for the Africans." Ultimately, Arthur Elmes may have best expressed the evolving sentiment among the "talented tenth" toward the Garvey movement:

> It does not do to treat Garveyism with detached indifference; it does not do to blame, decry, nor vilify in any sweeping, indiscriminate manner, nor yet "without sneering, others teach to sneer." Many an outsider, like myself, may be brought sooner or later to admit it: after all there was something to it.[33]

The *Negro World*, for the most part, on the front-page editorial graciously welcomed

> the remarkable attitude toward the persecution of the Hon. Marcus Garvey which has come to certain men and institutions here in America in recent days. Not only have they, while adding their voices to the chorus of appeal to the authorities for Mr. Garvey's release, been frank and strenuous in their condemnation of the orgy of chicanery and deceit which placed the famous leader in a prison cell, but with their special pleading have come belated, and so all the more striking, confessions of the correctness of the doctrines of the man, outspoken endorsement of the plans he formulated for the

redemption of his race—a tardy but complete realization that
happiness and progress and continued existence for the Negro
race lay only along the trail that Garvey blazed.[34]

In a separate article, *Negro World* Contributing Editor Samuel
Haynes even suggested "the immediate organization of a National
Committee of 100 and an International Committee of 50 to convince
the Department of Justice, and through them President Coolidge, of
the justice of our demand for executive clemency."[35] He recommended
inviting Dr. Mordecai Johnson, Professor Miller, Professor Locke, and
Professor and Dean Lucy Stowe, amongst many others, to join the
national committee.

Despite the outward display of congeniality and reconciliation,
some Garveyites remained suspicious and critical of the motivation
behind this sudden praise and sympathy for Mr. Garvey. Dr. Ferris,
the former *Negro World* editor, in a July 30th article in the *Pittsburgh
Courier* subtitled "Imitation Is Sincerest Form of Flattery Quoted as
Former Critic Accepts Principles He Denounced" and with the pull
quote "Garvey's Mantle Has Fallen on Du Bois," commented:

We find Marcus Garvey languishing in the Atlanta Penitentiary and we find some of the editors and organizations who
saw no worth whatever in Marcus Garvey, or the Universal
Negro Improvement Association which he organized, and
who created the adverse sentiment against the man and his
movement, which spurred the Federal Government to jail
Garvey, now capitalizing and exploiting some of the fertile
and vitalizing ideas which Garvey and his movement were the
first to champion, propagate and popularize. That the so-called
Garvey Movement was the expression of the soul of the aspirations and hopes of the real Negro is evidenced by the fact
that scores of erstwhile critics of the movement are now riding
triumphantly on the crest of the wave which it launched."[36]

Additionally, Haynes considered the decision to host the PAC in Harlem during the month of August, absent the UNIA convention, "a brazen attempt to steal the thunder of the UNIA," unmasking "a desperate desire to capture the imagination of the masses whom Garvey had awakened, ere Garvey returned."[37]

Negro World Editor T. Thomas Fortune also gave an unflattering report of the PAC in an editorial entitled "Mr. Garvey and the Pan-African Congress." Fortune became incensed when Howard alumnus Rev. Dougal Ormonde Beaconsfield Walker introduced the PAC resolution endorsing executive clemency for Mr. Garvey, only to have Dr. Du Bois maneuver it into a committee from which it never returned. Fortune candidly concluded, "Dr. Du Bois has no love for Marcus Garvey."[38] The editorial staff of the *Negro World* followed those remarks with a disclaimer, apologizing for accusing Du Bois of stealing Mr. Garvey's thunder, conceding, "The man is too small even to imitate Garvey successfully."[39]

The campaign for executive clemency did eventually pay off in November 1927 when President Calvin Coolidge commuted Mr. Garvey's sentence and immediately deported him back to Jamaica. From the promenade of the SS *Saramacca*, Mr. Garvey delivered an eloquent valedictory message to his American audience, assuring his followers of the righteousness of their cause, declaring his innocence of any crime and reminding everyone that "the Negro Intelligentsia double-crossed and framed me. They signed my name with a rubber stamp to documents on which I was convicted."[40] His departure, however, did not dissuade his followers from continuing the program.

Following Mr. Garvey's release and deportation, the exoneration campaign essentially ended. However, all was not quickly forgiven or forgotten. One of the students in Howard University's Garvey Club, Malcolm Nurse, better known as George Padmore, continued to register his indignation with the injustice meted against Mr. Garvey by militantly protesting the 1928 visit of Sir Esme Howard. Howard, the British ambassador to the US and primarily responsible for Mr. Garvey's deportation, was scheduled to speak at the dedication of the university's International House, located at 2447 Georgia Avenue NW, Washington, DC. During the demonstrations, Padmore is said to have thrown leaflets in Sir Esme's face and have referred to him "as the representative of history's most bloated empire."[41] The leaflets, directed to the student body, read in part: "We protest against your present misleaders who have, without your consultation and approval, invited the British Ambassador and other imperialists to officiate at your function."[42]

Out of the Shadow of History

As African and Caribbean nations began gaining their independence in the 1950s and 1960s, largely inspired by the anti-colonial crusade of Mr. Garvey, efforts to properly honor this patriot and martyr for racial justice commenced. In 1957, the newly independent nation of Ghana honored the Right Excellent Marcus Garvey by placing a black star in the center of their national flag, in honor of the Black Star Line. On November 11, 1964, the government of Jamaica declared him their first National Hero and subsequently conferred upon him the Order of National Hero. Senegal formally recognized Mr. Garvey as a "pioneer thinker" who helped blaze a trail to Africa's independence by issuing the 1970 Marcus Garvey postage stamp in his honor.

In America, the trend continued. In 1980, the Washington, DC, headquarters of the Organization of American States installed a Marcus Garvey bust in their Hall of Heroes. This event was attended by the Garvey family and a host of Garveyites, including Baba Oduno A. Tarik, an original student member of Dr. Cain Hope Felder's Biblical Institute for Social Change at Howard University and founding president of the Washington, DC, Division No. 330 of the UNIA. Baba Tarik, who facilitated weekly sessions of the Our Own History Club on campus between 1979and 1982, also attended the 1987 Marcus Garvey hearing before the Subcommittee on Criminal Justice of the Committee on the Judiciary in the House of Representatives, initiated by then congressman Rangel's "concurrent resolution expressing the sense of the Congress that the mail fraud charges brought against Marcus Garvey by

the Federal Government were not substantiated and that his conviction
on those charges was unjust and unwarranted." Later that year, one of
the lead participants at the congressional hearing, Dr. Tony Martin,
received an award at a Howard University celebration hosted by the
National Black Student Unity Council, honoring the centennial of Mr.
Garvey's birth.[43] By 1988, *The Hilltop* began publishing updates on the
status of Rangel's House Resolution 84.[44]

Fifteen years later, TransAfrica and the National Council on
Caribbean Affairs hosted an event at the Bunche Center, featuring a
keynote address by Prime Minister PJ Patterson of Jamaica. Patterson
commended the Congressional Black Caucus for their "unswerving
advocacy in support of the resolution calling for the complete exoneration of Marcus Garvey." He extolled Mr. Garvey as one of the greatest
leaders and thinkers of the twentieth century and declared:

> This great Jamaican, this noble fighter for the dignity of peoples
> the world over, was not only an example to countless numbers
> of his countrymen, but inspired thousands in the United States
> and indeed millions around the world through his profound
> sense of internationalism and his deep commitment to social
> justice and human rights. Garvey's contribution, in retrospect,
> is made even more remarkable, given the fact that at the rela-
> tively young age of thirty-four, he already had thousands of
> followers throughout the hemisphere who were members of
> his Universal Negro Improvement Association. Garvey and
> the influence of these UNIA groups contributed to the later
> emergence of the civil rights movement in the United States
> and greatly benefitted the work of American stalwarts, such as
> the late Dr. Martin Luther King Jr.
>
> Still regarded by millions of African-Americans as among
> the ten most influential persons of the 20th Century, Garvey's
> influence and the power of his ideals continue to resonate here
> in the US.[45]

Dr. Julius Garvey, son of the Most Honorable Marcus Garvey, spoke before an audience of three hundred at Howard University in 2007, launching a campaign calling for the posthumous exoneration of his father by the US Congress and/or president of the United States.[46] In 2009, former HU law student and future HU professor Justin Hansford authored an article in the inaugural issue of the *Georgetown Journal of Law and Modern Critical Race Perspectives*, entitled "Jailing a Rainbow: The Marcus Garvey Case," explicating the court's partiality in the trial and conviction of Marcus Garvey for conspiracy to commit mail fraud. Seven years later, as attorney for the Garvey family, Hansford joined the campaign to exonerate Mr. Garvey and held a press conference at the National Press Club in Washington, DC, attended by the author. Among the esteemed panel of participants were Dr. Goulda Downer, chairwoman of the Caribbean American Political Action Committee (CPAC), assistant professor in the College of Medicine at Howard University, and head of the Howard University Telehealth Training Center; Nkechi Taifa, founding director of Howard University School of Law's award-winning Equal Justice Program; and, Quito Swann, professor of African diaspora history at Howard.

Following the press conference, the Justice for Garvey Campaign hosted a panel discussion at Howard University's Ralph J. Bunche International Affairs Center that included Dr. Emory J. Tolbert and invited participation from a host of Howard students.

In 2022, Dr. Julius Garvey—in conjunction with CPAC and a national coalition of Black booksellers, including Howard University's own Paul Coates, owner of Black Classic Press—relaunched the Justice4Garvey Campaign, calling for the exoneration of Mr. Garvey. Downer, Hansford, and Taifa all supported the campaign once again, and HU Alumnus Ambassador Curtis Ward and Professor Ta-Nehisi Coates also participated in the campaign that successfully gathered over one hundred thousand signed petitions to present to the White House.

Today, Howard University remains ever ready to defend the unimpeachable legacy and legal record of the Most Honorable Marcus Garvey from the ignominious stain placed on his record by less scrupulous men. As the HU community was among the first to oppose the unjust persecution and wrongful conviction of the Right Excellent Marcus Garvey, we are confident it will continue fighting until justice is won. When the story of Mr. Garvey's journey from wrongful incarceration to a full, posthumous exoneration is finally written, we are confident the heroic struggle of Howard University's relentless advocates will be inextricably woven between the pages.

The Honorable Mwariama Dhoruba Kamau is an international organizer, born and raised in the Banneker City Metropolitan Area (Washington, DC) and first introduced to the Universal Negro Improvement Association and African Communities League in 1997. By 2000, he was elected second vice president of Division No. 330 of the UNIA-ACL Rehabilitating Committee and appointed webmaster of the association's website and by 2001 had cofounded the Marcus and Amy Garvey Work-Study Group. He served as a delegate to numerous international conventions of the association and in 2003 was assigned vice chair of the Elder Commemoration Committee, after which he actively began researching the lost and forgotten history of the UNIA after Marcus Garvey's 1940 elevation.

In 2005, Mr. Kamau was elected president of the Washington Division, cofounded the Henrietta Vinton Davis Foundation, and cofounded the Universal Marcus Garvey Day Tribute and Celebration. He also joined the executive board of the Amy Garvey Institute as deputy chancellor of research. By spring 2006, he became special delegate to the parent body in laying claim to the Isaiah Morter Estate in Belize and by August earned the title international organizer of the UNIA.

Additionally, Mr. Kamau was an associate producer and consultant for *Mosiah*, the first-ever narrative short film based on the life of the Most Honorable Marcus Garvey Jr. He also educates communities across the globe about the UNIA through copious journal articles and social media pages.

He currently retains the title UNIA international organizer and vice president of the Washington Division No. 183. He also serves as a special representative to the president-general of the Marcus Garvey Institute in Chicago and commissioner of the Marcus Garvey Society in Raleigh, North Carolina.

Mr. Kamau currently resides in Accokeek, Maryland, and is a proud father of four wonderful children and six grandchildren.

Notes

1. Chandler Owen, "A Symposium on Garvey by Negro Leaders," *The Messenger*, December 1922, 550–52.
2. Theodore Kornweibel, *No Crystal Stair: Black Life and the Messenger, 1917–1928* (Ann Arbor: The University of Michigan Press, 1975), 139.
3. Amy Jacques Garvey, ed., *The Philosophy and Opinions of Marcus Garvey*, vol. 2. (Dover: The Majority Press, 1986), 294–300.
4. Marcus Garvey, "W. E. Burghardt Du Bois As A Hater Of Dark People," *Negro World*, February 17, 1923, 2. Incidentally, two Howard-trained attorneys turned law professors, Joseph H. Stewart and Lafayette M. Hershaw, did engage in a debate over the merits of the Garvey movement shortly after Du Bois's decline ("Plan Joint Debate," *The Evening Star* [Washington, DC], November 17, 1923, 13).
5. Garvey, *Philosophy and Opinion*, vol. 2, 309.
6. Kelly Miller, "Kelly Miller Says," *The Baltimore Afro-American*, February 21, 1925, A9.
7. Kelly Miller, "Kelly Miller Says," *The Baltimore Afro-American*, September 14, 1923, 1.
8. "Like Other Great Leaders Garvey Pays the Price," *Negro World*, June 30, 1923, 2, col. 4.
9. John Edward Bruce, "Bruce Grit's Column," *Negro World*, July 14, 1923, 4.
10. "Ask Harding to Aid Garvey: Negroes Would Have President Inquire Into His Trial," *The Washington Post*, July 7, 1923, 3.
11. Robert Hill, ed., *The Marcus Garvey and Universal Negro Improvement Association Papers* (*MGP*), vol. 5 (Berkeley: University of California Press, 1983), 390–94.
12. "Collect Money Here to Fight for Garvey," *The Washington Post*, July 7, 1923, 2.
13. "New Appeal for M. Garvey," *Negro World*, July 27, 1923, 17.
14. UNIA Washington Division Papers (UNIA–WDP), private collection, Washington Division No. 183 convention resolution to President Coolidge, August 27–29, 1923.
15. "A Warm, Hearty, Inspiring, Enthusiastic Welcome: Marcus Garvey Greeted With Acclamation Befitting An Emperor," *Negro World*, September, 22 1923, 2.
16. Albert Crofton Gilbert, "Howard University Faculty And Students Enthused Over Presentation Of UNIA Program By Hon. Marcus Garvey," *Negro World*, February 2, 1924, 2.
17. Marcus Garvey, "Old Leaders of Negro Race Must Give Way To Youth," *Negro World*, January 22, 1924, 1.
18. Kelly Miller, "Kelly Miller Says," *The Baltimore Afro-American*, February 21, 1925, A9.
19. Kelly Miller, "Kelly Miller Says," February 21, 1925, A9.
20. Kelly Miller, "Freedom of Speech Most Cherished Of Privileges," *The Baltimore Afro-American*, May 9, 1931, 2.

21. "Editorials," *The Messenger*, June 1924, 178.
22. Letter from UNIA delegation to President Calvin Coolidge, UCLA African Studies Center, American Series Sample, Volume VI: September 1924–December 1927, www.international.ucla.edu/asc/mgpp/sample06.
23. "Mr. Garvey's Incarceration Wrong, Says Prof. Hart," *Negro World*, March 28, 1925, 4.
24. Perri W. Frisby, president, Aaron P. Prioleau, trustee, Miss Katie Jenkins, secretary, Washington (DC) Division No. 183, Universal Negro Improvement Association, to President Calvin Coolidge, December 22, 1925, Office of the Pardon Attorney, Record Group 204, 1160B, Folder 3, National Archives at College Park, Md.
25. Maceo Dailey, Jr., "Calvin Coolidge's Afro-American Connection," *Contributions in Black Studies: A Journal of African and Afro-American Studies* 8, Article 7, (1986): 97.
26. Mary E. C. Drew, *Divine Will, Restless Heart* (Bloomington IN: Xlibris Corporation, 2010), 192. Apparently, Cobb's offer almost cost him a judgeship in 1926 when Attorney General Sargent viewed his "affiliation" with the Garvey movement as grounds to deny the appointment (*Hampton Review* 14, no. 1, [1988]: 41).
27. Judith Stein, *The World of Marcus Garvey: Race and Class in Modern Society* (Baton Rouge: Louisiana State University Press, 1986), 206; E. Franklin Frazier, "Marcus Garvey: Mass Leader," *Negro World*, August 21, 1926, 5. Although originally published in *The Nation*, *Negro World* editorial staff believed the article's attempt at impartiality while stating its bias made it worthy of circulating.
28. Stein, *The World of Marcus Garvey*; Frazier, "Marcus Garvey."
29. Kelly Miller, "Kelly Miller Says," *The Baltimore Afro-American*, May 7, 1927, 16.
30. W. E. B. Du Bois, *Dusk of Dawn: An Essay Toward an Autobiography of a Race Concept* (San Diego: Harcourt Brace & Company, 1940), 279.
31. Kelly Miller, "Why Marcus Garvey Should Be Pardoned," *The Baltimore Afro-American*, August 27, 1927, 7.
32. Hill, *MGP*, vol. 7, 541; Clifford L Miller, "'Bootleggers, Ministers Lead Race,' Student Speaker Says," *The New York Amsterdam News*, August 25, 1927, 7.
33. Arthur Elmes, "Garvey and Garveyism: An Estimate," *Opportunity: A Journal of Negro Life* 3 (May 1925), 141.
34. The Editors, "The Great Triumph of Marcus Garvey and the Cause," *Negro World*, September 3, 1927, 1.
35. Samuel Haynes, "Through Black Spectacles," *Negro World*, September 3, 1927, 3.
36. William H. Ferris, "'Garvey's Mantle Has Fallen On Du Bois,' Says W.H. Ferris," *The Pittsburgh Courier*, July 30, 1927, 1.
37. Samuel Alfred Haynes, "Of Interest and Moment In 1927," *Negro World*, January 14, 1928, 4.

38. Timothy Thomas Fortune, "Mr. Garvey and the Pan-African Congress," *Negro World*, September 3, 1927, 4.

39. "Garvey and Du Bois," *Negro World*, September 3, 1927, 2.

40. "Nearly 1,000 Bid Garvey Good Bye at New Orleans," *The Washington Tribune*, December 9, 1927, 1.

41. Rukudzo Murapa, *Padmore's Role in the African Liberation Movement* (DeKalb: Northern Illinois University, 1974), 15.

42. "Radical Literature Greets British Minister at Howard," *The Chicago Defender*, December 22, 1928, 4.

43. "Marcus Garvey Scholar Honored by Students," *Atlanta Daily World*, November 20, 1987, 3.

44. April Smith, "Garvey Bill Pulled Until October," *The Hilltop*, September 30, 1988, 3.

45. Jamaican Information Services, "PM Pledges Strong Support for Move in U.S. House to Clear Garvey's Name," *JIS Daily Newsletter*, October, 26 2003, http://jis.gov.jm/pm-pledges-strong-for-move-in-u-s-house-to-clear-garveys-name/ (accessed January 11, 2023).

46. Valencia Mohammed, "Marcus Garvey Exoneration Sought Locally, Nationally," *Afro-American* (Baltimore, MD.), February 24, 2007, B1.

III

GARVEY'S ACTIVISM IN JAMAICA

CHAPTER TEN

Garvey Fights Racial Capitalism of the British Empire in Jamaica

Rupert Lewis, PhD

> Every student of political science, every student of political economy,
> every student of economics knows that the race can only be saved
> through a solid industrial foundation.

—Marcus Garvey

THERE HAS BEEN a persistent tendency to dismiss the story of Garvey's life after his unjust deportation from the United States in 1927. What this does is curtail our understanding of his intellectual and political development in the decade of the 1930s, when race and class issues intertwined in a manner exacerbated by the economic depression in the United States. Increasing unemployment in the Caribbean and worsening social and economic conditions led to the emergence of radical labor upheavals throughout the English-speaking Caribbean in the mid- to late 1930s.

The conceptual significance of this period is that Garvey was engaging frontally with the British Empire as Black lives were subject to its imperial system. This system had its origins in Europe, the transatlantic slave trade, and plantation-industrial complexes that matured into world systems of production, especially in the United States. He combines recognition of the power relations in the global system with the need to develop policies and organizational initiatives specific to the conditions of Latin America and the Caribbean; West, Central, and

Southern Africa; the United States; and Europe. It is Garvey's understanding of the dialectic of the international and national that gives
Garveyism, when creatively applied, its dynamic capabilities.

The Caribbean dimension of the Garvey movement in Central
America and the Caribbean was a consequence of migration following
American capital investments.[1] Garvey was himself a migrant to Costa
Rica, Panama, and Guatemala. The Garvey movement in the 1920s and
1930s was active in Antigua, the Bahamas, Barbados, Bermuda, British
Guiana, British Honduras, Costa Rica, Cuba, the Dominican Republic,
Grenada, Guatemala, Haiti, Honduras, Jamaica, Mexico, Nevis, Nica-
ragua, Panama, Puerto Rico, Saint Lucia, Saint Vincent, Suriname,
Trinidad, Venezuela, and the Virgin Islands (Hill 1990, 997–1000).
To these territories must be added the Caribbean diaspora in Canada,
the United States, Britain, France, Holland, and Germany. The *Negro
World* newspaper acted as a clearinghouse for reports from the branches
in this region. So, the Caribbean dimension of the Garvey movement
was large and survived under racist colonial rule.

When Garvey returned to Jamaica in December 1927, the *Gleaner*
published "Trouble Coming." He stressed the inextricable links between
local and international sources of oppression in colonial systems and the
need to prepare and mobilize for freedom on all fronts.

Garvey's statement on his return was calm and deliberate: "I was
born in the beautiful parish of St. Ann near the falls of the Roaring
River. I grew with nature and drank much of her inspiration; hence
my soul is full of human love, and on this my return to Jamaica I shall
seek to do all I can for the mass of the population, who suffer most.
Anything that will help to solve the great world problem of the negro
with which I am particularly charged, by virtue of my position as President-General of the Universal Negro Improvement Association I shall
not fail to do."[2]

The system of British racial capitalism is an apt descriptor for how
capital accumulation took place under conditions of slavery and colonialism benefiting the British ruling classes and white populations and
because of centuries of African enslavement and colonialism destroying

the hopes and lives of millions of African people. But equally important for how we conceptualize the past and present was that these economic structures were embedded in governmental and private institutions of racial oppression and racist ideologies that continue to permeate the development of capitalism in Europe and later the United States.

The phenomenal growth of British racialized capitalist development in the late nineteenth century involved the colonization of huge chunks of Africa and Asia. This, of course, followed the transatlantic slave trade and plantation slavery from the seventeenth century to the third decade of the nineteenth century. Eric Williams, in *Capitalism and Slavery*, pointed to the inextricable relationship between the rise of industrial capitalism in Britain and the enslavement of Africans. And that line of research now underlies many databases strengthening the case originally made by Williams in his doctoral thesis at Oxford University. The reparation research done by Hilary Beckles in two volumes set out the economic wealth based on extraction of labor, resources, and centuries-long injustices. The first volume, *Britain's Black Debt: Reparations for Caribbean Slavery and Native Genocide*, provides data on how Britain was built by slavery and paid plantation owners a huge compensation when slavery was abolished. The second volume, *How Britain Underdeveloped the Caribbean: A Reparation Response to Europe's Legacy of Plunder and Poverty* discusses how, in the 1940s and 1950s, Britain deliberately set out to make independence fail through lack of finance in any meaningful way to meet the developmental needs of the region. This same policy was at work in the 1930s, and Garvey's challenge to Britain's leaders foreshadows the unsuccessful efforts of West Indian leaders in the 1940s–1960s to seek development financing from a country that had colonized the region for over three hundred years.

The period of great expansion for Britain in Africa and Asia was from the 1860s through to the partitioning of Africa in the 1880s. At the start of the twentieth century, England "controlled over 9.3 million square miles of territory obtained through war and plunder. Between 1884–1900 Britain acquired some 3.7 million square miles of colonial territory. The United Kingdom was in comparison only 121,000 square miles. The population of this empire was 431 million while that of the U.K. amounted to 60 million. On the eve of World War II Britain's Empire included ¼ of the world's area" (Lewis 1994, 81).

The British Empire was maintained by violence and ideological mechanisms that compelled subservience based on racial superiority.

"Forty-seven percent of Britain's foreign investment was in the Empire in places like Canada, New Zealand, India, Burma, Malaya, Ceylon, Africa and Latin America. British capitalists reaped huge profits from making loans at high rates of interest. It was through her finance capitalists that she met her frequent balance of payments problems" (Lewis 1994, 81.)

Walter Rodney's classic text, *How Europe Underdeveloped Africa*, is relevant to this discussion. The extraction of wealth from its colonies in the far-flung empire was key to British power and has had an enduring impact on Britain's position in the world today.

Public Policy in a Time of Crisis

The need for radical public policy changes to the systems established by global empires, principally the American and European structures, were at the heart of the philosophy and global actions of the Garvey movement. These principles and policy initiatives were set out in the 1920 Declaration of Rights of the Negro Peoples of the World at the historic Madison Square Garden Convention. Colonial public policies were antiblack, anti-poor; moreover, discriminatory and patriarchal practices ruined the lives of Black women and children. Too little attention has been placed on Garvey's adversarial relationship with the British colonial government in Jamaica. These relations were full of conflict on political, racial, cultural, legal, and economic grounds.

Garvey's focus in the 1930s was on Jamaican and Caribbean development, and his adversarial relations with the governor and the secretary of state for the colonies in Britain are crucial. The British had developed what was called, in their own phase, a "dove and serpent"[3] approach to anti-colonial protests and memoranda. They presented a dovelike posture at times, but the fierce serpent of colonial oppression was always there, sometimes in the background and many times in the foreground.

In the 1929 manifesto of the Peoples Political Party, we find the following policy positions.

Economic

1. Protection of native labor.
2. A minimum wage for the working and laboring classes of the island.
3. A law to protect the working and laboring classes of the country by insurance against accident, sickness, and death occurring during employment.
4. An eight-hour working day throughout Jamaica.
5. Land reform.
6. A law to encourage the promotion of native industries.
7. A law to compel the employment of not less than 60 percent of native labor in all industrial, agricultural, and commercial activities engaged in on this island.
8. The establishment by the government of an electrical system to supply cheap electricity to such growing and prospering centers as are necessary.
9. The compulsory improvement of urban areas from which large profits are made by trusts, corporations, combines, and companies.
10. A law to prevent criminal profiteering in the sale of lands in urban and suburban areas to the detriment of the expansion of healthy home life of citizens of moderate means, profiteering such as has occurred in lower St. Andrew by heartless land sharks.
11. A law to empower the parochial boards of each parish to undertake, under the direction of central government, the

building of model sanitary homes for the peasantry by a
system of easy payments over a period from ten to twenty
years.

12. A law to empower the government to secure a loan of three
million (or more) pounds from the imperial government,
or otherwise, to be used by the Government, under the
management of a department of the director of agriculture
in developing the Crown lands of the island, agricultur-
ally and otherwise, with the object of supplying employment for our surplus unemployed population and to find
employment for stranded Jamaicans abroad and that the
government purchase such ships as are necessary from time
to time, to facilitate the marketing of the produce gathered
from these Crown lands, and at the same time offering an
opportunity to other producers to ship and market their
produce (Lewis 1994, 91–94).

There were other areas, such as greater political and civil liberties,
judicial reform, and social, cultural, and educational development.
Many of the points were put forward in the Kingston and St. Andrew
Council, of which Garvey was a member from 1930 to 1935. Because
of the limited franchise, he was unsuccessful in his bid for a seat on the
legislative council.

Garvey's Continued Advocacy for Public Policy Reform

The rest of this chapter is concerned with Garvey's memoranda of 1934
and 1938 to Governor Denham of Jamaica and the British secretary of
state for the colonies, which continued his advocacy for public policy
reform.[4] These documents are to be found in Colonial Office files from
1934 and 1938 and include the Memorandum of the Permanent Jamaica
Development Convention to Governor Edward Denham and the notes
of several civil servants advising the governor on his response. I also

draw on Garvey's letter in 1938 to the Right Honourable Malcolm MacDonald, the secretary of state for the colonies.

Among the initiatives Garvey took before leaving the island for good in 1935 was the establishment of the Permanent Jamaica Development Convention (PJDC) in 1934. The PJDC held an all-island convention in the parish of St. Andrew from September 3 to September 12, 1934, "which was attended by delegates from the different parishes, and which discussed most seriously and thoroughly the social, economic and educational conditions of the Island."

This convention took place on the centenary of the West Indies' emancipation from slavery in 1834. It was therefore an initiative that was anchored in the politics of freedom that the colonial system had deliberately frustrated. It also demonstrates the importance of consultation with the people as a central element in Garvey's work of representation.

The memorandum outlined a development program for Jamaica and a request for a loan of £10 million, which in current value would amount to £656,821,656.07. This was to be a long-term loan of some forty years that would partially be paid for by a tax "on all properties sold in this island or transferred from one owner to the next within the period of the loan." Garvey was chair of a seven-member team, which led the civic grouping. The establishment of the PJDC came at the end of the 1934 Convention of the UNIA in Kingston, where particular attention was given to Jamaican issues.

The context to the memorandum was the impact of the economic crisis caused by the Depression throughout the West Indies. Government intervention was necessary. While the colonial government was opposed to the memorandum and to the loan request, it took the labor uprisings throughout the region in the 1930s—and in the case of Jamaica, the 1938 upheaval—to secure a response from London using the instrument of a Royal Commission chaired by Lord Moyne (Beckles 2021, 109–119).

The preamble to the 1934 memorandum contended "the conditions socially and economically now prevailing in Jamaica are of such as to be regarded with alarm, seeing that tens of thousands of the inhabitants are

out of employment and other hundreds of thousands are almost desti-
tute and hopeless in their condition, and whereas, socially, the bulk of
the population falls below the standard of the people of other communities in our present civilization by virtue of the fact that they are not
able to provide themselves with healthy, sanitary and congenial means
of living the Convention called for a loan of £10,000,000."[5]

The background to this crisis was the global capitalist depression of
1929–33. Industrial output in the capitalist world shrank by 38 percent.
"Agricultural output dropped by over one-third. Thousands of banks
crashed and currency depreciated in 56 countries. Unemployment in
the capitalist world rose to 35 million. This included 16 million in
America, 5.5 million in Germany, 3 million in Britain and 2.8 million
in Japan; for the colonies it meant that the prices received for agricultural raw materials and food dropped considerably in value on the world
market... thousands of migrants were returning from the United States,
Cuba and the Central American republics. Between 1930–1934 over
28,000 migrants returned to Jamaica to live in further misery" (Lewis
1994, 83).

The core points of the platform of the PJDC to meet the crisis were
as follows.

Education

The appendix to the PJDC pointed out that "more than fifty per cent
of the children of schoolable age are outside of the schools and that a
large percentage who are attending schools do so irregularly and are
generally in a poor state of health, caused chiefly through malnutrition
and diseases resulting therefrom."[6] The British argued that the number
was about 47 percent, which was still alarming. The official who was preparing the response to the memorandum for Governor Denham noted
that, "the figures in the 1931/32 Education Report show that out of a
child population, of 7–14 years of age, of 185000, 136000 are attending
'controlled' primary schools. This would give 49000, i.e. a percentage of
27% not in 'controlled' schools. If to the primary school enrolment is

added the number of non-school going pupils in uncontrolled schools and in secondary schools the number of non-school going children would probably be about 45000. The Governor's estimate of 50000 is, I think, rather over the mark."[7]

Top of Garvey's crisis plan was education, and £150,000 was to be spent annually for "improved education including vocational training." Also proposed was the development of a "Board of Lecturers, especially trained to lecture on subjects of Social Sciences, Political Economy, Economics, Ethnology and Sociology, and that one lecturer be allotted to each parish to travel through that parish regularly as his employment, lecturing from day to day in villages, districts, towns and all convenient centres, thereby reaching the entire population of the parish within a reasonable period of time each month." Garvey was primarily concerned with raising the educational level of the mass of the population, not only with the cultivation of a few bright scholarship winners but also that "education be improved to include the elementary teaching of the Science of Government, Economics, Sociology, and Ethnology and a special department for teaching character building."

The PJDC charged that "elementary children leave the schools between fourteen and fifteen without much training, and complete their educational course at that, they naturally grow to become adults without the proper preparation for civic, social and cultural contact, hence their behaviour as adults become more criminal than cultural, adding greatly to the expense of the criminal administration of the country, which as a fact is more than three times in expense to that of the educational administration." There are definite parallels with the crisis we faced of getting our children back into schools after two years of so many being out of the system as a result of COVID-19.

In the internal assessment, the British opposed this idea of social science teaching, saying that it would only "result in a large crop of Marcus Garveys."[8]

Garvey's memorandum called for the establishment of a Jamaica University with a capital of £1 million "to prosecute complete courses in the Sciences and the Arts." The British response was, "I should hardly think that Jamaica would be ready for this for a good many years to come."[9] The island's leading newspaper had opined, in an editorial a few years before, "The whole crux of the problem lies, not in the question as to where the money is to be found to establish a university that will be worth the name, but in the question as to what value will be attached to [a] Degree granted by second-rate men in the West Indies . . . So long as the London degrees are obtainable in the West Indies we cannot see any reason for this Island, which cannot even afford to pave all the streets of its capital properly, to go to the enormous expenditure which the establishment of a University involves."[10]

So, from the 1920s, Garvey advocated for radical reform in education from what was then known as elementary school to the tertiary level. Colonial education assumed that there should be a reservoir of cheap labor for the plantations; hence, it was out of the question to talk about developing a university.

Land Settlement

Since emancipation in 1838, the land question has been at the heart of rural and urban poverty and has contributed significantly to what George Beckford referred to as "persistent poverty." Garvey had campaigned in 1929–30 for land reform in Jamaica, which was a network of large sugar and banana plantations with small proprietors on hilly lands with difficult access to local and foreign markets. The memorandum called for "a land settlement scheme to provide agriculturists and peasant proprietors with the opportunity of securing cultivable lands on such terms as may be arranged by the Government and that the Government also place at the disposal of such agriculturists and peasant proprietors any additional Crown lands available for the expansion of such a scheme."[11] One million pounds or 10 percent of the loan was to be spent on land settlement.

Garvey went on to explain that £1 million was

> a modest amount considering how many agriculturists and
> peasants are deprived of the opportunity of engaging in

agriculture and the development of the land, because of the
absence of the possibility of obtaining lands under conditions now existing. These agriculturists and peasants would
ultimately become proprietors contributing much to general
revenue, from the products of their plantations and the estab-
lishments of their homesteads. Jamaica being an agricultural
country and land being the source of the wealth of the country,
it seems illogical that the land should go to waste, and the
people remain idle when they otherwise could profitably
engage themselves for the good of the Government and the
good of the community. When it is considered that most of
the valuable lands of Jamaica contribute very little to taxation,
but remain idle and in waste, the Government has good reason
for overhauling the land situation of the country and utilizing
as much of the available waste lands as possible for settlement
and development, so that at least tens of thousands of indus-
trious and homeless people may become proprietors in their
own rights to contribute to the upkeep of Government and
their own independence.[12]

Linked to this question of homelessness was a proposal for the
construction of model homes based on the fact that "the mud huts of
the people of the parochial districts and over-crowding of the people
in the poorly constructed homes and tenements of towns and the
city reveal a terrible state of our social life." Poor housing conditions,
Garvey continued, would impair health, as they were "breeding grounds
of disease, that will ultimately spread all over the land, affecting all
classes. At the present time tuberculosis has become a social problem,
in that, because of breeding grounds of the disease, it is being spread all
over the island. One million pounds spent therefore in the direction of
model homes will help a great deal to lessen the danger resulting from
the present conditions."

Connected to housing was health care. Hospital improvements
were also called for as "the sufferings, deformities and physical imper-
fections experienced among the common people as resulting from

improper attention at childbearing, ought to suggest to Government
the need for better maternity attention for the accommodation of these
people."

Financing

Garvey also called for a central industrial bank "to give to agriculturists
and possible industrialists the opportunity of securing assistance for the
development of their lands and businesses." Britain was not interested in
land reform and was committed to maintaining the plantation system
and the large holdings of land by the Crown.

The land question remains a critical one in Jamaica in the twenty-
first century, with squatters estimated to be anywhere between seven
hundred thousand and one million people. Since independence, respective governments have failed to develop comprehensive land reform.

Infrastructure

One million pounds was to be designated for irrigation and the start
of an island-wide water scheme. Garvey went on to deal with road
infrastructure. He argued that "making safe our dangerous roadways
is very necessary as Government can realize, because in all sections
of the country travellers by motor vehicles are exposed to imminent
danger through high embankments, unprotected sidings and at times
impassable rivers and gullies that cross roadways. During the time of
rain, travellers are also threatened by the possibility of landslides which
may overwhelm them." Road infrastructure, and its deterioration as a
result of the mountainous terrain and climatic conditions, remains a
burning question.

Garvey also advocated for a national steamship line, which the
British dismissed as uneconomical. Garvey proposed that a national
steamship service was necessary "to give impetus to agriculture and the
development of native industries, because the object behind this is to
find markets in other countries for these products. Naturally therefore,

there must be means of conveyance to these markets and Government transportation could be better relied on by the agriculturists and producers than private concerns that are likely to take advantage of opportunities as they arise.

Trade Commissioners, Marketing, and Advertising

In order to encourage trade, the memorandum called for the "maintenance of commissioners and marketing and advertising agencies in foreign countries.". He called for £1 million for island irrigation and an island water scheme and added that there was "no argument on this because everybody realizes the need of the better distribution of the water power of the island for all purposes." Garvey's idea was part of an infrastructure project that would include piers, docks, and harbors, based on increased trade from the productivity derived from the land settlement proposal.

Tourism

There are proposals on tourism, where Garvey argues that the "development of the seashore places for attraction would be a wonderful asset to this island." The memorandum mentioned the parishes of St. Ann, Trelawny, Westmoreland, and St. Thomas. But there was also an emphasis on health tourism, where he called for "the improvement of the baths at Milk River and St. Thomas" as that could result "in a source of great revenue." The response by the governor was that this should be left to the private sector.

Garvey Ignited the Jamaican Masses

The British did not accept Garvey's proposals of 1934, but in 1938, with the labor protests, they had to take stock. Garvey's 1938 letter to Malcolm MacDonald, British secretary of state for the colonies, written when the Jamaican workers were protesting conditions, pointed out:

If you will turn to the file of your Department, you may find
that I was instrumental in laying before your Department in
November 1934 a scheme for Jamaica, involving the Government raising a loan of ten million pounds to assist in the development of the country and in finding work for its numerous
unemployed. The scheme was discussed with the then new
Governor Sir Edward Denham to which he replied with the
obtaining of a loan of two million pounds, but which loan has
apparently been badly used for the purpose that was outlined
in the scheme, as most of the money has been spent in securing
materials from abroad, thereby defeating the bigger aim of
relieving local conditions."

The Jamaican masses had now intervened and were decisive in changing
the fate of the island. The decades between 1938 and independence in
1962 saw the shaping of a politically more democratic Jamaica. The main
markers for this were universal adult suffrage in 1944, the formation
of mass parties (the Peoples National Party in 1938 and the Jamaica
Labour Party in 1944), and the transition to greater local responsibili-
ties in governance and independence. Hilary Beckles points out in his
book *How Britain Underdeveloped the Caribbean* that the British, after
over three hundred years of extracting slave labor and low plantation
wages, opposed any reasonable financial request to help the transition to
independence. The political leaders of Jamaica and Trinidad and Tobago
were treated in the same manner as Garvey was by the governor and
secretary of state for the colonies.

Garvey's letters of 1934 and 1938 set out a template for initiating
reforms that are still relevant today. Aspects of this policy template have
been taken up by governments in the independence era but without
the kind of land reform that was necessary. However, while the 1938
working-class storm in Jamaica triggered the path to universal adult
suffrage in 1944 and independence in 1962, there was ambivalence
about blackness and the racial uplift core of Garvey's philosophy was not
at the heart of development. Goals were developed to serve the nation,
ignoring the need for reparative justice and to affirm the 90 percent

Black population. The burdens of self-hate, racial discrimination, and psychological insecurities, stemming from centuries of slavery and colonialism, were not adequately addressed in the educational system.

Those challenges remain for us to solve, along with the pressing economic and social challenges, in the twenty-first century.

Rupert Lewis, PhD, is professor emeritus of political thought in the Department of Government, University of the West Indies (UWI), Jamaica. He is a member of the advisory board of the PJ Patterson Institute for Africa-Caribbean Advocacy at UWI. In 2018, his biography of Marcus Garvey was published in the UWI Press Caribbean biography series, and his biography of Walter Rodney is forthcoming. He is author of *Walter Rodney's Intellectual and Political Thought* and has edited books on George Padmore, the Trinidadian-born Pan-Africanist, and Richard Hart, the Jamaican Marxist. He is a member of Jamaica's National Council on Reparation.

Notes

1. This paper was first presented as a plenary talk at the Caribbean Studies Association meeting, University of the West Indies, Jamaica, June 1, 2022.
2. *The Daily Gleaner*, December 12, 1937, 1.
3. See comment referring to the governor: "If his reply contains the necessary blend of dove and serpent, the S/S (Secretary of State) need never be bothered with the thing at all," 27.1.35.
4. All quotations from the memorandum sent to Governor Denham, the letter Garvey sent to the Right Honourable Malcolm MacDonald, and the responses from the governor and other officials in Jamaica and London in this paper can be found in CO 137 827 1113773, BRITISH LIBRARY.
5. Memorandum from Permanent Jamaica Development Convention, November 8, 1934, to His Excellency Sir Edward Brandis Denham K.C.MG.K.B.E., Governor of Jamaica and The Rt. Hon. Secretary of State for the Colonies.
6. Appendix of Explanation to Items of Memorandum presented by Deputation of Permanent Jamaica Development Convention to His Excellency, 2.
7. See document by Arthur Mayhew, 22.1.35.
8. Mayhew 11.12.1934.
9. See file dated 11.12.34.
10. *The Daily Gleaner*, January 8, 1929, 12.
11. PJDC, 6.
12. PJDC, appendix.

CHAPTER ELEVEN

Lewis Ashenheim's Legal Defense of Marcus Garvey in Jamaica

Lynda R. Edwards

> Marcus Garvey was one of the greatest mass leaders of all time. He was misrepresented and maligned, but he brought to the Negro people for the first time a sense of pride of being Black.
>
> —Adam Clayton Powell

UPON MARCUS GARVEY'S return to Jamaica following his deportation in 1927, a concerted effort was made by the colonial government to silence him once and for all. Leading the charge was Chief Justice Fiennes Cecil Arthur Barrett-Lennard.

In 1927, George Osborne Marke, a Sierra Leone national living in the United States, was a member and employee of the Universal Negro Improvement Association (UNIA) New York. After helping to oust Marcus Garvey during his imprisonment in Atlanta, Marke successfully sued the UNIA New York branch for unpaid salary. Winning the case, he then discovered the branch was insolvent and could not pay the judgment awarded to him by the American court.

When Marke learned of UNIA assets in Jamaica, under the leadership of Marcus Garvey, he brought the matter to the Jamaican Supreme Court, applying for final judgment and seeking to seize whatever property he could to satisfy his claim.

Chief Justice Barrett-Lennard, a colonial stalwart, heard the case in Jamaica. He was appointed chief justice of Jamaica in 1925 and knighted the following year.

He was as English as breakfast tea and loyal to the Crown.

On July 20, 1929, Chief Justice Barrett-Lennard ruled against Marcus Garvey, and wasting no time, he ordered the seizure and sale of all property associated with Marcus Garvey and the UNIA in Jamaica. He directed Bailiff John Cargill to immediately sell all goods and premises needed to satisfy the debt, including the Blackman Publishing Company printing office, a newspaper owned by Marcus Garvey with no legal ties to the UNIA.

Jamaican Attorney Takes the Case of Garvey's Blackman Press

The seizure of property of another society of Jamaicans—the African Communities League (ACL), under the leadership of Mr. A. V. Hague—brought noted Jamaican attorney Lewis Ashenheim into the fray. In a letter to the Colonial Foreign Office in England, Lewis explained why he took the case:

> On or about the 10th day of August 1929, a deputation of persons of the Negro Race waited for me at my office, and after making representations that the property of themselves and co-members had been levied on by the Bailiff in respect of the alleged Judgement debt of the foreign Negro Improvement Corporation (with which they had no connection of any kind) and that the property seized has been purchased by means of funds raised and contributed in Jamaica by themselves and co-members, they earnestly pressed me that I should professionally represent their interests as Solicitor in defense of their rights and property.

Lewis went on to say, "The deputation conveyed to me their belief that the litigation was part of a concerted plan of the capitalist class of Jamaica to keep the Negro Race subjugated and, for their own selfish purposes, to thwart or delay their efforts to uplift themselves and to handicap and persecute those undertaking or sympathetic to, Negro advancement. The proceedings and decisions given in the suit were bitterly questioned, and my help to obtain justice for the Negro was fervently demanded."

Lewis was able to discover that the colonial government of Jamaica had carefully monitored the conduct and speeches of Marcus Garvey since his deportation from America but could find no wrongdoing. The actions of his UNIA Jamaica had, in fact, led to an improvement in the orderliness and behavior of the Jamaican Negro population in direct contrast to what the colonial secretary, A. S. Jelf, had predicted in a report to Sir Vernon Kell, head of the British Security Services in England.

It was clear to Lewis that a grave injustice was being perpetuated and one that would have severe consequences for Jamaica's social, political, and cultural development. He wrote,

After careful consideration of the situation in both its legal and sociological aspects, and in the interests of the removal of class feelings, and in order to evidence the erroneous character of the impression that there existed any adverse sentiment of the white race against the black population, or that a white man would be unwilling to assist the Negroes to obtain justice, and having reached the opinion that there had been no inquiry into the property rights, if any, of the foreign corporation and that the Negroes in Jamaica, who claimed they were an entirely separate entity were entitled to have a full judicial inquiry into their claims to property rights and that the seizure of the property claimed by them under the executive order issued against the Corporation was improper.

From the moment Lewis and Chief Justice Barrett-Lennard stepped into a courtroom together, it was apparent that they had very different views on interpreting the case law surrounding this judgment. A fact

Lewis did not refrain from pointing out when he asked for a trial by jury instead of having Chief Justice Barrett-Lennard decide the outcome of the case in question.

Lewis's position was that the property seized could not be used to pay the debts of the insolvent American corporation because a branch in Jamaica, even of a foreign corporation, is separate from the corporation in its principal home. The New York judgment was between the foreign corporation and George Marke.

Lewis wanted a jury to decide if the defendants named, including Marcus Garvey, were to be held personally liable for the foreign debt. He argued that Chief Justice Barrett-Lennard's determination that UNIA Jamaica was indistinguishable from UNIA New York was erroneous and that a Jamaican jury was needed to decide the matter, adding that the individuals being personally held liable were not members or in any way associated with UNIA New York.

Lewis and Chief Justice Barrett-Lennard faced off in a courtroom in late August 1929. Lewis asked for a stay of execution because Marcus Garvey and his fellow defendants intended to appeal the verdict. In his haste to dispose of the case, Chief Justice Barrett-Lennard ordered the bailiff, John Cargill, to immediately sell all the assets at auction.

In referring to the Blackman Press, whose assets were solely owned by Marcus Garvey, Lewis argued that "individuals are distinct from a corporate body. It does not matter how an individual blends his funds or intermixes their resources. It does not matter whether the same people controlling a corporation control a subsidiary body. A corporation is defined as limiting its property to paying its debts, thus limiting creditors and excluding property of any individuals connected with it."

Lewis accused John Cargill of taking the side of George Marke and not doing his due diligence in the matter of securing an indemnity, suggesting the application was made by the bailiff on behalf of George Marke. "I submit it would require very exceptional reasons for allowing a foreign plaintiff to come into an English Court and sue Jamaicans under the jurisdiction of the English Court without protecting them from the consequences of a claim wrongly made against them."

John Cargill was so offended by the charge that he appealed to Chief Justice Barrett-Lennard for relief from Lewis's attacks. Chief Justice Barrett-Lennard retaliated by denying the appeal and ordering that all seized assets be sold immediately. Undaunted, Lewis made known his intention to take the appeal further and asked that the bailiff be instructed not to sell any of the goods seized until the Court of Appeal rendered their judgment. This, too, was denied.

Lewis then wrote a letter to Herbert Cox, the bailiff in charge of the auction, informing him that the case was on appeal, and if successful, Cox could be held personally liable as a trespasser and a wrongdoer for all losses suffered by Marcus Garvey and his fellow defendants.

Lewis wrote, "If you proceed to sell after this warning, without a complete indemnity covering you against all costs, you must not complain if you have personally to make good to our clients any loss suffered by them."

The bailiff went straight to Chief Justice Barrett-Lennard, complaining that he felt intimated in performing his lawful duties. Enraged, Chief Justice Barrett-Lennard charged Lewis with three contempt of court charges based on his letters to the bailiff and fined him £350.

What came next turned the legal profession on its ear. While the contempt action was pending, Chief Justice Barrett-Lennard was overheard discussing the matter at the Jamaica Club, where he loudly proclaimed his threat to send Lewis to prison when he appeared for the resolution of the matter. Several other attorneys overheard his remarks and were concerned about the harshness of Chief Justice Barrett-Lennard's rhetoric. Fearing civil liberties were at stake, including all solicitors' interests in performing their duty to represent their clients, several solicitors rallied to Lewis's defense, asking Governor Stubbs to be on standby to release Lewis from prison if Chief Justice Barrett-Lennard did, indeed, order his arrest.

Undeterred by these threats, Lewis prepared the appeal, showing that the property seized and sold by the bailiffs belonged to persons and entities with no connection with UNIA New York and with no legal obligation to assume its debts. On September 9, 1929, Lewis filed the notice and grounds of appeal.

Lewis attacked the findings of Chief Justice Barrett-Lennard by saying the bailiff's levy on the goods of the Judgement Debtor Corporation was unsupported by any legal evidence and was, in fact, contrary to the evidence presented and was arrived at without a fair trial or legal inquiry. Lewis went as far as to say the findings by Chief Justice Barrett-Lennard were not only contrary to the evidence but also contrary to the law and contrary to the express provisions of the Civil Procedure Code of 1888.

Lewis's most compelling argument, however, was that the property of the individuals could not lawfully be seized under a writ of seizure and sale issued against a corporation judgment debtor. In addition, George Marke was an alien permanently residing out of Jamaica with no assets on the island from which either damages or costs could be recovered. In these grounds for appeal, Lewis further stated, "The advertisement for sale, the particulars of the sale, and the conditions of sale approved by the Court was an illegal and prejudicial attack against the indefeasible title of my clients in the said registered land."

Victory on Appeal

Justice Henry Isaac Close Brown was president of the appeal court when the appeals were heard. Unlike Chief Justice Barrett-Lennard, Justice Brown was born and raised in Jamaica. His mother was a white woman from England, the daughter of a minister. His father was a mixed-race man and a solicitor in Montego Bay. During his distinguished career, he acted as chief justice on several occasions, including for this case, where he was called upon to review the findings of the now controversial Chief Justice Barrett-Lennard.

In his findings, he arrived at the following conclusion. "A foreign corporation cannot be said to be here unless there are facts from which it can be inferred that, like an individual, it is residing here, and in the case of a trading corporation, residence means the carrying on of its business. Therefore, the judgment would have to be against the incorporated Association against which the judgment has been obtained in America."

Justice Brown agreed with Lewis's assertion that UNIA New York was separate from UNIA Jamaica and should not be held liable. "The affidavit in support of the claim discloses a strong prima facie case that the claimants represent separate and distinct bodies from the foreign defendant corporation and that those bodies and their property are not liable to pay the debts of the U.N.I.A New York."

In a speech made by Leslie Ashenheim in May of 1979, Leslie recalled his father's reaction to the news. "I was a young solicitor of some five-year practice and was fully involved in the fight. The appeals were fully argued, resulting in a clear victory for our side with most of Chief Justice Barrett-Lennard's illegal orders set aside with costs, but it was too late—the goods and premises had already been sold by then. The Jamaican Division of the U.N.I.A. was fully cleared of all involvement in the financial affairs of the American Corporation. The fight waged by Marcus Garvey to preserve the Jamaican assets had been won—even if all the lost assets were not recovered."

While the appeal was ongoing, George Marke, having never set foot in Jamaica, died in the United States. The Blackman Printing Company, Liberty Hall, and the goods and premises of Edelweiss Park had already been sold on the orders of Chief Justice Barrett-Lennard and executed by John Cargill. George Marke received nothing, and Marcus Garvey lost his movement. The fallout continued when Chief Justice Barrett-Lennard tried to have Lewis disbarred.

Lewis knew he had the support of his fellow solicitors and the Jamaican judges in the court. He pushed back in a letter to the Colonial Foreign Office, where he, without caution, detailed the failures of Chief Justice Barrett-Lennard and his inability to act fairly and without prejudice in his rulings, stating, "The character of the case did not justify the hostile and angry view of the Chief Justice. Subsequently, on the 31st of October 1929, Sir William Morrison informed me that Chief

Justice Barrett-Lennard told him that I should resign my position on the Solicitors Committee or risk being forcibly removed."

Chief Justice Barrett-Lennard was enraged by Lewis's audacity in his letter to the Foreign Office and wrote his own letter to the governor with the following warning: "Your Excellency will see that the end of British rule is reached if the Government tolerates such a letter. In no properly governed country ought such a letter to be possible. The truth is that lawlessness is only too common here. I hope your Excellency will direct action to be taken at once."

The Colonial Foreign Office declined to overturn the contempt of court convictions against Lewis Ashenheim, which still stand on his record to this day. Instead, they allowed Chief Justice Barrett-Lennard to retire in 1932. After returning to England, he alleged that his retirement was forced upon him by ill health, resulting from having been poisoned while in Jamaica.

In denying the request to overturn the contempt of court convictions, Sir John Risley of the Colonial Foreign Office wrote, "Suffice it to say there seems to me to be some degree of doubt as to what Chief Justice Barrett-Lennard decided or ordered, and I do not believe Mr. Ashenheim acted with conscious impropriety. He seems to have been the victim of the lax standard of professional conduct which obtains in Jamaica, and I fear in many other colonies."

Lewis Ashenheim and Marcus Garvey remained friends after the trial. Marcus Garvey even campaigned for Lewis in his ill-fated political attempt in 1935. Marcus Garvey's support for Lewis was controversial. In 1930s Jamaica, Marcus was still considered a dangerous agitator, and several of the political meetings in which he attended resulted in violent disturbances.

The rise of Justice Henry Isaac Close Brown to the position of chief justice was one of the greatest successes of this case. He was described as a man who applied thoughtful application to his work. Absent from his demeanor was a display of superiority; instead, he exuded courtesy and fierce adhesion to justice and fair play principles and whose judicial opinions and decisions won profound respect. He was the embodiment of the Jamaica that Marcus Garvey and Lewis Ashenheim envisioned.

Lynda R. Edwards is a Jamaican writer. She has written three novels, *Redemption Songs, Friendship Estate,* and *I Am Cuba.* She is Lewis Ashenheim's great-grand niece.

IV

GARVEY LIVES

CHAPTER TWELVE

Beyond Trauma, the Whirlwind, and Redeeming the Soul of Humanity
Linda James Myers, PhD

> Let the sky and God be our limit, and Eternity our measurement.
> There is no height to which we cannot climb by using the active intel-
> ligence of our own minds. Mind creates and as much as we desire in
> nature we can have through the creation of our own minds.
>
> —Marcus Garvey

THE VISION OF the Marcus Garvey Institute for Human Development
is to educate humans toward the realization of their full potential and
purpose. This represents the continued manifestation of an unparalleled
African-centered worldview traceable from the first ancient Nubian/
Kemetic writings of classical African civilization to present day. Our
beloved Honorable Marcus Mosiah Garvey, along with other venerated
ancestors, has shown us the path, shedding light on the way forward
against the odds, cautioning that we must know our history or be like a
tree without roots. The focus here will be on the continued reemergence
of the genius of our ancestors' understandings in the wisdom tradition
of African deep thought, which have sustained us over the centuries and
remain requisite for healthy development and growth.

Beyond Trauma

The aim will be to illuminate how we can ensure our roots flourish by
nourishing the deep structure (understandings with regard to the nature

of reality, knowledge and how one knows, identity, values, planes of existence, and so on) of our cultural inheritance embracing all the surface structure (language, rituals, music, dance, diet, dress, etc.) manifestations emanating from those roots to bring forth harmonious balance. Optimal psychology emerges across time and space from the deep structure of this African wisdom tradition, reiterating and bringing forward the cultural insights for life and the soul needed to support the shifting of our consciousness toward harmonious and balanced holistic integration and to supply the depth of understanding required for healthy development, growth, self-determination, and unitary consciousness in the face of strife-ridden chaos and discordant imbalance (Myers 1988; Myers et al. 2018, 2022).

Using an Africological cultural lens established in the wisdom tradition of African deep thought from classical African civilization as the basis for the organizational structure, optimal psychology (OP), or optimal conceptual theory (OCT), expands our capacity to embrace a truly comprehensive understanding of humanity. Going back to our earliest historical records, we can bring forward insights relevant for escape from today's current morass. The cultural rootedness of this feat becomes even more relevant as we follow the science through the most current biogenetic, linguistic, archeological, and anthropological evidence to the realization that Africa is the birthplace of all human culture and civilization (Bynum 1999). The Euro-western suboptimal cultural worldview prevailing in this society and proliferated globally has been central in creating the current discordant and chaotic state of affairs and crises currently facing humanity. The challenges facing humanity require careful examination from a cultural frame of reference capable of offering holistic, integrative, cohesive, and coherent analyses contributing to the production of psychological knowledge leading to wisdom and viable solutions to the problems of life. OP has demonstrated such capacity.

Failing to overcome the lack of knowledge of our true history and phenomenal cultural heritage utilizing the insights of our ancestors thwarts our development and the salvation of humanity. Most people do not likely know of this history and its cultural richness, which has now come full circle to be confirmed by contemporary scientific undertakings in quantum mechanics and neuroscience. The truth has deliberately been kept from them because it would set them free, making them no longer susceptible to the social engineering of the dominant Euro-Western cultural worldview or controlled by its exploitive materialist manipulations. So despite the convergence of knowledge across cultural groups, missing in the prevailing Euro-Western worldview is awareness of the implications of this "scientific" knowledge for harmonious balance in daily life, individually and collectively on all planes of existence. This realization remains for the most part absent for the reasons mentioned previously, but also because to do so most effectively would require a culture grounded in what our African ancestors called Maat, the science of life, or the principles and regulations governing form (composition of energy) and producing the healthy growth and development of the whole. Believed by the ancient ones to have been present from the beginning and remaining unchallenged, Maat maintains that the purpose of humanity is its maintenance on the earthly plane. Thus, humans as the highest manifestation of divine creativity were charged with the development of civilized living within society, respecting the sacredness of all life, the interrelatedness and interdependence of all its facets and planes of existence, and doing that which is true, just, right, and good. We find these teachings common among the vast majority of groups acknowledging African ancestry.

The most essential system informing human consciousness is from the deep structures of culture, those philosophical assumptions and principles giving birth to one's reality. It determines the patterns of interpreting reality and designs for living known as one's conceptual system. Its nature becomes accessible through critical thinking, introspection, self-examination, and reflection. OP's corollary psychoeducational/psychotherapeutic process, Belief Systems Analysis (BSA; Myers 1988, 1993), looks to history to provide the evidence-based method for clarifying and optimizing one's conceptual system. With roots traceable from the wisdom tradition of African deep thought identified with the classical African civilization of Nubia/Kmt, we see its proliferation across the continent and the globe (Bynum 2021).

It also accounts for the survival and perseverance of non-immigrant Africans kidnapped and trafficked to the Americas, who emerge as the moral and spiritual leaders of the movement for justice and democracy after experiencing two and a half centuries of the most brutal, dehumanizing system of enslavement ever known and a century and a half of domestic terrorism. One must wonder how these people accomplished this feat, a miracle of modern times. OP posits that awareness of the true nature of being as unitary consciousness, or the oneness of all that is, enabled them to look beyond appearances and tap into a transcendent reality of knowing, sustainability, and perseverance. Such an optimal psychological understanding is expressed at a very high level by Marcus Garvey when he states, "Look for me in the whirlwind or the storm, look for me all around you, for, with God's grace, I shall come and bring with me countless millions of black slaves who have died in America and the West Indies and the millions in Africa to aid you in the fight for Liberty, Freedom and Life."

The Whirlwind

OP provides the depth of analysis called for by the Honorable Marcus Mosiah Garvey, founder of the Universal Negro Improvement Association (UNIA) and leader of the largest mass liberation movement of Black people throughout the diaspora in contemporary times. Garvey emphasized the necessity for Black people to emancipate themselves from mental bondage or control of their minds—perceptions, thoughts, feelings, actions, and experience. Describing the mind as sovereign and our only ruler, he acknowledged the primacy of mind in human experience long before mainstream Western psychology. A master metaphysician, Garvey understood that none but oneself can free one's mind. Garvey made clear in his teachings that the person who fails to develop and use their own mind to think and create for themselves is bound to be subjugated by those who do. If an individual follows the fragmented suboptimal worldview imposed on their thinking and that of others in this social context, a double bind is created. The social engineers, leaders of the dominant group imposing their will, are aware that the nature of the suboptimal worldview they are propagating conceptually incarcerates its adherents to a very limited, disempowered mindset. Discouraging thinking for themselves, they recognize that their targets will not likely be able to discern that what is being sold to them is not in their best interest. Tapping into the ancient African dictum of self-knowledge as the basis of all knowledge, the Honorable Marcus Mosiah Garvey noted that we can only be destroyed by ourselves, from within and not from without. He reiterated the victory is to be won from within and can be lost only from within.

BSA is designed to facilitate and support progress in making the shift from a fractured, suboptimal conceptual system to a restored, optimal one. Although a developmental process, with careful examination of the current set of assumptions informing one's perception, thoughts, feelings, behaviors, and experience, one can make a conscious decision about which conceptual system one seeks to pursue. If it is the optimal one that is chosen, a self-correcting, self-perpetuating process of optimization can be put in place (Myers 2004).

Such shifting of consciousness from the lower to the higher realms will lead to the eradication of the roots of systemic racism, as well as other societal isms, and inoculation against their toxic pathogen and processes. The suboptimal worldview, associated with lower consciousness due to the outcomes of its fragmented, disintegrative nature, leads to insecurity, fearfulness, addictions, violence, materialistic greed, spirit alienation, and embedding systems of dehumanization (racism, sexism, classism, elitism, and so on). The optimal worldview, associated with higher consciousness due to the outcomes of its holistic and integrative nature, has been found to lead to an intrinsic sense of worth and security; a multidimensional sense of self connected to ancestors, nature, community, and future generations;

and ultimately the totality of existence, or Ntr, within which there is no death. The principles of Maat embrace diunital or both/and reasoning; for example, masculine/feminine dualities are understood to be complementary, both being needed for the greater good of the whole. The seven principles of Maat commonly articulated out of love and peace are truth, justice, righteousness, reciprocity, balance, harmony, and order. The means by which their advancement will be achieved is through ntu'ology, or human and spiritual networks (Dixon and Nichols 1983).

All human beings have the potential and capacity to inhere the tenets of either lower (suboptimal) or higher (optimal) consciousness. However, if people do not think for themselves, they will likely submit (either consciously or unconsciously) to the suboptimal mindset given them by the dominant Euro-Western cultural (mis)socialization. Due to its cultural and intellectual imperialism that conceptually incarcerates due to the epistemic violence perpetrated by the social engineers committed to perpetuating their agenda of personal materialistic self-interest and control/power, it is not easy to escape. Psychological liberation is made possible by making a conscious, deliberate choice about what one believes/knows to be true and pursuing that individually and/or collectively. Given the choice, an optimal conceptual system, engaging in a self-correcting, self-perpetuating ordered process of optimization that decolonizes the mind is the most viable option. When engaged in that process, challenges and negativity in human experience are accepted as part of a cyclic system for the purpose of growth and edification for self-mastery, ensuring development toward conscious awareness as divine being becoming (Myers 2003). It is beyond the purview of this essay to further detail the processes and strategies of BSA, but suffice it to say here that it has been practiced and utilized for over thirty-five years by many and transformed lives. Among them, a behavioral health practice in the Midwest has used it as their primary therapeutic modality for their agency for over twenty-five years with tremendous success, destigmatizing seeking help in a pathological social context (Myers et al. 2018).

Redeeming the Soul of Humanity

Optimal theory posits that it is the ontologically flawed and faulty sub-optimal cultural worldview underpinning systemic racism that afforded its creation, perpetuation, and the current crises seen in American society and across the globe. Although some progress has been made, the relative ease and popularity of accepting/adopting false narratives, impaired moral reasoning and ethics, limited spiritual acumen, and materialistic greed currently so flagrant and pervasive are simply the continuation of the pattern set.

For example, the American Psychological Association (APA) has as its tag line, "advancing psychology to benefit society and improve lives," but overall, very little movement in that direction seems to have been accomplished in the real world, given the present abominable state of affairs. America has come to a place where almost half of its voting public denies the truth of its most recent presidential election. The legal system is failing, exemplified by the fact that its highest court has no standard of ethics by which the "justices" must abide or be held account-able and by the absence of a just, equitable system that holds all citi-zens to the same standards, equally accountable for their wrongdoings despite their race and socioeconomic class, particularly in light of the systems of dehumanization on which this nation and the Western world was built, without any restorations. The degree of economic inequity is at an all-time high, and elected officials have historically enacted social policies that have benefited the wealthy to the detriment of the masses. A clear example that has continued repercussions is the bailing out of financial institutions whose illicit practices led to crises for which the American taxpayer had to pay. Missing has been the cultural grounding needed to critically reflect and make the comprehensive examination required. OP brings forth an alternate cultural point of view capable of providing insight, understanding, and the wisdom for forward move-ment (Myers et al. 2022).

Unity around beliefs, values, and behaviors that contribute to creating a just, sacred, and sustainable world will save the soul of humanity. Enough people choosing not to succumb to the oppression of others and themselves by exposing, confronting, and rectifying the driving forces behind inhumane treatment can do it. Echoing the same sentiment of Marcus Garvey decades later in his 1967 keynote address to the APA, Martin Luther King Jr. shared the requirements for overcoming systemic racism that still ring true today. Stating liberation from ideological dependence on dominant white society is requisite, he noted that its philosophy and morals are not holy or sacred but often degenerate and profane. Describing the inability to question and defy the fundamental precepts of the larger society as the worst aspect of the oppression of Black people, King foresaw and applauded the critical trend of Black thought returning to its roots. Now, fifty-five years later, a new yet ancient understanding of OP is affirmed; it encourages all who have internalized the destructive ideology of systemic racism to free themselves, promoting the creation of a just, sacred, and sustainable world for all.

It is apparent the soul of humanity is in total jeopardy without a stable, culturally grounded framework for determining what is right versus what is wrong. The confusion is so compounded and extensive that some in society would argue there is no such thing as right and wrong, as the distinctions are arbitrary. Further, others suggest it is offensive to call people out and hold them accountable for being. The list could go on and on. With the attempted coup and insurrection of January 6, 2021, inspired by former president Trump to stop the electoral process; the blatant white supremacist agenda to prevent the teaching of the nation's true history; and fear of so-called white replacement by people of color, resulting from the long historical pattern of white people replacing people of color in whatever lands they find them, this current state of affairs has not only put hope for American democracy's future at total risk but also redemption of its soul and impossibility. It will be only those committed to truth, justice, moral integrity, and decency who take a hard stand who will save the possibility for this nation to become the democracy once hoped and fought for. These outcomes have a doubly hard impact on those already targeted for disenfranchisement due to race, gender, or socioeconomic status. This does not mean that these groups are astute and mindful of the challenges, as they, too, have taken on the suboptimal worldview of their socialization, and to a great extent may have internalized oppression.

A shift in consciousness toward holistic, integrative, moral elevation, and illumination of the soul is required. Here, turning to the evidence provided by history showing that Black people have been the moral and spiritual leaders of this nation's movement toward civil rights, democracy, and justice for all will be most helpful. Careful investigation reveals the deep structure of the African cultural worldview Black people brought with them, passed on, and held strong prior to the most concerted onslaught of cultural disruptions of the past several decades. Rather than strengthen these vital cultural roots, inappropriate and failed social policies and practices of community disruption and denigration were imposed. Yet an optimal psychology has been identified, which supported the capacity of these Black people to navigate two and a half centuries of historically unprecedented systems of dehumanization and another century and a half of the continued struggle for equal civil rights. What of relevance today can be learned about how this feat was achieved against all odds through morally grounded peaceful protest? Research developing optimal psychology provides tried and true substantiation of its power for perseverance and resilience in the face of tremendous struggle for justice, creating what Congressman John Lewis called good trouble, standing up for that which is true, just, and honorable.

Moving away from the fractured, exploitive, suboptimal materialist cultural worldview that now prevails is essential for the sustainable well-being of humanity. There are four basic challenges that must be faced and mastered if this nation is to get on course for redemption and fulfill any of the high ideals on which it was supposedly founded. Not only have they never been realized, but with the current push of promoters of the suboptimal way of life taking away civil rights, advancing economic inequity, and setting back social advancements, if their efforts are not reversed, along with great suffering it is also ensured they never will be. Therefore, the first challenge to be dealt with is the requirement of increased self-knowledge. A long, hard look into our own hearts and minds must be taken honestly to evaluate the values and beliefs we hold. Increasing knowledge of self around the assumptions and principles, or conceptual system, informing our own perceptions, thoughts, feelings, behavior, and experience is essential. For clarity regarding worldview correction and enhancement, we can go within our own spirit and seek direction, finding a sense of peace and love realizing our oneness and intrinsic worth. Among other things, we can truly follow the science in terms of what is known about the nature of reality itself from quantum mechanics and neuroscience now affirming the teachings of the wisdom tradition of African deep thought known to many acknowledging African ancestry through ancient sacred texts and experience. The spiritual aspect of being becoming is primary and proactive in the transcendent consciousness of human experience.

A materialistic, spiritually alienated orientation disrupts human connection to a vital spiritual anchor and essential moral compass. OP speaks to these truths outside of the context of religious doctrines—allegorically the goal is to have our heart/mind (consciousness) be as light as a feather when weighed on the scale of eternal truth (Myers 2004). Should we so choose, we each can access our best selves, higher consciousness, and eternal beingness that is one with creative life source. All of humanity originated in the continent we now call Africa, according to the most current biogenetic, linguistic, anthropological, and archaeological evidence. A truly comprehensive understanding of human evolution and development must be inclusive of this cultural knowledge for which we have evidence thrived for at least six thousand years and spread globally. From this awareness, we are compelled to hold high values for truth, justice, and righteousness and to take a stand for them.

A second challenge and necessity is honest truth telling, to speak the truth. Truth is the only solid foundation for alignment with supremely good or divine spirit, on which good, healthy, sustainable outcomes can be built. The truth sets aside false ego and simply acknowledges what happened, what has been done. The claim that we are a nation with freedom and justice for all can no longer apply to only an unjustly advantaged group inhering the human diversity markers of being white (racism), male (sexism), and materially benefited (classism), to name a few most often favored. Learning to think critically and deeply, no longer dissuaded by labels assigned by the media and others, focus should be on the substantive values and ethical standards for which people stand. All too often labels such as liberal, conservative, progressive, moderate, socialist, and so on are used deceptively with the intent that listeners take stands on particular issues not in their best interest. Demand the honest specifics of what the stand is on each issue of concern to you, and do not accept the red herrings frequently thrown to distract and dissuade from the most important issue at hand. For example, if one is pro-birth and has no interest in or sense of responsibility for the child after birth, they should not be allowed to dishonestly claim to the identity of being pro-life.

Transferring focus from being politically correct to being morally correct is essential to enhancing authenticity and integrity development. The idea of disallowing the true history of this nation or any people to be told is a major red flag and tactic of those dealing as masters of deception. Do not allow such flagrant manipulation to go unaddressed any longer. For too long the history and role of Black and Brown people in this country have been silenced and marginalized. Now some in political leadership want to wipe it out completely because it is so wretched and shameful. What parents who do not want the truth of Black history to be taught are really asking for is that American history not to be taught correctly. The social outcomes we are witnessing today reflect what happens when lies are used as a key strategy for social engineering. Much of the citizenry grows up believing lying, deceiving, and manipulating are not only acceptable but also the best ways to achieve power and control over others.

Building good character is not taught as a part of formal education, nor is it modeled by many of those in roles of political leadership. Denied the access to a comprehensive history and understanding of humanity, social anarchy, decline, and regress are inevitable. The Maatian nature of spiritual law from the psychohistorical perspective of OP is that the truth always comes to light, now or later; in actuality, from a holistic integrative standpoint, the sooner the truth comes out and can be addressed, the better. Less toxicity and pathology will have been created and ingested, and the doorway to movement toward health and wholeness will be opened more quickly. The longer the delay, the deeper the hole dug for self and future generations, and when lessons created by a false sense of self are not mastered, they come back around only more difficult and troubling than before.

Developing the capacity for advanced moral reasoning is essential and mandatory and is the third challenge. Decades ago, leading Euro-Western psychologists and researchers discovered that the capacity for moral reasoning of members of this society was quite low (Kohlberg 1972). While not surprising, given the nation's history, we have seen and continue to see little collective progress. Regarding systemic racism, for each apparent step forward, there is always backlash, eroding progress and preventing any progress to be made in many areas of life. One limiting factor characteristic of the dominant suboptimal cultural worldview is its penchant for dichotomous logic, which restricts reasoning to either/or conclusions. The diunital logic of an optimal conceptual system encourages the expansion of reasoning toward both/and conclusions, acknowledging that two things can be true at the same time, contingent on perspective. For example, from the micro level of refined subatomic observation, it is evident that particles and waves are always in constant motion; from the more macro level of five sense observation, matter may appear to be still and not moving. Both are true at the same time when increased knowledge and perspective is factored into the analysis. In terms of interpersonal relationships, this addition of perspective taking to moral reasoning encourages the increased likelihood of empathy and compassion.

While wrong may be wrong, all wrongs are not the same in terms of degree of scope, impact, intention, long-term consequences, and/

or commitment to restitution, repair, and restoration. All may make regrettable decisions, but false equivalence for moral infractions must be recognized and not accepted. Despite what mainstream Euro-Western sociological thought leaders or others might say or understand to be true, there is a difference between social and moral infractions, and some are worse than others. Stealing an elderly lady's pocketbook and stealing her pension cannot be equated. While both acts are deplorable, in this society, which criminal will likely be imprisoned versus rewarded with a bonus worth millions of dollars for which the tax-paying public will have to pay? As seen with the decision that was made regarding banks being too big to fail, the economically advantaged are also the legally and politically advantaged given current social policies and practices. Those seeking to demonstrate commitment toward fulfillment of humanity's promise could make significant movement by taking a stand in support of racial, economic, political, and legal equity. Additionally, allocation of resources toward meaningful restoration, not just reparations, for the descendants of those caste chattel enslaved non-immigrant Africans in the Americas, on whose backs the wealth of the Euro-Western world was built, must be implemented.

The fourth challenge that must be overcome and the understanding that must be embraced and pursued for sustainable well-being and illumination of the soul is that of developing unitary consciousness capable of recognizing that all existence is Ntr. In so doing, the double consciousness of which W. E. B. Du Bois spoke, the idea of two warring minds in one body, exists in only the service of self-edification. The suboptimal and optimal conceptual systems of OP mirror orientations to the lower and higher consciousness in the wisdom tradition of African deep thought. The achievement of unitary consciousness fosters peace, inner security, and the sustainable well-being that cannot be achieved through the false, illusory, and temporal nature of externalized materialistic identification and dependence. Because self-love based on one's true identity as spirit being becoming is the basis of all love, absence of love for oneself will manifest in denial; projection of one's own feelings, motives, and thoughts onto others; and a lack of love, appreciation, and compassion for the multiple dimensions of self, inclusive of those who came before (ancestors), future generations, nature, and community. Be it within-group conflict or between-group conflict, the defining issue must be examined in terms of not how whomever is appearing but rather what energies they are representing in their heart/mind or consciousness field and whether Maat can be identified there.

As human beings, we are always expressing the forces that exist within us—we cannot be spewing hated and anger if such energies do not first exist within us. While the suboptimal worldview fosters such negative feelings, as well as being prone to violence and addictions, alienation from spirit and insecurity are the underlying cause, along with ignorance and immaturity. Each of us inheres a variety of human diversity markers, and appreciation of each of our own markers, even those mainstream society would encourage us to devalue, can give us insight into our own being and appreciation of true diversity. In the suboptimal cultural worldview, difference is almost always equated with deficiency. Such a deficit mentality not only misses the fullness of life and richness of humanity, but it also precludes the realization of oneness of the totality of which all are a part (unitary consciousness). A value for civility, true diversity, equity, and inclusion going beyond the superficial difference of appearance is essential for full realization of what it means to be human. The assumptions and principles informing diverse thinking and backgrounds can enhance collective progress when they are centered in truth, justice, and righteousness. A group of people who look different but think alike in the suboptimal mainstream will yield little movement toward real cultural diversity. Functional cultural inclusion must go beyond the surface structures of culture, such as language, dress, diet, and so on, to the deep structures of culture, those assumptions and principles shaping the conceptual system, worldview, ideology, and values and informing our moral compass.

Embracing hearts and minds that enhance justice versus just maintaining the status quo is wise, bringing peace, joy, and fellowship. Unity around beliefs, values, and behaviors that contribute to creating a just, sacred, and sustainable world will save the soul of humanity. Enough people as members of the global community choosing to withdraw their power from belief in the suboptimal and not to succumb to the oppression of others and themselves, but rather inhere the lived tradition of the optimal, will lead humanity toward salvation. By exposing, confronting, and rectifying the driving forces behind inhumanity, we are in a position to embrace and enhance the illumination of the soul, which can only serve to uplift our understanding of what it means to be human with harmonious balance, as we grow healthy and develop together.

Linda James Myers, PhD, is an internationally recognized thought leader, author, and scholar whose Africological perspective in the production of psychological knowledge places the wisdom tradition of African deep thought at the forefront of the science of life and the paradigm shift supported by contemporary science, Eastern philosophies, and the African common sense of Ntr, around which the heights of knowledge across cultural groups converge. Her research articulating optimal psychology (OP), or optimal conceptual theory (OCT), deepens our understanding of the higher stages of human development and how to achieve them.

References and Further Reading

Allen, Amani M., Yijie Wang, David H. Chase, Melisa M. Price, Wizdom Powell, Teneka C. Steed, Angela Rose Black, Firdaus S. Dhabhar, Leticia Marquez-Magaña, and Cheryl L. Woods-Giscombe. 2019. "Racial Discrimination, The Superwoman Schema, and Allostatic Load: Exploring an Integrative Stress Coping Model Among African American Women." *Annals of the New York Academy of Sciences*, 1457 (104–27).

Bynum, E. B. 1999. *The African Unconsciousness: Roots of Ancient Mysticism and Modern Psychology*. New York: Teachers College Press.

Byrd, W. Michael, and Linda A. Clayton. 2000. *An American Health Dilemma: A Medical History of African Americans and the Problem of Race: Beginnings to 1900*. New York: Routledge.

Consoli, Andres J., and Linda James Myers, eds. 2022. "Alternate Cultural Paradigms in Psychology: Long Overdue Recognition and Further Articulations. Special Issue on Alternative Cultural Paradigms in Psychology." *Journal of Humanistic Psychology* 62 (4): 471–87.

Dixon and Nichols 1973. Philosophical Aspects of Cultural Difference. (unpublished presentation) Marcus Garvey Quotes. https://blackalliance.org/marcus-garvey-quotes/.

Myers, L. James. 1988, 1992. *Understanding an Afrocentric World View: Introduction to an Optimal Psychology.* Dubuque, IA: Kendall/Hunt.

———. 2003. *Our Health Matters: Guide to an African (Indigenous) American Psychology and Cultural Model for Creating a Climate and Culture of Optimal Health.* Columbus: Ohio Commission on Minority Health.

———. 2004. *Blessed Assurance: Deep Thought and Meditations in the Tradition of Wisdom from our Ancestors.* Gahanna, Ohio: The Institute for Optimal Transformation and Leadership.

———. 2011. "The Metaphysics of Optimal Psycho-social Functioning in Eliminating Abuse. In *Healing Black Women from Violence: Reclamation and Peace,* edited by L. Rodgers-Rose, and Z. Zai'mah. Norfolk: Traces Publications.

———. 2013. *Restoration of Spirit: An African-Centered Communal Health Model. Journal of Black Psychology.* Thousand Oaks: Sage Publications.

———. 2013. "Healing, Coping, & Transcending the Legacy of Racism, Sexism, & Classism." In *Afrikan American Women: Living at the Crossroads of Race, Gender, Class, and Culture,* edited by H. Lowman-Jackson, 387–96. San Diego: Cognella Academic.

Myers, L. James, and M. Anderson. 2013. "Mental Health Assessment and Treatment of African Americans in Cultural Context." In *Handbook of Multicultural Mental Health,* 2nd ed., edited by F.A. Paniagua and A. Yamada, 256–81. Chennai, India: Elsevier.

Myers, L. James, Michelle Anderson, Tania Lodge, Suzette Speight, and John Queener. 2018. "Optimal Theory's Contributions to Understanding and Surmounting Global Challenges to Humanity." *Journal of Black Psychology,* 50th Anniversary Issue 44(8), 747–72. https://doi.org/10.1177/00221678211048114.

Myers, L. James, Tania Lodge, Suzette Speight, and Kristee Haggins. 2022. "The Necessity of an Alternative Paradigm in Africana/Black Psychology, Special Issue on Alternative Cultural Paradigms in Psychology." *Journal of Humanistic Psychology* 62 (4): 488–515. https://doi.org/10.1177%2F00221678211048568.

Myers, L. James, and D. Shinn. 2010. "Appreciating Traditional Forms of Healing Conflict in Africa and the World." *Black Diaspora Review* 2 (1): 2–14.

Myers, L. James, and S. L. Speight. 2010. "Reframing Mental Health and Psychological Well-Being among Persons of African Descent: Africana/Black Psychology Meeting the Challenges of Fractured Social and Cultural Realities. *Journal of Pan African Studies* 3 (8): 66–82.

United Nations. 2021. *Annual Report of the United Nations High Commissioner for Human Rights and Reports of the Office of the High Commissioner and the Secretary-General: Racism, Racial Discrimination, Xenophobia and Related Forms of Intolerance, Follow-Up to and Implementation of the Durban Declaration and Programme of Action, July 2021.*

Poem Penned by Marcus Garvey in 1927 in Prison in Atlanta

Hail! United States of Africa—free!
Hail! Motherland most bright, divinely fair!
State in perfect sisterhood united,
Born of truth; mighty though shalt ever be.

Hail! Sweet land of our father's noble kin!
Let joy within thy bounds be ever known;
Friend of the wandering poor, and helpless, thou,
Light to all, such as freedom's reigns within.

From Liberia's peaceful Western Coast
To the foaming Cape at the Southern end
There's but one law and sentiment sublime,
One flag, and its emblem of which we boast.

The Nigerias are all united now.
Sierra Leone and the Gold Coast, too.
Gambia, Senegal, not divided.
But in one union happily bow.

The treason of the centuries is dead,
All alien whites are forever gone;
The glad home of Sheba is once more free,
As o'er the world the Blackman raised his head...

Over in Grand Mother Mozambique,
The pretty Union Flag floats in the air,
She is sister to good Somaliland,
Smiling with the children of Dahomey...

There is no state left out of the union—
The East, West, North, South, including Central,
Are in the nation, strong forever,
Over Blacks in glorious dominion.

Hail! United States of Africa—free!

Country of the brave Black man's liberty;
State of greater nationhood thou hast now,
A new life for the race is just begun.

BIBLIOGRAPHY

MANY BOOKS HAVE been written that detail my father's triumphs and trials and the successes and failures of the UNIA and ACL's programs. A few such authors are Essein Udom, Rupert Lewis, John Henrik Clarke, Tony Martin, Randall Burkett, and Robert Hill (who edited the multivolume series). As mentioned in my introduction, my mother, Amy Jacques Garvey, also adeptly compiled my father's writing.

Many lessons remain to be learned from my father. His ideas are still relevant and are the basis for the African Renaissance. The forces that opposed him are also still extant today. Read his work and let us work together to finish the work Marcus Garvey began.

"29 Famous Marcus Garvey Quotes (Confidence, Race, God)." Black Alliance. Accessed May 14, 2021. https://blackalliance.org/marcus-garvey-quotes/.

African American Literature Book Club (AALBC). "The Largest Site Dedicated to Books by or about People of African Descent." AALBC.com. Accessed January 24, 2018. https://aalbc.com/.

Afrika, Llaila O. *African Holistic Health.* Silver Spring, MD: Sea Island Information Group (Adesegun, Johnson & Koram Publishers), 1990.

Alexander, Michelle. *The New Jim Crow: Mass Incarceration in the Age of Colorblindness.* Revised Edition. New York: The New Press, 2012.

Asante, Molefi. *Afrocentricity.* Trenton, NJ: Africa World Press, 1988.

———. *The Afrocentric Idea.* Philadelphia: Temple University Press, 1988.

Asante, Molefi Kete, and Karenga Maulana, eds. *Handbook of Black Studies.* New Delhi: Sage Publications, 2006.

Azikiwe, Nnamdi. *My Odyssey: An Autobiography.* London: Hurst and Company, 1970.

Barnard, Harry. *The Forging of an American Jew: The Life and Times of Judge Julian W. Mack.* New York: Herzl Press, 1974.

Beckford, George. *Persistent Poverty: Underdevelopment in Plantation Economies of the Third World*. Morant Bay, Jamaica: Maroon Publishing House, 1983.

Beckford, George L., and Michael Witter. *Small Garden—Bitter Weed: The Political Economy of Struggle and Change in Jamaica*. Morant Bay, Jamaica: Maroon Publishing House, 1982.

Beckles, Hilary. *How Britain Underdeveloped the Caribbean: A Reparation Response to Europe's Legacy of Plunder and Poverty*. Kingston: The University of the West Indies Press, 2021.

Bethune, Mary McLeod. *Mary McLeod Bethune: Words of Wisdom*. Edited by Chiazam Ugo. Bloomington, IN: AuthorHouse, 2008.

Black Classic Press. "Black Classic Press." https://www.blackclassicbooks.com/.

Blain, Keisha N. *Set the World on Fire: Black Nationalist Women and the Global Struggle for Freedom*. Philadelphia: University of Pennsylvania Press, 2018.

Bolland, O. Nigel. *The Politics of Labour in the British Caribbean: The Social Origins of Authoritarianism and Democracy in the Labour Movement*. Kingston: Ian Randle Publishers, 2001.

Brathwaite, Edward Kamau. *Folk Culture of the Slaves in Jamaica*. London: New Beacon Books, 1981.

Browder, Anthony T. *Nile Valley Contributions to Civilization*. Washington, DC: Institute of Karmic Guidance, 2007.

Brown, DeNeen L. "Descendants of Marcus Garvey Press Biden for Posthumous Pardon." *Washington Post*, December 4, 2021. https://www.washingtonpost.com/history/2021/12/04/marcus-garvey-biden-pardon/.

Bryan, Patrick, and Rubert Lewis. *Garvey, His Work and Impact*. Trenton, NJ: Africa World Press, 1991.

Byrd, W. Michael, and Linda A. Clayton. *An American Health Dilemma: A Medical History of African Americans and the Problem of Race: Beginnings to 1900*. London: Taylor & Francis, 2012.

Bynum, Edward Bruce. *The African Unconscious: Roots of Ancient Mysticism and Modern Psychology*. New York: Teachers College Press, 1999.

Campbell, Horace. *Rasta and Resistance: From Marcus Garvey to Walter Rodney*. Trenton, NJ: Africa World Press, 1987.

Césaire, Aimé. *Discourse on Colonialism*. New York: Monthly Review Press, 1972.

Chevannes, Barry, ed. *Rastafari and Other African-Caribbean Worldviews*. New Brunswick, NJ: Rutgers University Press, 1998.

Coates, Ta-Nehisi. *The Beautiful Struggle: A Father, Two Sons and an Unlikely Road to Manhood*. New York: Spiegel & Grau, 2009.

———. *Between the World and Me*. New York: Random House, 2015.

———. *We Were Eight Years in Power*. New York: Penguin, 2018.

———. *The Water Dancer: A Novel*. New York: One World, 2019.

Consoli, Andres J., and Linda James Myers, eds. 2022. "Alternate Cultural Paradigms in Psychology: Long Overdue Recognition and Further Articulations. Special Issue on Alternative Cultural Paradigms in Psychology." *Journal of Humanistic Psychology* 62 (4): 471–87.

Cronon, E. David. *Black Moses: The Story of Marcus Garvey and the Universal Negro Improvement Association*. Madison: University of Wisconsin Press, 1960.

Diop, Cheikh Anta. *Civilization or Barbarism: An Authentic Anthropology*. New York: Lawrence Hill, 1991.

Dorman, Jacob S. *Chosen People: The Rise of American Black Israelite Religions*. Oxford: Oxford University Press, 2013.

Drew, Mary E. C. *Divine Will, Restless Heart*. Bloomington, IN: Xlibris Corporation, 2010.

Du Bois, W. E. B. *Dusk of Dawn! An Essay Toward an Autobiography of Race Concept*. San Diego: Harcourt Brace & Company, 1940.

Elkins, Caroline. *Legacy of Violence: A History of the British Empire*. New York: Knopf 2022.

Ewing, Adam. *The Age of Garvey: How a Jamaican Activist Created a Mass Movement and Changed Global Black Politics*. Princeton, NJ: Princeton University Press, 2016.

Ewing, Adam, and Ronald J. Stephens. *Global Garveyism*. Gainesville: University Press of Florida, 2019.

Fanon, Frantz. *Wretched of the Earth*. New York: Grove, 1968.

Foley, Barbara. *Spectres of 1919: Class and Nation in the Making of the New Negro*. Champaign: University of Illinois Press, 2003.

Garvey, Amy Jacques. *Marcus Garvey and the Vision of Africa*. New York: Random House, 1974.

———, ed. *Garvey and Garveyism*. New York: Octagon Books, 1963.

———, ed. *The Philosophy and Opinions of Marcus Garvey*. 2 vols. New York: Universal Publishing House, 1923 and 1925. Reprint, Dover: The Majority Press, 1986.

———. *Selected Writings from the Negro World, 1923–1928*, Ed. Louis J. Parascandola. Knoxville: The University of Tennessee Press, 2016.

Garvey, Marcus. *Philosophy and Opinions of Marcus Garvey or Africans for the Africans*. 2nd ed., 2 vols., Ed. A. J. Garvey. London: Frank Cass, 1967.

Garvey, Marcus. *Marcus Garvey Said—: A Collection of Quotations from Statements Made by Marcus Mosiah Garvey.* Edited by Ken S. Jones. Kingston, Jamaica: Ken S. Jones, 2002.

———. *Selected Writings and Speeches of Marcus Garvey.* Mineola, NY: Dover Publications, 2004.

Glissant, Édouard. *Caribbean Discourse: Selected Essays.* Charlottesville: University Press of Virginia, 1993.

———. *Poetics of Relation.* Ann Arbor: University of Michigan Press, 1997.

Grant, Colin. *Negro with a Hat.* New York: Oxford University Press, 2008.

Hansford, Justin. "Jailing a Rainbow: The Marcus Garvey Case." *Georgetown Journal of Law and Modern Critical Race Perspectives* 2 (2009).

Haugen, Brenda. *Marcus Garvey: Black Nationalist Crusader and Entrepreneur.* Minneapolis: Compass Point Books, 2008.

Helly, Dorothy O., and Susan M. Reverby. *Gendered Domains: Rethinking Public and Private in Women's History.* Ithaca, NY: Cornell University Press, 2018.

Hill, Marc Lamont. *Nobody: Casualties of America's War on the Vulnerable.* New York: Simon & Schuster, 2016.

Hill, Robert, ed. *The Marcus Garvey and Universal Negro Improvement Association Papers.* 7 vols. Berkeley: University of California Press, 1983–2006.

Hill, Robert A. *Dread History: Leonard P. Howell and Millenarian Visions in the Early Rastafarian Religion.* Chicago: Research Associates School Times Publications/Frontline Distribution International, 2001.

Hill, Robert Abraham. *The Marcus Garvey and Universal Negro Improvement Association Papers, Vol. X: Africa for the Africans, 1923–1945.* Berkeley: University of California Press, 1983.

Holt, Thomas C. *The Problem of Freedom: Race, Labor, and Politics in Jamaica and Britain, 1832–1938.* Baltimore: Johns Hopkins University Press, 1992.

Hudson, Cheryl Willis, and Wade Hudson, eds. *We Rise, We Resist, We Raise Our Voices.* New York: Random House Children's Books, 2018.

Hudson, Cheryl Willis, and Wade Hudson, eds. *The Talk: Conversations about Race, Love & Truth.* New York: Random House Children's Books, 2020.

Hudson, Wade. *Journey: Poems.* Chicago: Third World Press Foundation, 2020.

———. *Defiant: Growing Up in the Jim Crow South.* New York: Random House Children's Books, 2021.

———. *Invincible: Fathers and Mothers of Black America.* New York: Astra Publishing House, 2023.

Hudson, Wade, and Valerie Wilson Wesley. *Book of Black Heroes from A to Z*. New York: Scholastic, 1948.

Jackson-Lowman, Huberta, ed. *Afrikan American Women: Living at the Crossroads of Race, Gender, Class, and Culture*. Solana Beach, CA: Cognella, 2022.

Jamaican Information Services. "PM Pledges Strong Support for Move in U.S. House to Clear Garvey's Name." *JIS Daily Newsletter*, October 26, 2003. http://jis.gov.jm/pm-pledges-strong-for-move-in-u-s-house-to-clear-garveys-name/.

James, C. L. R. *Nkrumah and the Ghana Revolution*. Durham, NC: Duke University Press, 2022.

James, Winston. *Holding Aloft the Banner of Ethiopia: Caribbean Radicalism in Early-Twentieth Century America*. London: Verso Books, 1998.

Karenga, Maulana. *Selections from the Husia: Sacred Wisdom of Ancient Egypt*. Los Angeles: University of Sankore Press, 1984.

———. *Selections from the Husia: Sacred Wisdom of Ancient Egypt*. Los Angeles: University of Sankore Press, 1989.

———. *The Book of Coming Forth by Day: The Ethics of the Declarations of Innocence*. Los Angeles: University of Sankore Press, 1990.

———. *Kawaida: A Communitarian African Philosophy*. Los Angeles: University of Sankore Press, 1997.

———. *Odù Ifá: The Ethical Teachings*. Los Angeles: University of Sankore Press, 1999.

———. *Maat, The Moral Ideal in Ancient Egypt: A Study in Classical African Ethics*. Los Angeles: University of Sankore Press, 2006.

———. *Kwanzaa: A Celebration of Family, Community, and Culture*. Los Angeles: University of Sankore Press, 2008.

———. *Kawaida and Questions of Life and Struggle: African American, Pan-African, and Global Issues*. Los Angeles: University of Sankore Press, 2008.

———. *Introduction to Black Studies*. Los Angeles: University of Sankore Press, 2010.

———. *Essays on Struggle: Position and Analysis*. Los Angeles: University of Sankore Press, 2015.

Langley, J. Ayodele. *Pan-Africanism and Nationalism in West Africa, 1900–1945: A Study in Ideology and Social Classes*. Oxford: Clarendon Press, 1973.

Lentz-Smith, Adriane. *Freedom Struggles: African Americans and World War I*. Cambridge, MA: Harvard University Press, 2009.

"Letter from Harry H. Pace et al., to Harry M. Daugherty, United States Attorney-General." http://www.pbs.org/wgbh/amex/garvey/filmmore/ps_go.html.

Lewis, Rupert. *Marcus Garvey: Anti-colonial Champion*. Trenton, NJ: Africa World Press, 1988.

———. *Walter Rodney's Intellectual and Political Thought*. Detroit: Wayne State University Press, 1998.

Lewis, Rubert, and Maureen Warner-Lewis. *Garvey: Africa, Europe, the Americas*. Trenton, NJ: Africa World Press, 1994.

Madhubuti, Haki R. *Black Pride*. Detroit: Broadside Press, 1968.

———. *Think Black*. Detroit: Broadside Press, 1968.

———. *Don't Cry, Scream*. Detroit: Broadside Press, 1969.

———. *We Walk the Way of the New World*. Detroit: Broadside Press, 1970.

———. *Taught by Women: Poems as Resistance Language New and Selected*. United States: Chicago: Third World Press, 2020.

Maglangbayan, Shawna. *Garvey, Lumumba, Black Nationalists Separatists*. Chicago: Third World Press, 1979.

Malcolm X. *The Autobiography of Malcolm X*. New York: Grove, 1965.

———. *Malcolm X Speaks*. New York: Merit, 1965.

———. *The Speeches of Malcolm X at Harvard*. New York: William Morrow and Company, 1968.

———. *By Any Means Necessary*. New York: Pathfinder Press, 1970.

Manela, Erez. *The Wilsonian Moment: Self-Determination and the International Origins of Anticolonial Nationalism*. Oxford: Oxford University Press, 2007.

Martin, Tony. *Race First: The Ideological and Organizational Struggles of Marcus Garvey and the University Negro Improvement Association*. Westport, CT: Greenwood, 1976.

———. *Race First: The Ideological and Organizational Struggles of Marcus Garvey and the Universal Negro Improvement Association*. Dover: Majority Press, 1986.

McKittrick, Katherine. *Demonic Grounds: Black Women and the Cartographies of Struggle*. Minneapolis: University of Minnesota Press, 2006.

"Memorandum from J. Edgar Hoover to Special Agent Ridgely (Oct. 11, 1919)." http://www.pbs.org/wgbh/amex/garvey/filmmore/ps_fbi.html.

Mintz, Sidney Wilfred, and Richard Price. *The Birth of African-American Culture: An Anthropological Perspective*. Boston: Beacon Press, 1992.

Mitchell, Michele. *Righteous Propagation: African Americans and the Politics of Racial Destiny After Reconstruction*. Chapel Hill: University of North Carolina Press, 2005.

Murapa, Rukudzo. *Padmore's Role in the African Liberation Movement*. DeKalb: Northern Illinois University, 1974.

Myers, Linda James. *Understanding an Afrocentric World View: Introduction to an Optimal Psychology*. Dubuque, IA: Kendall/Hunt, 1992.

———. *Our Health Matters: Guide to an African (Indigenous) American Psychology and Cultural Model for Creating a Climate and Culture of Optimal Health*. Columbus: Ohio Commission on Minority Health, 2003.

———. *Blessed Assurance: Deep Thought and Meditations in the Tradition and Wisdom of Our Ancestors*. Gahanna, OH: Institute for Optimal Transformation and Leadership, The Center for Optimal Thought, 2004.

Myers, Linda James, and Michelle Anderson. "Mental Health Assessment and Treatment of African Americans in Cultural Context." In *Handbook of Multicultural Mental Health*, edited F.A. Paniagua and A. Yamada, 256–81. Chennai, India: Elsevier, 2013.

Myers, L. James, Michelle Anderson, Tania Lodge, Suzette Speight, and John Queener. "Optimal Theory's Contributions to Understanding and Surmounting Global Challenges to Humanity." *Journal of Black Psychology*, 50th Anniversary Issue 44(8), 747–72. https://doi.org/10.1177/00221678211048114.

Myers, L. James, Tania Lodge, Suzette Speight, and Kristee Haggins. "The Necessity of an Alternative Paradigm in Africana/Black Psychology, Special Issue on Alternative Cultural Paradigms in Psychology." *Journal of Humanistic Psychology* (2021). https://doi.org/10.117 7%2F00221678211048568.

Nelson, Stanley, dir. "Marcus Garvey: Look for Me in the Whirlwind." *American Experience*. Aired February 12, 2001, on PBS. https://www.pbs.org/wgbh/americanexperience/films/garvey/#transcript.

Nkrumah, Kwame. *Ghana: The Autobiography of Kwame Nkrumah*. Edinburgh: Thomas Nelson, 1957.

Office of the Pardon Attorney. "Pardon after Completion of Sentence." 2023. US Department of Justice. Accessed March 15, 2023. https://www.justice.gov/pardon/apply-pardon.

Page, Melvin E., and Andy McKinlay. *Africa and the First World War*. New York: St. Martin's Press, 1987.

Perry, Jeffrey Babcock. *Hubert Harrison: The Voice of Harlem Radicalism, 1883–1918.* New York: Columbia University Press, 2009.

Robinson, Cedric J. *Black Marxism: The Making of the Black Radical Tradition.* Chapel Hill: University of North Carolina Press, 2000.

Rodney, Walter. *The Groundings with My Brothers.* London: Bogle-L'Ouverture, 1969.

———. *How Europe Underdeveloped Africa.* London: Verso Books, 2018.

Rogers, Robert Athlyi. *The Holy Piby.* Auckland: Floating Press, 2009.

Rosberg, Carl Gustav, and John Cato Nottingham. *The Myth of "Mau Mau": Nationalism in Kenya.* Stanford, CA: Hoover Institution on War, Revolution, and Peace, 1966.

Shakur, Assata. *Assata: An Autobiography.* London: Zed Books, 1987.

Sheller, Mimi. *Democracy after Slavery: Black Publics and Peasant Radicalism in Haiti and Jamaica.* Gainesville: University Press of Florida, 2000.

Stein, Judith. *The World of Marcus Garvey: Race and Class in Modern Society.* Baton Rouge: Louisiana State University Press, 1985.

Stoddard, Lothrop. *The Rising Tide of Color Against White World-Supremacy.* New York: Scribner, 1920.

Taifa, Nkechi. *Black Power, Black Lawyer: My Audacious Quest for Justice.* United States: House of Songhay II, 2020.

———. *Reparations on Fire: How and Why It's Spreading Across America.* United States: House of Songhay II, 2022.

Taylor, Ula Yvette. *The Veiled Garvey: The Life and Times of Amy Jacques Garvey.* Chapel Hill: University of North Carolina Press, 2002.

———. *The Promise of Patriarchy: Women and the Nation of Islam.* Chapel Hill: University of North Carolina Press, 2017.

Thiong'o, Ngũgĩ wa. *Moving the Centre: The Struggle for Cultural Freedoms.* London: James Currey, 1993.

Toure, Sekou. *Toward Full Re-Africanization.* Paris: Présence Africaine, 1959.

Washington, Booker T. *Up from Slavery: An Autobiography.* Boston: Houghton Mifflin, 1928.

West, Michael O., William G. Martin, and Che Wilkins Fanon. *From Toussaint to Tupac: The Black International Since the Age of Revolution.* Chapel Hill: University of North Carolina Press, 2009.

White House Historical Association. "Homepage." 2019. https://www.whitehousehistory.org/.

Williams, Chad L. *Torchbearers of Democracy: African American Soldiers in the World War I Era.* Chapel Hill: University of North Carolina Press, 2010.

Wright, Richard. *Black Boy.* 75th anniversary ed. New York: HarperCollins, 2020.